*The Metamorphoses of Landscape and Community
in Early Quebec*

In the seventeenth and eighteenth centuries French settlers radically transformed the landscape of the St Lawrence river, creating strong local communities that became the crucibles of a New World nationalism. Drawing on the insights and methods of cultural history, Colin Coates examines the seigneuries of Batiscan and Sainte-Anne de la Pérade, recreating the social relations between individuals and ethnic groups that inhabited the area. He shows that successive waves of immigrants sought to appropriate the landscape of the New World and replace it with a physical and cultural reality much closer to their European roots and traditions.

French settlers distanced the indigenous people and flora and fauna to create a landscape that by the mid-eighteenth century had become recognizably European. British industrialists and landowners attempted similar appropriations with far less durable results and the area remained a heartland of French-Canadian life, with a sense of cohesive community. This community spirit, rooted in the agrarian landscape, was channelled into the developing sense of colonial nationalism of the 1820s and 1830s.

Drawing on maps by explorers and surveyors, correspondence documenting the conflict between a backwoods priest and his parishioners, a gentlewoman's sketchbook, and the documents of a bitter court case between a seigneur's wife and a local priest, Coates illuminates the development of the region and the social, cultural, and economic ties and tensions within it, providing insights into the often hidden values of a rural community.

COLIN M. COATES is director of the Centre of Canadian Studies at the University of Edinburgh.

STUDIES ON THE HISTORY OF QUEBEC/
ÉTUDES D'HISTOIRE DU QUÉBEC

John Dickinson and Brian Young
Series Editors/Directeurs de la collection

Habitants and Merchants in Seventeenth-Century Montreal
Louise Dechêne

Crofters and Habitants
Settler Society, Economy, and Culture in a Quebec Township,
1841–1881
J.I. Little

The Christie Seigneuries
Estate Management and Settlement in the Upper Richelieu Valley, 1760–1859
Françoise Noël

La Prairie en Nouvelle-France, 1647–1760
Louis Lavallée

The Politics of Codification
The Lower Canadian Civil Code of 1866
Brian Young

Arvida au Saguenay
Naissance d'une ville industrielle
José E. Igartua

State and Society in Transition
The Politics of Institutional Reform in the Eastern Townships, 1838–1852
J.I. Little

Vingt ans après *Habitants et marchands,*
Lectures de l'histoire des xviiᵉ et xviiiᵉ siècles canadiens
Habitants et marchands, Twenty Years Later
Reading the History of Seventeenth- and Eighteenth-Century Canada
Edited by *Sylvie Dépatie, Catherine Desbarats, Danielle Gauvreau,
Mario Lalancette, Thomas Wien*

Families in Transition
Industry and Population in Nineteenth-Century Saint-Hyacinthe
Peter Gossage

The Metamorphoses
of Landscape
and Community
in Early Quebec

COLIN M. COATES

McGill-Queen's University Press
Montreal & Kingston · London · Ithaca

Legal deposit 1st quarter 2000
Bibliothèque nationale du Québec

Printed in Canada on acid-free paper

This book has been published with the help of grants from the Publishing
Fund of the International Council for Canadian Studies, the History
Group of the British Association of Canadian Studies, and the
Association internationale des études québécoises.

McGill-Queen's University Press acknowledges the financial support of
the Government of Canada through the Book Publishing Industry
Development Program (BPIDP) for its activities. We also acknowledge the
support of the Canada Council for the Arts for our publishing program.

Parts of this manuscript have appeared in different form in *The Canadian
Historical Review* 74, no. 3 (1993): 317-43 (reprinted by permission of
University of Toronto Press Incorporated); *Histoire sociale/Social History*
22, no. 43 (1989): 65-90; and Donald Fyson, Colin Coates, and Kathryn
Harvey, eds., *Class, Gender, and the Law in Eighteenth- and Nineteenth-
Century Quebec: Sources and Perspectives*, 81-97 (Montreal: Montreal
History Group, 1993).

Canadian Cataloguing in Publication Data

Coates, Colin MacMillan, 1960–
    The metamorphoses of landscape and community in early Quebec
    Includes bibliographical references and index.
    ISBN 0-7735-1896-7 (bnd)

    1. Canada – History – To 1763 (New France) 2. Land settlement patterns
    – Quebec (Province) – History. 3. Nationalism – Quebec (Province) –
    History – 19th century.
    HN110.Q8C518 1999   971.4'01   C99-900810-2

This book was typeset by Typo Litho Composition Inc.
in 10/12 Palatino.

Contents

Maps, Tables, and Figures

FIGURES

ix   Maps, Tables, and Figures

Preface

In the midst of the winter of 1811, Benjamin Joseph Frobisher, co-proprietor of the Batiscan Iron Works Company, ordered a copy of Ovid's *Metamorphoses*.[1] We cannot know what consolations this compendium of classical Roman mythology brought to him in the isolated industrial village that had grown around the ironworks. The assurances of continuity in change, of the possible positive outcomes of wrenching metamorphoses, that are recounted in the book may have alleviated in a small way what were to be difficult years for the company. In late 1813 Frobisher's business partner, John Craigie, died and the forges' furnaces were extinguished, never to be lit again.

Probably the book reminded Frobisher of his youth, spent at a boarding school in England, far from his Canadian family. In the late eighteenth century Ovid's *Metamorphoses* was a staple of the schoolboy's learning.[2] It remains today, as one critic puts it, "a book of changes, a great poem explaining the origins of the world, of human personality, and of organized society all through the image of change."[3] Did Frobisher think of his personal transformations? The son of an English fur-trading father and a French-Canadian mother in the French-speaking but British-dominated colony, he had been sent to study in England. As a young adult, he returned to the world of the fur trade, an active political life in the colonial legislature, and an ill-fated venture into industrial activity. Within a few years of the closure of the Batiscan ironworks, Frobisher was again on the fur-trading frontier, where he suffered from the increasingly violent competition between the North West Company and the Hudson's Bay Company.[4]

Like Frobisher, we can rely on Ovid's *Metamorphoses* to chart a course through a period of important changes.[5] This book, one of the few that can be placed in this rural region during this period, provides leitmotifs that all the people of the area would have understood on some level. Recounting traditional Roman myths, Ovid details the harrowing changes, the apparent changes, the unsuccessful changes, that humans and gods experienced and wrought. Living his later years in exile from the imperial centre, he might even have felt some kinship to the people of this isolated North American colony.

The theme of metamorphoses of the landscape, from aboriginal territory to French small-scale agriculture, provides the compass which this book will use to explore the region's history. As in all such societies, the predictable seasonal cycles of agrarian society sometimes masked larger transformations. This area, the seigneuries of Sainte-Anne de la Pérade and Batiscan, a heartland of rural French Catholic society, delineates the growth and challenges experienced by rural dwellers in early Quebec.

Acknowledgments

The process of completing a PhD dissertation and then turning it into a book involves the collaboration of many friends and colleagues, and it is a pleasure to recognize so many debts. In the final stages of this process, the support and comments of my colleagues and friends Brian Young, Ged Martin, Grace Owens, and Adam Fox have been invaluable. In its earlier incarnation as a thesis, this work benefited from the comments of the members of my committee: Fernand Ouellet, T.J.A. LeGoff, Ramsay Cook, Marilyn Silverman, and Cornelius Jaenen. The encouragement of my supervisor, Fernand Ouellet, through all stages has been most generous. His good-humoured and incisive comments on my work helped me through to its completion. The thesis was supported financially by York University, the Social Sciences and Humanities Research Council, and the Ontario Government Queen Elizabeth II Scholarship.

Parts of this book have appeared in different form in *The Canadian Historical Review* 74, no. 3 (1993): 317-343; *Histoire sociale – Social History* 22, no. 43 (1989): 65-90; and Donald Fyson, Colin M. Coates, and Kathryn Harvey, eds., *Class, Gender and the Law in Eighteenth- and Nineteenth-Century Quebec: Sources and Perspectives* (Montreal: Montreal History Group, 1993), 81-97.

Colleagues who have shared research materials with me include Thomas Wien, Roger Hall, Gilbert Gignac, Eva Major-Marothy, René Hardy, Allan Greer, Rénald Lessard, and Patricia Kennedy. Yves Otis kindly prepared the graphs and maps for this study. John Bateman and Renate Henschel checked my translations of German material.

Elizabeth Hulse's careful copy-editing has improved the final version of this work. My friends John Lutz, Robert Penrose, Lise Fradet, Tom Keirstead, Deborah Laing, and Kenneth Coates all shared ideas that are reflected in this book.

Together with many friends, my parents have always supported my studies and my arcane interests. I wish that my father could have seen this completed book. I am delighted to show it to my mother.

Megan Davies has been part of my life for just a little longer than Madeleine de Verchères. I cannot begin to acknowledge the myriad of ways in which she helped this project: reading more drafts than a human should ever be forced to, counting numbers of baptisms in parish registers, and most important, reminding me, with help from our children, Mab and Bryn, that history is only one of our shared passions. With love, I dedicate this book to her.

The Metamorphoses of Landscape and Community
in Early Quebec

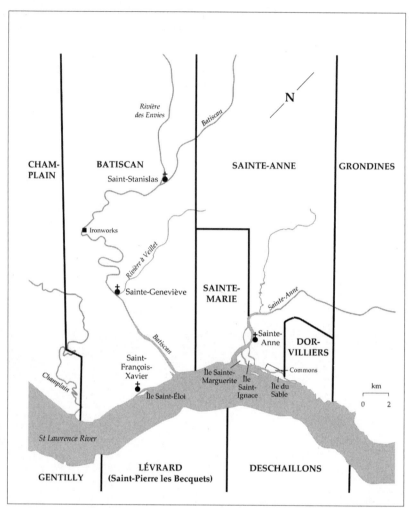

Map 1   Batiscan and Sainte-Anne

Introduction: The Rivers

And every other stream whose eddying course,
Rolls to the main its tributary force.

Ovid, Metamorphoses, 36

The two rivers flowed laggardly and sometimes seemingly without direction. Rising to the northeast of what would become Quebec City, they wound their way, almost parallel in places, between the jagged peaks and through the endless valleys of the Laurentian hills, before finally sensing their destiny in the great St Lawrence River and rushing towards it.

As in so many other parts of Canada, the Batiscan and Sainte-Anne rivers provided the initial focuses for the people who came to inhabit the territory. They were the roads, inefficient in some ways yet still passable. As they descended from the heights of the Canadian Shield, they produced rapids that would hinder movement upstream. Nevertheless, for aboriginal peoples, for hunters and fur traders, and for timber workers they facilitated travel deep into the interior.

These were only two of the many rivers that rise deep in the Laurentian shield to launch themselves into the St Lawrence River, a river so grand that in French it merited the epithet *fleuve* to distinguish it from a mere *rivière*. Before adequate roads could be built and long before railways would ensure passage, the rivers attracted the attention of travellers. Beginning in the late seventeenth century and over some one hundred and fifty years, they held out new promises to immigrants who established permanent homes on their banks. In addition to providing water, fish, and transport, they represented an energy supply for small-scale grist milling and lumber cutting. For a brief period, the Rivière Batiscan permitted the experiment of industrial development when a dam was used to power an ironworks.

The landscapes near the mouths of the rivers were transformed in the space of those one hundred and fifty years. A mid-nineteenth-century travellers' handbook would take pains to point out that there was nothing particularly interesting to see at the mouth of the Rivière Batiscan. The fact that boats might call there on the way between Montreal and Quebec should not encourage the traveller to think otherwise, the 1857 publication implied.[1] Batiscan was just another rural settlement along the banks of the St Lawrence – unremarkable, perhaps even typical.

The unremarkable aspect of Batiscan is testimony to the success of the metamorphosis of it and other areas on the shores of the St Lawrence. From banks of trees to Europeanized, settled farmland, the landscape reflected the travails of successive generations of habitant farmers in carving out a new terrain. This agrarian landscape would survive other attempts to introduce an industrial focus and slightly later a picturesque English idyll. For these were ideal landscapes that the various participants attempted to foist on the land; only the back-breaking and seasonal labour of the family farm would perdure in the area. This labour infused the landscape with meaning and passion.

This was a process of displacement – of aboriginal peoples, plants, and animals. It is not often adequately recognized how successful the displacement was. Even through a second wave of attempted British colonization of the St Lawrence valley, even in the face of military and political domination, the local French-Canadian society survived. This does not mean that nothing changed in this area or others in the valley. Rather, the transformations in social structure that occurred under the British regime served to establish the political, economic, demographic, and social basis for what we can call "nationalism," although at this level the more accurate term may be "community." Two British attempts at metamorphosis occurred in this period, but with relatively few long-term effects. It is the purpose of this book to examine the successive visions of ideal landscapes, and to account for the ultimate victory of the habitant landscape over all others.

This study attempts to chart new historiographical territory. While there have been many solid contributions to the understanding of the social structure of the St Lawrence valley,[2] few studies have tried to examine how the people within the communities made sense of their own world. This book focuses on the cultural history of the region, taking a broad anthropological view of "culture." I examine how people argued with each other, how they tried to make sense of their lives and their surroundings. In looking for different meanings in traditional documents, the study applies new historiographical models, best exemplified in the work of German historian David Warren Sabean.[3] Cultural developments are firmly rooted in the socio-economic context which influenced them and which they influenced.

Moreover, in linking socio-economic structures and cultural meanings, this study elucidates one of the key transformations in early Quebec: the growth of nationalist sentiment. By the end of the period under study, a stronger sense of locality had emerged in which these physical settlements were also "imagined" communities.[4] Through the processes of economic differentiation and the activities of a flourishing lay elite, the French-Canadian communities identified themselves as different to their British co-territorials, and they acted upon those distinctions.

1 Aboriginal Landscapes

The lofty pine, torn from the mountain's brow,
Stem'd not the billows with adventurous prow
In search of climates distant and unknown,
For mortals knew no climate but their own.

Ovid, *Metamorphoses*, 10

In 1663 the earthquake struck. "Reports were heard as of brazen cannon, and of frequent and horrible thunders, which, mixed with the crashing noise of shattered trees – falling together by hundreds, and loudly dashing into one another, – caused to stand on end the hair of those who were either present at those spectacles, or heard such an unusual din from a distance." The very fact that the great earthquake of the summer of 1663 was later reported by the Jesuits indicates a European presence along the Rivière Batiscan: "One of the Frenchmen ... had made his cabin there with the barbarians."[1] The chance occurrence brought the area, if only briefly, to the attention of the Jesuits' audience in Europe. The entry in the *Jesuit Relations* reveals the French missionaries' interest in the aborigines north of the St Lawrence, and it suggests fur-trade activity. On two counts, religious and economic, the French had turned their attention to Batiscan.

Within a decade the solitary European was replaced by a sedentary French population, and chroniclers soon ceased to refer the Amerindian population of Batiscan. However, aboriginal people did not disappear from the region. In the early nineteenth century, occasional travellers through the area remarked on Amerindian encampments on the shores of the Batiscan and Sainte-Anne rivers.[2] Otherwise, Native people became almost invisible in the historical record, withdrawing deep into a landscape that, only one hundred and fifty years previously, had been an unequivocal part of their migratory routines.

ABORIGINES

It is still a common assumption that the landscapes which the original explorers saw were "natural" ones: environments that aboriginal peoples lived in but had not attempted to modify. However, in many cases North American Natives purposefully manipulated their own environment. Through controlled burning, for instance, they encouraged the growth of specific edible plants.[3] Despite this transformative attitude, aboriginal peoples did not share Judeo-Christian perspectives on the world. They perceived the local landscape in a way different from all but the earliest French fur traders.

Archaeological studies of the region reveal an aboriginal settlement during the first millenium BC in an area not far from the Rivière Batiscan. The vestiges include pottery shards, projectiles, scrapers, and animal remains,[4] pointing to a hunting and gathering economy, with some indication of metal use but not of agricultural techniques. This occupation involved the temporary settlement of a nomadic people whose use of the area was restricted to a camping site, probably part of a perpetual migration.

Some two thousand years later, during Champlain's lifetime, Algonquins used the river for trapping, trading, and travelling.[5] This aboriginal people still occupied the region through the 1660s, trading furs and foodstuffs to the French.[6] The new trade opportunities clearly encouraged the Amerindians to hunt more intensively than ever before. But even without the incentives afforded by European commerce, the aboriginal economy had an impact on the landscape.

The Algonquins' use of their environment went far beyond trapping. In addition to hunting, fishing, and gathering, they also practised swidden agriculture. This small-scale burning of the forest permitted the cultivation of certain grains and vegetables, such as maize, beans, squash, and peas.[7] But swidden agriculture implied only short-term sedentary activity. Thus the techniques employed by the aboriginal people fit into a larger program of nomadic occupation of the land.

Nomadism, because of its extensive nature, involves different perceptions of landscape than does sedentary agriculture. Concerning the aborigines of Australia, one scholar points out that aboriginal appropriation of land contrasts sharply with European concepts. "The Aborigine," he argues, "travelled in order to stay where he was."[8] Or in the Canadian case, according to a seventeenth-century Jesuit, "In these great forests, the road is everywhere."[9] The Algonquins' landscapes were broad, much vaster than the comparatively small plots of land that future European settlers would occupy.

Moreover, the aboriginal people did not only exist within the land-scape; they were part of it. Of the Amerindians living to the north of the St Lawrence, the Jesuits wrote, "Their life is nothing but a contin-ual hunt."[10] Indeed, it was a large part of the Jesuit mission to turn these aboriginal people into sedentary dwellers.

It would have been impossible for the aborigines to imagine them-selves outside of their environment, and the Europeans also linked ab-original people and what they termed "savage" nature inexorably. The European appropriation of the St Lawrence valley landscape therefore involved overshadowing the Amerindians' presence and stressing their rootlessness. Champlain commented on the temporary nature of the settlement of the Algonquins and Hurons who came to meet him near Île Saint-Éloi, where "some two or three hundred Indians ... were encamped."[11] Documents providing evidence of aboriginal-white con-tact in Sainte-Anne in the 1660s stress the homelessness and helpless-ness of the aboriginal people. In one instance, Amerindians were forced to sleep outside in January 1667 when Jean Cusson refused them admittance into his cabin.[12] In a symbolic fashion, the French docu-ment recording this event expressed the belief that the aboriginal peo-ple had no other "home" where they could take refuge. And if they had no home in this area, it could be appropriated for French purposes.

With European settlement, Amerindians receded into the shadows. Although they continued to travel to the mouths of the Batiscan and Sainte-Anne rivers into the nineteenth century,[13] their presence in documents was restricted largely to baptisms – in other words, to events in which they seemed, from a European perspective, to aban-don some of their "Indianness."[14] For most non-aboriginals the land-scape had become unquestionably European.

EXPLORERS

In a fashion similar to that of aboriginal people, the official explorers travelled in order to occupy. Their projects, beginning with those of Jacques Cartier in 1535, inescapably involved an appropriation of landscape for European uses. The very descriptions of the explora-tions made the new continent fit for new purposes. The projects themselves, rooted as they were in European culture and history and decided in advance of leaving the home harbours, determined much of the future of the continent.

Explorers who wished to justify both their own enterprise and fu-ture explorations had to emphasize the richness of the natural re-sources of the "new" lands.[15] However, the shores of what would be christened the St Lawrence did not abound in obvious, exploitable mineral wealth. Instead, the explorers hinted at the agricultural possibilities of the St Lawrence valley, including the Batiscan and Sainte-Anne areas. In so doing, they implicitly stressed the similarities between old France and what would become the "New." Jacques Cartier's trip up the St Lawrence in 1535–36 led him past "as fine a country and as level a region as one could wish."[16] It was the evenness of the terrain that interested the sailor from western France, the Laurentian hills presumably hiding just out of sight under the forest cover. Similarly, he stressed the abundance of trees and birds, of which he enumerated a lengthy inventory, stopping only to add, "and other birds, the same as in France, and in great numbers."[17] For him this section of the St Lawrence, part of which later became Sainte-Anne and Batiscan, offered the natural resources of France and more.

Some seventy years later, Samuel de Champlain repeated Cartier's positive affirmations. The further one advanced up the St Lawrence, the more beautiful the land became.[18] Discussing the land to the north of Île Saint-Éloi, Champlain wrote that, "after penetrating a little way into the woods, the soil is good."[19] Likewise, he stated later, "The whole river from Ste. Croix upward [i.e., about thirty miles upriver from Quebec] is delightfully beautiful."[20] In general, Champlain linked positive statements about land and land quality with level terrain.[21] Thus his commentary encouraged an agrarian perception of the St Lawrence valley. Furthermore, he evaluated the landscape on the basis of home, implicitly assuming the grain-growing practices of western France.

In an even more dramatic fashion, Pierre Boucher's *Histoire véritable et naturelle ... de la Nouvelle-France*, published in 1664, represented a plea for the agrarian settlement of this part of the colony. He evaluated the land that by his time included the seigneury of Batiscan: "From the Sainte-Anne River to Trois-Rivières, about ten leagues, the land is very good and low; the banks along the great river are sand or meadows; the forests are very beautiful and very easy to clear."[22] The forests along the shore offered more by their eventual replacement with European crops than they did in their natural state. Boucher pointed to the promise implicit in the presence of numerous "prairies" in the area, precursors to agricultural development.

Two elements can be extracted from these three descriptions of this region. First, the perspectives were clearly taken from the St Lawrence River. The authors landed briefly, if at all, on the shore and made only short sorties into the forest. Secondly, all three were intellectually able to impose a new future on the area, to foresee the absence of the trees. The forests, which they deemed beautiful, could easily be removed and give way to promising agricultural terrain. This was not an immediate but a distant prospect. The forests were one of the omnipresent geographical features that demanded their attention. And yet forests held, in French culture, a number of cultural connotations: the home of "l'homme sylvestre," the man of the forest, the opposition between civilization and savagery, between hidden danger and wide-open perspectives.[23] The forests had to be removed in order to make the region habitable by settlers.

These authors appealed for the imposition of French techniques on the landscape of the colony. However, whereas Cartier and Champlain were not clear on who would actually see to this enterprise, by Boucher's time in the 1660s the grandiose failure of the French to assimilate the Amerindian population by turning them into sedentary farmers was becoming apparent. He appealed for the emigration of French settlers to the New World, the repopulation of the St Lawrence valley with a new race of inhabitants.

Thus the connection between the removal of much of the North American forest in the lowlands and its replacement with French settlers, plants, and animals was established by the mid-seventeenth century. Perhaps hoping that Christianized aboriginal people would populate the seigneury and clearly fearing the wrath of the Iroquois, the Jesuits did not take in hand the agricultural future of Batiscan for many years. When they finally took legal possession of the seigneury in 1662, some sixteen years after the initial grant, they performed a ritual to consecrate their ownership. They cut trees, made crosses on other trees, pulled up grass (herbes), and threw stones, "just as a real landowner is accustomed to do."[24] The symbols of possession thus implied deforestation, surveying, and clearing the land for agrarian purposes. The French had begun to create a new landscape. The first land grant, to the surgeon Felix Tuné du Fresne, occurred nineteen months later.[25]

FUR TRADERS

Until the axe and the plow wrought their changes on the land, the mere presence of Europeans in the area did not entail a revolution in the landscape. The earliest French activity in this territory did not differ fundamentally from aboriginal practice. In an initial phase the fur trade had led Europeans to the area: in 1657 eight Frenchmen left Trois-Rivières with twenty canoes of Algonquins. They travelled up the Rivière Batiscan and returned less than three months later, their canoes "filled with beaver pelts."[26] French fur traders lived among the Amerindians or established temporary posts in both Batiscan and

Sainte-Anne. In the 1660s, for example, Île Saint-Éloi served as a meeting place.[27] The earthquake of 1663 surprised some French traders who had established themselves in an aboriginal encampment along the Rivière Batiscan. The Jesuit chronicler of the disaster likened the French and Native reactions to the event: "The barbarians, at those prodigies, raised horrible shouts, along with our countrymen of like superstition, and discharged their guns to drive away those aërial demons, and rout them from their borders."[28] For the Jesuit, the close connections between impious French traders and Amerindians were not serving to "civilize" the latter.

Aboriginal-white trade was not limited to the Batiscan area. The merchant Michel Gamelain, the first seigneur of Sainte-Anne, had by 1667 established a trading post along the river where he exchanged brandy and merchandise for pelts and foodstuffs. Many of the early tenants in his seigneury were in fact fellow traders whose main activities led them up the Ottawa, Saint-Maurice, and Sainte-Anne rivers. The first clearings of the forest took place in Sainte-Anne seigneury during this period.[29] Nonetheless, Amerindians maintained a presence in the region.

By 1674 the governor had expressed concern that Amerindians in the area were trading their guns and clothes for liquor, "which most often reduced them to such a state of nudity that they found themselves unable to continue hunting."[30] Consequently, the colonial state tried to suppress the liquor trade with the Natives, or at least to centralize it in the towns.[31] It did not look kindly on the relatively benign presence of Europeans – benign at least in regard to aboriginal control of the territory. Instead, the colonial government fostered agrarian land use in the seigneuries. Intendant Jean Talon, supported by imperial directives, encouraged seigneurs to establish settlers on their land. This settlement of the French and displacement of the aboriginal peoples to areas where fur-trade activities were the only option for them represented a major change in the landscape of the St Lawrence valley.

By the 1680s the fur trade had become less important in the locality. However, participation in the trade persisted. Habitants of Batiscan and Sainte-Anne obtained *congés* (permissions) to trade furs along the Ottawa River.[32] Even though agriculture came to form the basis of the local economy, the fur trade continued to attract the attention of the French settlers. For a long time, men from Sainte-Anne and Batiscan, but particularly the latter, were involved in the activity and worked as *engagés* (contract employees).

The north shore of the St Lawrence from Champlain to Deschambault represented one of the major sources of labour in the fur trade. At the beginning of the eighteenth century a high percentage of *engagés* came from the seigneuries of the Trois-Rivières government. According to one estimate, up to 30 per cent of the adult male population on the north shore of the district was active in the fur trade.[33] Family networks influenced participation. For instance, the extended family of the Rivards of Batiscan provided a total of fourteen *engagés* between 1708 and 1717.[34] Participation in the fur trade could on occasion lead to permanent migration away from the seigneury. Claude Gouin decided in 1750 to leave his land in Sainte-Anne and establish his family at Detroit. His brother Joachim, who stayed in Sainte-Anne, advanced him supplies for expeditions in 1751 and 1752.[35]

The main labour pools for the fur trade moved progressively towards the seigneuries near Montreal. However, even in the late eighteenth century, men from Batiscan continued to sign up for work. Between 1773 and 1781 fur magnate Lawrence Ermatinger hired ten men from Batiscan.[36] Two years later the militia captains in Batiscan seigneury proposed the consolidation of the companies of Sainte-Geneviève and Saint-François-Xavier because of the large number of adult men absent from the latter parish: "Captain Lanouette ... has no more than twenty-two militiamen, of whom the majority are voyageurs."[37]

In this way, like many other rural parishes, Batiscan and to a lesser extent Sainte-Anne represented a labour pool for workers in the fur trade. These temporary seasonal and yearly migrations undoubtedly allowed some accumulation of capital. Young men could acquire enough to hasten their marriage and agricultural establishment in the seigneury; married men could obtain cash for commercial purchases. Obviously, this movement was strictly limited to males. It became less important over time, as the fur trade changed its focus. But unlike other voyageur parishes, where reliance on the waged labour in the seigneury ultimately contributed to a general impoverishment,[38] in Batiscan the decline in this external labour market was compensated by local developments.

Important as the fur trade might be to individual fortunes, the vast majority of the French inhabitants of Batiscan and Sainte-Anne seigneuries focused their economic strategies around agriculture. The relatively small number of fur traders, with their propensity to fit into Amerindian perspectives of landscape, was fated to decrease over time. The future lay in agrarian landscapes, and this would be the first and the only complete revolution in the St Lawrence valley.

2 Seigneurial Landscapes

Land was no longer free as air or light,
A fixed division mark'd each owner's right.

Ovid, Metamorphoses, 12

In the three hundred years following Jacques Cartier's first sighting of the area that became the seigneuries of Batiscan and Sainte-Anne de la Pérade, the landscape underwent irrevocable change. In contrast to the shields of forests that had confronted the early European explorers and settlers, it became possible by the early nineteenth century to compare the land to European landscapes and to use European artistic conventions to capture it on paper. The changes that occurred were long-term ones caused by different perceptions and uses of the land. At least in the areas close to the St Lawrence, the landscape became essentially European, with a visible hierarchy of land use.

The appropriation of the landscape by French settlers involved the importing of new animal and plant species and obviously a new race of humans. This process entailed the distancing of the native animals, plants, and humans from the new settlements. There was a dual process in the transformation of the landscape. In the first place, the French colonial state and the seigneurs played important roles in an overall restructuring of the land; the respective importance of the seigneurs and the state varied over time. Even more important, the practical labour of generations of habitants irrevocably altered the bases of society.

REDEFINING THE LAND

Naming

One of the most important ways in which the colonial state initially made its presence felt in Batiscan and Sainte-Anne de la Pérade was through attempts to redefine the land, to draw and redraw borders around the areas.[1] The first act of appropriating the territories in the name of the French king was to name them (or properly speaking, re-name them).

The origins of the word "Batiscan" are obscure, though it doubtless has an Amerindian derivation. Samuel de Champlain first mentioned "a river called Batiscan" in his account of his 1603 voyage.[2] Among the various geographical phenomena that he saw during his explorations, he found rivers particularly noteworthy. This interest illustrates the bias of the typical explorer, intrigued by geographical phenomena which demarcate journeys as well as those which promise future explorations.[3] However, the ambiguous chronology surrounding its mention in the account leaves open the possibility that the name does not necessarily refer to the same river as today. Indeed, Champlain's 1612 map placed the "contrée de bastisquan" to the west of the Rivière Saint-Maurice. By contrast, Marc Lescarbot's map of 1609 illustrated and named the "R. Batescan" in the same area as the present one. Even if, in reporting the earthquake of 1663, the Jesuits alluded to "the river which the barbarians call Batiscan,"[4] it was a French decision whether or not to adopt the name.

The river with the Algonquin name formed the symbolic locus of future French settlement. The title "Batiscan" was extended to the seigneury, indicating that early French interest in the area lay, not in the land itself, but in the river and the transportation that it provided into the interior and into fur-trading areas. Over time, French settlers populated the territory and placed more importance on the land than the river. They even occasionally domesticated the aboriginal origin of the name. In 1783, for example, the habitants living along the river drew up a petition in which the name was given as "Baptiste Camp."[5]

In his account of the 1609 voyage and on his 1612 map, Champlain had named the river to the east of the Batiscan the Sainte-Marie. This name later came to refer to the seigneury on the west bank of the river, and the river itself took on the name of an island at the mouth, Île Sainte-Anne.[6] As in Batiscan, the river's name was extended to both the seigneury on the east bank and the parish, which included settlers on both sides. The names Sainte-Marie and Sainte-Anne, linked as they were to Christian beliefs and particularly to the Marian cult of the Catholic Counter-Reformation, illustrated another imperial aim: the propagation of the faith.

But the region owed its territorial names not only to explorers and their imperial initiatives. Local seigneurs also made their imprint. To distinguish it from the other Sainte-Annes in the colony, the seigneurial patronymic La Pérade gradually replaced *près Batiscan* (near Batiscan) in the eighteenth century. Likewise, in Batiscan the choice of the Jesuit pioneers for the parish names of Saint-François-Xavier and Saint-Stanislas surely reflect the order's ownership. Finally, when the Jesuits' agent sold businessman Thomas Coffin an *arrière-fief* (a fief within a larger seigneury) in Batiscan in 1795, it is not difficult to imagine the inspiration for the name Saint-Thomas. In these ways seigneurs replicated for their own purposes the state's initial process of imposing names on the region.

Distributing Fiefs

Conceded as seigneuries at different times, Batiscan and Sainte-Anne illustrate two important moments in the distribution of fiefs during the seventeenth century. According to its charter, the Compagnie de la Nouvelle France was compelled to establish a French population in the colony. In 1636 it conveyed ten leagues of land downstream from the Rivière Saint-Maurice to Jacques de La Ferté, the king's confessor. Three years later, La Ferté conceded part of the immense tract in *arrière-fief* to the Jesuits. The shape of Batiscan seigneury resembled other land grants of the period: a long trapezoid with relatively little waterfront.[7]

Jacques de La Ferté "for the love of God" conveyed the area around the Rivière Batiscan to the Jesuits, the religious order leading the Counter-Reformation and one of the largest landholders in the colony. The Jesuits' deed stipulated the width of the seigneury – from one-quarter league beyond the Batiscan to one-quarter league beyond the Rivière Champlain – but left its depth ill-defined.[8] It may have been Champlain's reference to an aboriginal population in the Batiscan area that led to the decision to concede it to the Jesuits. According to the deed, the seigneury was intended for Christianized Amerindians, but their lack of interest and hostility delayed settlement for decades. The Jesuits' intention was clearly to create a new France in the New World, preferably with converted Natives. However, agents of the order did not perform the ritual taking symbolic possession of the seigneury until 1662.

Batiscan seigneury represented one of the larger land grants in the colony. Nonetheless, the exact boundaries were not immediately defined. In 1667 the Jesuits claimed, in vague fashion, ownership of "a space of land between the Rivière Batiscan and the Rivière Champlain."[9] Ten years later it was acknowledged that the breadth consisted of two leagues of river frontage from the east bank of the Rivière Champlain to a quarter league beyond the Rivière Batiscan.[10]

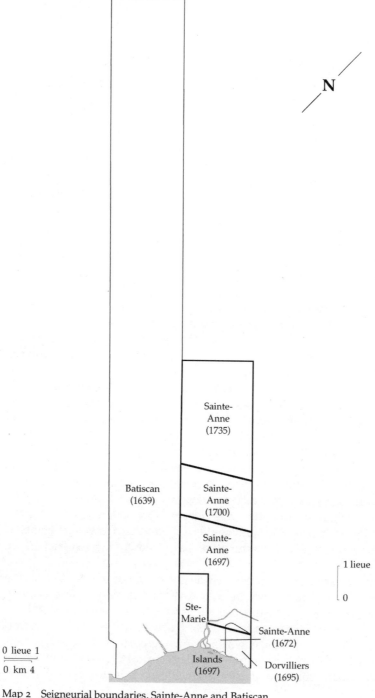

N

Sainte-
Anne
(1735)

Batiscan
(1639)

Sainte-
Anne
(1700)

Sainte-
Anne
(1697)

1 lieue

0

Ste-
Marie

Sainte-Anne
(1672)

Islands
(1697)

Dorvilliers
(1695)

0 lieue 1

0 km 4

Map 2   Seigneurial boundaries, Sainte-Anne and Batiscan

The seigneury extended twenty leagues into the interior, representing some 282,240 arpents (one arpent equals .342 hectares). Batiscan did not appear in the colonial census of 1663, but many settlers received land grants in the following decade.[11] According to the seigneurs, confirmed deeds of settlement had been delayed by two main factors, the Iroquois menace and the absence of established authority – "having no regular or established form of justice in the area."[12] From the beginning, European settlement required the authority of the colonial state.

Changes in royal policy account for the difference in size of the concessions of Batiscan and Sainte-Anne. After Louis XIV assumed direct control of the colony in the 1660s, he expressed the desire to limit the size of seigneurial grants and to curtail the granting of seigneuries to religious orders. The details of the granting of Île Sainte-Anne to Michel Gamelain, probably in 1666, are not known,[13] but it is clear that the seigneury extended over only a tiny area. Gamelain used this property to establish a fur-trade post, but he nonetheless did concede some land on the island.[14]

Intendant Jean Talon pursued the king's policy more thoroughly, granting smaller seigneuries, many of them to officers of the Carignan regiment.[15] This desire to facilitate the creation of a noble military-seigneurial class led to Talon's approval of the purchase of Gamelain's land by Edmond de Suève and Thomas de Lanouguère. In 1672 the intendant officially recognized the purchase and further conceded land to a depth of one league between the Rivière Sainte-Anne and the seigneury of Grondines to the two noble officers. As he stated, this grant was given "in consideration of the good, useful, and praiseworthy services that they have rendered to His Majesty in different places, both in Old France and in New France since they passed to the latter on His Majesty's order, as well as in consideration of the services that they intend to render in the future."[16] The intendant explicitly justified the officers' status as seigneurs by mentioning their service to the monarch. Members of the de Lanouguère family subsequently carved out a long career of service to their king, regardless of the throne on which he sat.

The co-owners of Sainte-Anne divided the seigneury into two distinct sections. In 1695 de Suève willed his half to Edmond Chorel de Champlain, who passed it into the hands of his brother, François Chorel d'Orvilliers. As in the western part of Sainte-Anne, the seigneurial family names over time came to identify the area. However, the seigneurs who owned the eastern section did not reside there. The d'Orvilliers family lived principally in Champlain seigneury during the French regime, and subsequent seigneurs of Sainte-Anne Est in the early nineteenth century were also absentee owners: Moses Hart, a merchant in Trois-Rivières, and Pierre Charest, a merchant at Saint-Joseph de Soulanges.[17]

From time to time boundary disputes set the seigneurial families of the two parts of Sainte-Anne against each other, but by the 1730s it was clear that de Lanouguère's son, Pierre-Thomas Tarieu de La Pérade, enjoyed greater local prominence. He and his mother had successfully petitioned for the extension of the original boundaries in 1697, 1700, and 1735.[18] The two smaller fiefs on either side, Dorvilliers to the east and Sainte-Marie to the west, found themselves bounded on the north by the expanded seigneury. By 1735 Sainte-Anne seigneury encompassed some sixty square leagues. Although the Tarieu de Lanaudière family was by no means always present at its seigneury, it seems to have participated actively in local issues. Like the Jesuits in Batiscan, its members exercised their seigneurial privileges at certain times and provided a link to the world of the colonial state.

Hierarchy in the Landscape

In contrast to the aboriginal occupation of the territory, the French landholding system entailed a hierarchical view of society. The king, in whom ultimate title rested, distributed tracts of land to seigneurs and preserved certain rights on that land, particularly concerning minerals and timber. The seigneur in turn distributed lots to tenants (*censitaires*) but placed limits on the tenants' control of their property.

When the seigneurs began to distribute land in their seigneuries, it was of course impossible for them to know that immigration would remain negligible over the next century. They could not know that future population growth and the concomitant increase of their seigneurial revenues would depend almost exclusively on natural demographic trends. Therefore in an examination of the way in which seigneurs preferred their landscape to take shape, the earliest years of French settlement are the most revealing.

The seigneurs' attempts to structure their space appear most clearly in their decisions concerning manors, mills, and churches. In both Batiscan and Sainte-Anne the early seigneurs first directed their proprietorial interest towards small islands in the St Lawrence, perhaps because these were more defensible. In Batiscan the *aveu et dénombrement* (list of landholdings) of 1677 designated Île Saint-Éloi, along with a nearby concession on the mainland, as the "demesne and seigneurial manor."[19] The first windmill, constructed in 1668, and the parish church were erected nearby on the mainland. Since this tract of land lay in the middle of the concessions along the St Lawrence, we can speculate that the Jesuits attempted thereby to provide a symbolic centre for the early seigneury, one dominated by the religious power of the church, the practical economic functions of the windmill, and the legal authority of the seigneur. An early deed of concession referred to this area as "le village de batiscan," which, given the low density of settlement at that date, represented more a wish than a reality.[20]

In Sainte-Anne, Michel Gamelain first granted concessions on Île Saint-Ignace, at the mouth of the river. He reserved Île des Plaines for himself, and over time, subsequent seigneurs regained most of Île Saint-Ignace for themselves.[21] These islands would remain in the hands of the seigneurs for the next century and a half, but they chose to establish their manor on the mainland. Unlike Batiscan – or for that matter, neighbouring Sainte-Marie and Dorvilliers – none of the habitants' concessions fronted on the St Lawrence. In Sainte-Anne the seigneurs reserved this privilege to themselves, establishing their manor a short distance away from the river and only sharing the frontage with a common.[22] Consequently, from the perspectives afforded by the rivers, the seigneurs of Sainte-Anne dominated their landscape: anyone sailing along the north shore of the St Lawrence or travelling up the Sainte-Anne would first come into view of seigneurial lands. The Lanouguères enjoyed the clearest view of the St Lawrence from their land, while the principal axis for the habitants' concessions would be the Rivière Sainte-Anne.[23]

The seigneurs of Sainte-Anne also encouraged the founding of a village. Disputing the location of the parish church with the seigneur of adjacent Sainte-Marie, they were ultimately able to establish the church on the east bank of the river.[24] In 1691 de Suève granted to the parish land for a church and a presbytery and permitted the construction of a village on the remaining property, transferring the rents for this land to the church.[25] By the time of James Murray's 1760 map, a rather diffuse village had taken shape, largely to the south of the parish church.[26] It probably owed its existence in part to chance: it served as an important relay post along the royal road, one day's journey from Quebec. In general, the habitants in both Sainte-Anne and Batiscan avoided dense settlement.

Given the fact that Lanouguère, de Suève, and the Jesuits could not have known how slow the rate of settlement would be, we must speculate as to the nature of the ideal landscape that they wanted to establish. It was one in which the seigneurs wished to occupy central and strategic places. From the land that they maintained as a demesne, they could closely watch over the development of their respective seigneuries. The Jesuits' control centred around the church and the mill; that is, it was based on both religion and economy. The lay seigneurs of Sainte-Anne dominated the view of the St Lawrence and therefore the access to the external world.

After Gamelain's initial, and short-lived, focus on fur-trading activities, subsequent seigneurs turned their attention to a local agrarian economy. But the early attempts to structure the landscape illustrate their desire to assert their ascendancy and reveal the symbolism of land distribution.

SEIGNEURS AND THE STATE

The Lanaudière Family

The local elite ensured the connection of their society to the external world: seigneurs, priests, local state officials (judges, notaries, bailiffs, and militia captains), and military officials all played a role, but in Sainte-Anne the seigneurs enjoyed pre-eminence during the French regime. The colonial state relied on this noble elite to represent it in rural areas and provided privileged access to patronage and favours. For the Tarieu de Lanaudière family, this treatment persisted into the British regime.

For many seigneurial families, military commissions and concomitant fur-trade privileges provided the economic basis of their status. The Lanaudières always remained a military family. All the adult males up to the early nineteenth century held commissions in either the French or the British army, and a couple of the women were famous for their exploits with firearms too.[27] Through the five generations of Lanaudières who owned Sainte-Anne, the family profited from its connections to governing officials to obtain trade licences and other lucrative privileges.

After Sainte-Anne was granted to de Suève and Thomas de Lanouguère, the former managed the seigneury while the latter, with Governor Louis de Buade de Frontenac's support, participated in the fur trade and exercised the military command in Montreal.[28] From an early date the seigneurs defended their rights; in 1673 they appealed to their seigneurial judge to force their tenants to pay their dues.[29] After his death in 1678, Lanouguère's widow, Marguerite-Renée Denys, assumed control of the western half of the seigneury. A 1685 census enumerated 114 residents. In 1704 Denys abandoned, in exchange for annual payments of 400 livres, ownership to her second son, Pierre-Thomas, under the assumption that his long-absent elder brother was dead.[30]

In the 1720s and 1730s Pierre-Thomas and his wife Madeleine de Verchères, initiated a number of court cases as they attempted to enforce their legal rights and ensure their social and economic prominence in the growing seigneury. In 1728, for example, they accused the local priest and several habitants of contravening the requirement to take grain to the seigneur's gristmill. The judgment in this case validated the seigneur's seizure of wheat and required the habitants to take their grain to the seigneurial mill in the future. To add prestige to the economic gain, the intendant ordered that the seigneur should serve as arbiter in any disputes over measurement.[31] In other cases, the family sought confirmation of its exclusive rights over fishing and hunting and for the privilege of first pew in the parish church.[32]

During this time it appealed to the government for other concrete recognitions of its status. In 1731 Madeleine de Verchères requested, through the governor and the intendant, an increase in the royal pension that she received for her youthful heroism in defending her family fort at Verchères from the Iroquois.[33] Although Pierre-Thomas's application in 1729 for the position of chief road officer and his request the following year for a military promotion were not granted,[34] he continued to hold military posts, which he was able to use to profit from trade. Despite his activity outside the seigneury, Pierre-Thomas and in particular his wife were very active in local social relations. Their heirs, however, became less involved in the seigneury.

In the last decades of the French regime, Pierre-Thomas's son, Charles-François de Lanaudière, became even more closely tied to state officials in Quebec. Diarist Élisabeth Bégon described his wife as the intendant's "princesse."[35] Charles-François and his younger brother formed part of Intendant François Bigot's retinue, following him on his travels through the colony.[36] Charles-François, while serving as an officer in the colonial troops, earned the cross of the order of Saint-Louis in 1759. He served the governors on a number of occasions in a police capacity: compiling a roll of militiamen and requisitioning provisions from the peasantry for the sustenance of French troops during the Seven Years War.[37] He also participated in the fur trade, establishing lucrative accounts with merchants in La Rochelle, selling seal furs and oil, and importing wine and brandy.[38] In 1750 Lanaudière was granted the seigneury of Lac-Maskinongé, presumably in recognition of the successes of his military career. The official favour that Lanaudière enjoyed in the period before the Conquest confirmed his status in society, but it also drew him away from the seigneury of Sainte-Anne. The estate inventory drawn up after the death of his first wife in 1762 noted that there was no seigneurial manor.[39]

After the Conquest, Sainte-Anne might have passed out of the hands of the Lanaudière family. Charles-François and his only surviving child, Charles-Louis, both sailed to France following the military defeat. However, they did not emigrate definitively. Charles-François, like others in his situation, discovered the difficulties of acquiring a good position in the French army, of maintaining his trade contacts in the newly redefined North America, and of establishing a son who lived more expensively than he could afford. With the direct trade to Canada blocked, Charles-François pursued trading possibilities through the French island of Miquelon off Newfoundland and through Louisiana, dealing in merchandise such as cloths, nails, and sealing lines, but this venture took many years to come to fruition and proved less lucrative than he had foreseen. Charles-François's subsequent correspondence with La Rochelle merchants focused on investing his capital in securities. He hesitated for a while about settling in France, but the news that Canadian officers found it difficult to acquire positions in the French army must have been discouraging.[40]

Charles-François returned to Canada in 1762, after the death of his first wife. Two years later he married Marie-Catherine Le Moyne de Longueuil, with whom he had ten children. Over time, his eldest son, Charles-Louis, developed an interest in Sainte-Anne seigneury, one which appeared to be tied up with noble sentiments and with an assertion of his position among his father's offspring.

The father had attempted to establish Charles-Louis in a military career in the home country, though he was required to pay a high price for a captaincy in the marine corps.[41] This was not a time of his life about which Charles-Louis would later reveal many details; his nephew Philippe Aubert de Gaspé reported that his uncle did not like to talk about his European military career. "My uncle de Lanaudière ... never referred to his military career; I know that he was involved in wars on the continent, when he was again wounded rather severely ... 'I conducted in France,' he said, laughingly, 'very glorious exploits against smugglers.'"[42] Charles-Louis had returned to Canada by 1768, apparently because he was an inveterate gambler and had racked up so many debts that he had to leave France to escape his creditors. During his stopover in London he ran into more troubles and had to make a hasty return to Quebec.[43]

Back at home Charles-Louis de Lanaudière was able to acquire a position as aide-de-camp to General Guy Carleton, a position he relished. As he informed his father in 1770, "one cannot be happier than I am with my sire the general."[44] In this position, he returned to England and Europe on many occasions, during which he attempted to enhance his trading activities. But his father was less than pleased with his son's comportment, which Charles-Louis characterized as only that of any young man of his noble status. He had, he later claimed, only "enjoyed the pleasures of life and of good company, as is very natural for a young man to do."[45] His companions cost him and his father much money, and tensions increased when Charles-Louis again returned to visit his father.

According to Charles-Louis, a hunting trip with three English friends awakened his interest in the paternal estate of Sainte-Anne. The English aristocratic predilection for country estates and in particular for hunting privileges is well recognized.[46] Charles-Louis de Lanaudière undoubtedly came to share these tastes. He asked his father for title to the seigneury, which was granted to him less Île des Plaines (or Île Sainte-Marguerite) in an agreement signed in 1772.[47] Nonetheless, he did not establish permanent residency at Sainte-Anne. His activities led him to spend much of his time in Quebec, but the letters that Charles-Louis wrote from Sainte-Anne indicated that his presence at the seigneury was not restricted to any one season.[48] A German officer stationed at Batiscan and Sainte-Anne during the winter of 1776–77 remembered Lanaudière's hospitality: "Our 'seigneur' of Sainte-Anne, a relatively rich man, 'Chief Inspector of Forests and Royal Waters' and 'aide-de-camp' to General Carleton, has visited us many times with his friends, among whom were ladies of the city."[49] Despite his occasional notable appearances on his seigneury, Lanaudière paid much less day-to-day attention to its administration. He entrusted the management of the seigneury to the Gouin family. By the 1810s he was concentrating his demesne farming on sheep, hay, and wheat.[50] Nonetheless, he still maintained a paternalistic interest in his tenants.

Obviously, Lanaudière would have appreciated the steady, if not elevated, income that the seigneury provided. However, his main projects, such as fur-trading ventures, took place elsewhere.[51] But his principal field of activity was his connection with the new rulers of the colony. He was appointed to the sinecure of surveyor general of forests and rivers in 1771. He demonstrated his loyalty to the British crown in 1775 when he tried to raise militia to fight the American invaders and provided protection for Governor Carleton. Charles-Louis received his share of patronage and social recognition as a result, being appointed to the Legislative Council and to the position of overseer of highways.

Like British grandees of the period,[52] he saw the position of surveyor general as an opportunity to bend rules to his own profit. In 1778, for example, he sent a proposal to his cousin, François Baby, to cut timber from his seigneury and the neighbouring ones for sale in Quebec. Taking advantage of his position and his connections to the government, he suggested supplying the garrison in Quebec with wood: "As the government must use its authority to cut the wood – I propose this, if I can be given the parishes of Deschambault, Grondines, Sainte-Anne, and all of Batiscan – which never supply wood, with the power to command the men whom I will require for this work."[53] The government's ability to demand a corvée (required labour) would even release him personally from the necessity of hiring workers to cut the trees. He added in a subsequent letter, "in conducting government business, I must also do my own."[54] For Lanaudière, state and personal affairs were not just compatible; they were mutually reinforcing.

He and other members of the family continued to use whatever influence they could muster to support the colonial government. In the 1792 elections for the House of Assembly, for example, Lanaudière campaigned in favour of William Grant, a candidate who favoured strong British rule.[55] Almost two decades later, his half-brother Xavier-Roch presented himself for election in Sainte-Anne, an act which sister Agathe applauded in trying to convince her other brother Gaspard to do the same: "it is the duty of all men who are attached to their king to make this effort."[56]

The Lanaudière family, in particular Charles-Louis, had obviously made an easy transition to the new regime. It is possible that its members counted among the most successful French nobles in this regard.[57] In doing so, Charles-Louis adopted many of the viewpoints of the new rulers, in particular those concerning land tenure. In 1783 he attempted to attract Loyalist settlers to his seigneuries. He offered ten years free of rent and four years during which they would not be charged dues on their wheat; they would also benefit from the free sawing of boards at his mill.[58] This policy seems to have had some success, since in 1788 the priest in charge of Saint-Stanislas asked for guidance in dealing with the *bastonnais* (Yankee) families who had recently taken up land in a part of Sainte-Anne close to the chapel.[59]

Earlier that same year Lanaudière had demonstrated that the Loyalists were not arriving in the numbers he wished. He petitioned the government to suppress seigneurial tenure on his properties. His appeal referred to the desire to increase the colony's population, particularly the wish to attract Loyalists: "can we ... believe that these same people who have left their homeland to take up land in this province will give preference to our seigneuries for settlement when these are regulated by a legal system that horrifies them and that they cannot understand."[60]

In 1790 Lanaudière submitted his opinions on seigneurial tenure to the Executive Council. After drawing a somewhat exaggerated picture of seigneurial privileges, he concluded, "The honorary, as well as pecuniary duties and dues are evidently complex, arbitrary, injurious. Can anything further be necessary to induce a benevolent monarch and nation to destroy them, and to grant in their stead that certain and determinate tenure of King Charles the Second, free and common socage, which the other subjects of His Majesty King George the Third enjoy, and with so much reason boast of."[61] The printing of Lanaudière's petition in 1791 in the *Gazette de Québec* launched a heated public debate with Abbé Thomas-Laurent Bédard over the advantages of free and common socage. Lanaudière reviewed the movement of settlers to other parts of North America and claimed that if he could not alter the tenure on his lands, "I ran the risk of remaining alone with my family and the few *habitans* who have settled themselves on it; and that the remaining part might lie uncultivated." Lanaudière continued his appeal by referring to the superiority of English social and economic conditions: "An english farmer discovers liberty in his very figure and air … He consumes more in one month than three fourths of your farmers [i.e., habitants], even of those at their ease, in six."[62] Of course, Lanaudière's wish was not granted. Nonetheless, he did not give up on his idea of abolishing seigneurial tenure on his lands.

In the meantime he defended his seigneurial privileges, for example, justifying his rights over the Sainte-Anne ferry by exhibiting his titles.[63] But in 1810 he renewed his petition, "having always ardently wished to hold his land in free and common socage in preference to feudal tenure."[64] In this light, Lanaudière occupies a rather singular place as an anti-seigneurial Canadian seigneur, preferring English land tenure to French.

A number of visitors to the colony met with Lanaudière and recorded his pro-British sentiments. John Lambert commented that Lanaudière "is sincerely attached to the British government, and in his conduct, his manners, and his principles, appears to be, in every respect, a complete Englishman."[65] He certainly was one noble with close connections to the government, and he tried to use these to his best advantage. As it had during the French regime, the Lanaudière family supported the colonial rulers and benefited from its connections. For instance, just as the colonial government and the English elite tried to encourage hemp growing, Lanaudière addressed an appeal to his tenants to grow the plant, offering to purchase all their production at the highest market prices.[66] During his intermittent presences in Sainte-Anne, Charles-Louis worked hard to defend the policies of the British rulers. No French seigneur could have better represented the British colonial state.

The Jesuits

While a noble seigneur's ties to the state are readily apparent, the role of a corporate religious seigneur is more complex. The relationship between tenants and such a seigneur was obviously different from the personal connections that one might have with a powerful family. Nonetheless, the Jesuit owners of Batiscan were no less implicated in the running of the colonial state. In their general relations with the colonial government, they defended a specific elitist and state-oriented view of the social order, one in which religion represented the supreme virtue. Like that of the Lanaudière family, the history of the Jesuits' seigneurial title was linked to their relations with the colonial government.

Historians have shown that ecclesiastical seigneuries were managed with much astuteness and flexibility. This generalization applies to Batiscan also, at least during the French regime. The first concessions there date from 1664, and they multiplied thereafter. The Jesuits had begun to comply with the royal edicts compelling them to see to the settlement of their lands. According to the census of 1685, 261 people lived in the seigneury by that date.

Early riverfront concessions to individuals in the eastern part of the seigneury often accompanied grants of land in the western part. "The Jesuits," concludes the most detailed analysis of Jesuit policy in Batiscan, "could thus solidly establish the colonists by assuring them from the beginning a plot on which to settle their sons." An agent (*procureur-général*) for the Jesuits' interests resided in Batiscan during the French regime. By the eighteenth century the order had taken advantage of a larger population base to enforce control over land-granting practices, not conceding land in pioneer zones until some clearing had occurred.[67] The seigneurial court, established definitively at Batiscan after 1726, provided a means for ensuring adherence to the Jesuits' policies. In 1745, for instance, the agent summoned Antoine Trottier to the court in order that he be dispossessed of land that he had worked without proper title for the previous five years.[68]

The Jesuits also constructed mills on their seigneury. A map from about 1726 depicts two windmills along the St Lawrence and a sawmill situated in the depths of settlement on the Rivière Batiscan. The Murray map of 1760 indicates the existence of a windmill on the St Lawrence and a watermill on the Batiscan. As shown by their land-granting policy and their construction of mills, the Jesuits' active role in the running of the seigneury continued up to the time of the Conquest.

Although the Conquest did not lead to a fundamental redefinition of land title and obligations in the old seigneuries, when the British

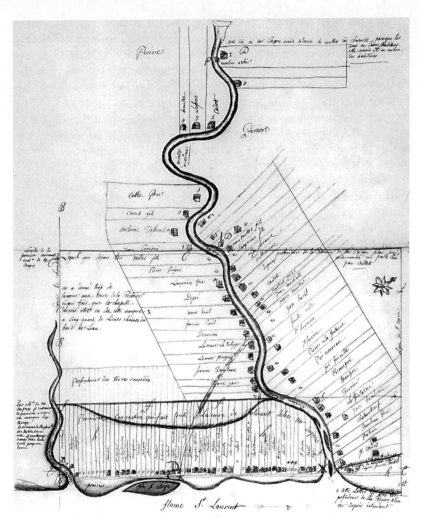

Map 3   A cadastral map of Batiscan, drawn up about 1726 to change the boundaries of Saint-François-Xavier parish. (Courtesy of the National Archives of Canada; original held at Les Archives nationales de France, Colonies G1, vol. 4G1 / NMC 0001725)

abolished seigneurial courts, they destroyed a powerful instrument for enforcing the seigneur's will at the local level. Moreover, the Jesuits suffered more than other seigneurs when Canada was lost.[69] General Jeffery Amherst, the supreme British military commander in North America at the time of the Conquest, refused to grant protection to the property of the Jesuits and the Recollets until the Crown had pronounced on the future status of those orders in the colony. British aversion to the Jesuits in particular was reinforced by the movement in other countries to suppress the order. In 1764 a royal decree dissolved the Jesuits throughout France and its colonies. Nine years later Pope Clement XIV suppressed the entire order. The consequences for Jesuit properties in Canada were complex. In 1775 the British government outlined a policy concerning the Jesuits. Although the order was suppressed, the surviving members would be provided for during their lifetimes. Ultimately, this policy came to mean that they were to enjoy the profits from their properties, but that title would revert to the Crown on the death of the last member of the order.

Meanwhile, General Amherst had requested a grant of the Jesuit lands in recognition of his services to the Crown, and King George III had promised him this recompense. Subsequent attempts to acquire the titles persisted beyond his own lifetime. His nephew and heir, the second Lord Amherst, pressed the claim in the declining years of the last Jesuit, Father Jean-Joseph Casot. Ultimately, the second Lord Amherst received monetary compensation for the king's promise, but he never acquired title to the estates themselves. In 1800, upon Casot's death, the lands previously belonging to the Jesuits reverted to the Crown.

During this period of uncertainty over the disposition of the Jesuit estates (which launched a century-long political debate concerning the use of public funds for education and the relationship between church and state), the Jesuits continued to employ agents to manage their seigneuries. The principal agent for Batiscan, François-Xavier Larue, lived in Pointe-aux-Trembles, near Quebec. In general, the Jesuits now seem to have been less attentive to the management of Batiscan than in the period before the Conquest. However, they were more vigilant than the government itself would be when it ultimately took control.

Judging by the mills, the single most lucrative of the seigneurial privileges, the Jesuits through their agents continued to attend to their property. The 1781 *aveu et dénombrement* made reference to a mill in the process of being built in the seigneury.[70] The windmills along the St Lawrence were replaced over time by watermills along the Batiscan. A report prepared at the end of the Jesuits' administration noted two mills in operation, one built of stone on the northeast shore of the Rivière Batiscan at Sainte-Geneviève and the other built of wood on the Rivière des Envies.[71] The mills apparently remained functional and at least partially fulfilled the needs of the habitants: a seigneurial agent later reported that the mills "still worked and were in relatively good order at the time of the last Jesuit."[72] In providing relatively lucrative banal mills, the Jesuits maintained a traditional seigneurial monopoly, one that offered at least a minimum of required services to their tenants.

However, the Jesuits were much less attentive in their management of land grants in Batiscan seigneury. The numbers of titles conceded provide at least a general overview of their stewardship. From 1763 to 1790 only twenty-two concessions were awarded.[73] The Jesuits' agents were no longer facilitating settlement of the seigneury.

Another measure of the Jesuits' interest in their property is provided by their collection of seigneurial dues. Information concerning the amount collected is available for only a few scattered years. In 1768 the Jesuits acknowledged receiving 1,291 *livres tournois* in rents. Thirteen years later, in 1781, different copies of the general recapitulation of the Jesuits' properties indicate between 988 and 1,285 *livres tournois* in *cens et rentes*.[74] The reasons for the discrepancies in these figures, which relate to the same document, are not clear. It is possible that land-granting policy limited the amount of seigneurial dues paid up to that point. However, by 1790 the revenues had about doubled, although the population had increased by only about 40 per cent. Batiscan earned about £94 sterling in *cens et rentes*, or 2,256 *livres tournois*. The banal mill earned another 1,200 *livres tournois*. Even with this increase, Batiscan was not a particularly lucrative Jesuit seigneury: it provided less than 7 per cent of the total receipts for the estates, much less than other properties such as La Prairie and Sainte-Geneviève near Montreal and Notre-Dame-des-Anges near Quebec.[75]

In the final years of life of the last Jesuit, the land-granting policy changed dramatically. A large portion of the seigneury fell into the hands of English-speaking entrepreneurs. In the 1790s the rhythm of concessions picked up markedly. Between 1795 and 1800, 83 concessions were granted, 53 in 1798 alone. Most of these involved small amounts of land and probably entailed the recognition of land already occupied by tenants. However, among the concessions were huge grants to businessman Thomas Coffin, made under the dubious circumstances surrounding the disposition of the Jesuits' properties. In 1795 Coffin received the *arrière-fief* of Saint-Thomas, comprising all of the seigneury north of the Rivière des Envies, in exchange for 300 sols annual rent. In 1798 he added three ill-defined "compeaux" of land, "being the remainders between conceded land, that he [Coffin] is obliged to have surveyed, and pay one 'sol' per arpent."[76]

This vast land grant, with its timber and iron resources, held much promise for profit, since Coffin and his partner, the deputy commissary general John Craigie, were able to establish a new ironworks.

Not all colonial officials were pleased with such land grants. In July 1799, before the death of Father Casot, the attorney general, Jonathan Sewell, protested against the land grant, expressing to the agent, Desjardins, "the disapprobation of Government not only of that Concession but of all others (except perhaps the common Concession en roture to Habitans of small lots at the accustomary cens et rentes)."[77] Likewise, the local agent for the Jesuits' estates protested that Coffin had begun employing men to cut wood in the seigneury without permission.[78] Nonetheless, the owners of this Batiscan land were too well connected to be in danger of losing it.

When Father Casot died in 1800, title to the Jesuit estates reverted to the Crown, which appointed a commission to oversee the management of the property. Coffin and Craigie soon acquired a new partner in the Batiscan ironworks, Thomas Dunn, a former administrator of the colony, who sat on the Board of Commissioners of the Jesuit Estates. Lord Amherst's brother-in-law, John Hale, who anxiously watched over the family's interests in the colony, resigned from the Board of Commissioners when it became apparent that the property was not likely to be turned over to Amherst.[79]

According to Hale, the granting of land in Batiscan played an important role in Lord Amherst's failure to receive title to the estates. He wrote to Amherst in 1801, "I have lately discovered a fresh source, from which obstacles are likely to arise here. a Mr Craigie, who is [deputy] Commissary General, & one of [Governor] Sir R. Milnes's chief counsellors, has opened an Iron Mine, upon the Seigniorie at Batiscan, the right of which certainly is either with the Crown, or the Seignior ... he would be ruined were he called upon to pay for the Iron he had dug, or were to pay for it in future."[80] Using their connections to the colonial rulers, Coffin and Craigie opened an ironworks at the moment of uncertainty over seigneurial title.

For their part, the Jesuits' role in Batiscan seigneury had changed over time. Following their active involvement in its administration during the French regime, the complicated post-1763 struggle over the order's estates in Canada led to an increasing indifference towards Batiscan. As title shifted from the Jesuits to the Crown, a large section of the seigneury fell into private hands.

CONCLUSION

Seigneurial control over the land was undoubtedly an important aspect of the changes in landscape. It gave the localities their broad outlines, though it did not strictly speaking determine the nature of land use. This responded more to the exigencies of small-scale, family-oriented agricultural production. Superficially, the landscape projected a seigneurial presence, even though this faded the closer and the later one looked.

Since the mid-eighteenth century, commentators have argued over the degree to which seigneurial tenure was incompatible with profitable economic development.[81] But as Françoise Noël has demonstrated, "seigneurial tenure ... could be used by large proprietors to monopolize scarce resources."[82] The founding of the Batiscan ironworks rested upon seigneurial privileges granted in *arrière-fief* by an increasingly irrelevant seigneur.

Thus the lack of attention that seigneurs showed to their seigneuries could be equally determinant as when they did try to direct matters firmly. The increasing inattention during the British regime gave more rein to local elites to exercise control over social relations. It was during this latter period that the seigneurs had the least impact on the local landscape, marginalized as they increasingly became from local affairs.

3 Habitant Landscapes

Then all is bloom, fields laugh with gaudy flowers,
No strength of leaf yet shades the budding bowers.

Ovid, *Metamorphoses*, 569

More than the theoretical revolution of surveyors' lines, back-breaking agricultural work transformed the landscape and determined the limits of local society. For the first one hundred and fifty years of European settlement, agriculture captivated local energies. It did not preclude other endeavours, and indeed, its seasonal nature freed men and women for other activities. The nature of this agriculture shifted over time, but it had relatively few New World influences.

CONTROLLING ACCESS TO LAND

Historians have explored the influence of seigneurs over the nature and pace of rural settlement. Their evidence applies to seigneuries owned by individuals as well as those belonging to religious orders.[1] Among the latter, various Jesuit seigneuries, including Batiscan, have received attention, each historian arguing that the order closely directed the development of the seigneuries.[2]

Most of these historians have emphasized evidence culled from notarial records. However, in assuming that deeds of concession are evidence in themselves of what actually occurred in the seigneuries, these scholars downplay the normative nature of these records and the ability of the habitants, within limits, to pursue their own choices of action. The seigneurs' power was at times restricted by the habitants' passive or active resistance to their wishes.

The early seigneurs of both Batiscan and Sainte-Anne did indeed try to structure the landscape. Moreover, they enjoyed a strong legal position vis-à-vis the habitants, not only because the law was weighted in their favour but also because, given their class connections to colonial leaders, they were much more likely to receive state sanction for their causes. In this way, the seigneurs enjoyed much more *potential* power than the habitants, and this ability would come increasingly into play as populations grew in their seigneuries during the French regime.

In Batiscan, for instance, the Jesuits divided the seigneury along the St Lawrence into two sections, granting land in both parts to many of the tenants. This practice aimed at rooting the settlers more firmly by providing land for their sons.[3] Later cadastral maps reveal the extent to which this policy was fulfilled by the habitants themselves. Catalogne's 1709 map, drawn approximately one generation after the initial concessions, shows only five family names repeated in both sections. A more detailed map of the seigneury from about 1726 notes only three names common to both sections.[4]

From the beginning the seigneurs faced problems in asserting their authority over the territory: a shortage of qualified surveyors and the habitants' attitudes created difficulties. In Sainte-Anne, for example, the early deeds granted more land than the islands contained. Lanouguère and de Suève had to see to the redrawing of property lines and to buy out one habitant's claim to his concession.[5]

In Batiscan, early settlement raised larger conflicts. Disagreement with the Jesuits arose in the first instance over survey lines. Faced with a number of habitants requesting land, the Jesuit superior, Jacques Frémin, placed a surveyor's chain in their hands and permitted them to measure out two arpents of frontage in the seigneury. He cautioned them that if they took more than two arpents, they would lose the surplus. In February 1669 the seigneurs issued a warning to the habitants to keep to the survey lines mentioned in their concession deeds.[6] An official survey later that year revealed discrepancies in the boundaries, and found that habitants had worked their neighbours' land and in some cases had built their houses on property that did not belong to them. A number of habitants, led by Nicolas Rivard, Sieur de la Vigne, protested against the modifications that the new survey entailed. Rivard claimed that the surveyor had conducted his work in secret and without a compass. He demanded that the old lines be accepted as they were, keeping the habitants' definitions of the boundaries. The Jesuits responded by decrying Rivard's insubordination and demanding that he make atonement to them. In responding to Rivard's complaints, the Jesuits' representative sighed, "Oh it is deplorable to have to deal with ingrates and ill-formed minds."[7] In this case, the habitants argued over the legitimacy of established property lines as the seigneurs attempted to apply stricter legal definitions.

This problem of surveying uncleared land did not disappear after the first decades of settlement. As the agrarian population spread up the Rivière Batiscan, habitants on occasion came into conflict with seigneurial policy over the layout of new concessions. In 1745 the Jesuits summoned Antoine Trottier before the seigneurial court to stop him from illegally occupying land on the small Rivière à Veillet. Trottier, the seigneurial agent charged, had ignored a number of explicit orders to stop working the land and had opposed the official survey, which would have restricted him to the south side of the creek. Trottier responded that he had occupied the land for the past five years with the tacit agreement of the seigneurs. In reply, the agent accused him of being "rebellious and resistant to the king's orders."[8] Not surprisingly, Trottier lost his case before the seigneurial court, as he did his two subsequent appeals.

This case reveals another way in which the habitants occupied the land. They did not necessarily await official deeds before they began to clear it for farms – or indeed, before they felled trees for timber. By relying on deeds of concession, historians miss this dynamic in the history of settlement. In 1746 the Jesuits demanded that three habitants provide proof that their land had been surveyed, maintaining "that they have more land than they need." The habitants replied that their payments of rents provided proof enough of their rights.[9] Two years later the Jesuits nullified François Massicot's right to a piece of land, which he claimed he had worked for the past fifty years.[10] In the 1740s the Jesuits appeared to exercise control more fully and thus overturn the habitants' attempts to interpret land ownership in a more flexible fashion.

Following the Conquest and the suppression of the order, the habitants of Batiscan enjoyed less strict supervision. On the one hand, very few concessions were granted until the final years of Father Casot's life, although the Jesuits' agent himself began paying rent in 1792 on property for which he had no title deed.[11] After 1800, when the government agent refused to concede lands, and faced with the general lack in interest shown by the Board of Commissioners of the Jesuit Estates, habitants in Batiscan began, as in many other seigneuries, to occupy land before receiving legal title. Asked by a legislative committee in 1823 how they came to terms with the slow process of receiving title, the habitant James (Jacques) Lambert from Batiscan responded: "They [the young people] go upon those Lands without any Titles, make no Buildings, and a small clearing where they raise Corn [i.e., wheat] and Potatoes on a small scale, while they await the pleasure of the Agent to give them a Title."[12] In this way, habitants exercised claims to land which were not strictly legal but which revealed a belief in their right to settle new lots.

In Sainte-Anne, habitants made other claims concerning moral boundaries in the seigneury by arguing over lands held in common. They defended their access to the common and to the vegetation that grew on it, revealing that this area was not perceived merely as livestock pasture. In 1727 Madeleine de Verchères complained to the intendant that the priest Joseph Voyer of Sainte-Anne had ordered wood cut for him on Île du Sable despite its distance of more than a league from his presbytery. Moreover, this action was directly aimed at insulting the seigneur, she claimed, as he had cut a sugar maple tree used by the La Pérades. The priest, in what seems to have been a concerted defence of the habitants' pretensions, responded that the Île du Sable had always been considered a common.[13]

Likewise, in 1735 La Pérade summoned Jean Grimard to the seigneurial court at Batiscan to have him account for the hay that his children had cut and carted away from the common on the St Lawrence shore.[14] In the early nineteenth century, habitants continued to make use of the common, but not in an organized fashion. Consequently, a number of habitants petitioned the House of Assembly to permit them to choose trustees to manage the common, "to remedy the abuses that so often occur there."[15] By this time, the argument over proper use of the common took place among the habitants and no longer with the seigneur.

Of course, such records of disputes provide evidence not only of peasant actions and attitudes but also of seigneurial vigilance. The legal system supported the seigneurs' policies, particularly during the French regime. Nonetheless, habitants on different occasions contested their ability to define boundaries, geographical and moral, in the landscape. They did not question the foundations of seigneurial ownership, only their claims to determine land usage in particular areas.

HABITANTS AND NEW CULTURES

Both seigneurs and habitants agreed on the overall structure of the landscape. The creation of a "European" landscape in Batiscan and Sainte-Anne resulted primarily from the activities of generations of habitants. The vast majority of French colonists focused on the establishment of European agriculture. In doing so, they largely ignored the Amerindian examples that lay close at hand. Colonial agriculture followed, at least in part, the imperatives of local climate, topography, and economic conditions.[16] Equally important is the revolutionary nature of the choices made, which had more to do with economic and cultural traditions than local ecology.[17]

The first step in creating a European agriculture was to deforest the landscape. Only one generation into European settlement of Batiscan, Gédéon de Catalogne noted the absence of trees along the St Lawrence shore: "the first concessions lack wood. They are obliged to procure it in the depths of the seigniory and on the south side of the river."[18] Analysis of documents drawn up to produce the *aveu et dénombrement* for Batiscan in the 1720s suggests that about 29 per cent of the area of the concessions fronting on the St Lawrence was cleared for farmland ("labourable").[19]

The relatively small percentage of farmland obscures the scarcity of wood in Batiscan. Even if much of the land remained uncleared, wood became scarce at a short distance from the settlements at an early date. By the 1720s the seigneur of Saint-Pierre, across the St Lawrence from Batiscan and Sainte-Anne, complained that absentee tenants wanted lots only for the timber: "they intend merely to damage the forest."[20] The issue was not raised only by seigneurs. In 1740 two habitants of Batiscan argued over the right to cut trees. Pierre Gouin summoned Michel Stanislas Lapellé, *dit* Lahaye, to the seigneurial court to charge him with felling trees on Gouin's land during his absence and without his approval. Gouin stated that he had tried to maintain a stand of trees (*une futaie*) on his property, "given that wood is very rare in Batiscan."[21] Local inhabitants agreed that trees were a valid issue in claims of access to resources.

In this way, trees took on both economic and symbolic value for the habitants. Wood was needed for practical local purposes such as buildings, fences, and heating. The habitants defined their conflicts over trees by referring to the distances needed to travel to acquire wood and the properties of particular tree species. In fact, disputing the right to fell timber represented one strategy for launching disputes over boundaries. Thus in 1745 the felling of trees led the militia captain of Champlain to take a habitant of Batiscan to court over a boundary dispute involving the line between the two seigneuries.[22] Six years later the seigneur of Champlain and the militia captain of Batiscan fought a similar court battle.[23] The symbolic importance of trees during the first half of the eighteenth century was clearly local; access to timber raised issues concerning local perceptions of boundaries.

The removal of trees was linked closely to family life cycles. To a large extent, each farm's landscape reflected the demographic profile of the household. The 1765 census for Batiscan and Sainte-Anne

Table 3.1
Average arpents of cleared land by number of male children in household,
Sainte-Anne and Batiscan, 1765

Ages	No. in household	Batiscan		Sainte-Anne	
		Cases	Avg. arp.	Cases	Avg. arp.
Boys 15 and over	0	112	18.1	105	19.7
	1 or more	20	41.3	8	35.0
Boys under 15	0	51	19.6	29	16.9
	1	35	17.1	34	18.4
	2	23	27.5	26	23.3
	3 or more	23	27.0	24	25.9

Source: 1765 census for Batiscan and Sainte-Anne.

provides evidence that the amount of cleared land tended to increase
according to the number of male children in the family (table 3.1). The
German officer stationed in Batiscan and Sainte-Anne in 1776–77 described the method of establishing new farms and gave his opinion of
the consequences for the landscape: "The new habitant sets fire to as
many trees as must be uprooted for arable land ... All the habitations
have already made so much woodland over into arable land that they
have splendid expanses of fields, and the woodland is already one-
quarter league removed from their houses ... The woodland therefore
appears *scandaleux*; and one often thinks that fire must have fallen
from the heavens into the woods, when one sees half-burned, half-
barren, and entirely barren trees therein."[24]

In this way, the process of settlement conflicted with the presence
of the forest, a fact that bothered the sensibilities of the German officer to a certain extent and many subsequent English-speaking travellers. In the late eighteenth and early nineteenth centuries, British
and American travellers commented disparagingly on the lack of
trees near the habitants' homes. Joseph Sansom wrote, "The trees are
all cut away round Canadian settlements, and the unvarying habitations, stand in endless rows, at equal distances, like so many sentry
boxes or soldiers' tents, without a tree, or even a fence of any kind to
shelter them."[25] The ideal landscape envisioned by this class of writers included many more trees than did the Canadian habitants'; they
themselves were more concerned about reducing mosquito populations near their houses.

Thus the habitants' appropriation of the landscape in Batiscan and
Sainte-Anne de la Pérade implied a distancing of the forest. The exemplary landscape for these farmers was open and flat. In this, it did not
differ much from the ideal landscapes of the French administrators

and seigneurs, though both would have appreciated a more central-
ized human population. Of course, this ideal found a justification in
the extensive agriculture which the habitants practised. The requirements of this use of the land explain Joseph Trepanier's statement to a
legislative committee in 1823: "There are few better Lands than the
Waste Lands in the Seigniory of Batiscan, they are perfectly level."[26]

The replacement of native species by imported ones is apparent
both in the distancing of the forest and in the selection of crops. With
the important exception of the sugar maple tree, over which seigneurs tried to assert their control,[27] the typical habitant seems to have
had little use for plants native to the continent.[28] Having removed the
indigenous foliage from the farm landscape, the settlers quickly filled
it with new elements. They built houses and fences and dug ditches,
in asserting the changes they wished to impose. They also repopu-
lated the land with European plants and animals.

Apart from certain garden vegetables, such as squash and some
beans, the only food crop native to North America which was
adopted by the habitants was maize. Potatoes returned to the continent after their introduction to Europe. All the other crops recorded
by census takers (wheat, barley, rye, buckwheat, and flax) were imported species brought along with European farming techniques (tables 3.2 and 3.3). Only maize offered an alternative foodstuff to the
European crops. Yet in Sainte-Anne the volume of maize grown never
represented more than 8 per cent of the total amount of wheat produced. In Batiscan, with the exception of two years (1726 and 1727),
the proportion of maize to wheat production remained less than 3 per
cent.[29] In both seigneuries the ratio, never large to begin with, declined over time. Agriculture was destined to become increasingly
European in inspiration. Establishing the supremacy of Old World
staples was an historical process followed in many New World European settlements.[30]

European animal species represented a third element of the peasant
landscape of Sainte-Anne and Batiscan. In the first years of settlement, native species of animals undoubtedly formed a large part of
the habitants' diet. In 1668, for example, the surgeon Louis Pinart was
willing to accept moose and pigeons as payment for treating the
former soldier and habitant of Batiscan Jean Larieu Lafontaine.[31]
However, by deforesting the land near their settlements, the habitants
destroyed the natural habitats of many of the native species. Although they obviously continued to hunt and trap some animals,
their diet soon relied much more on livestock. In 1707, a little more
than one generation after the first agrarian settlement of the area,
Noël Trottier La Bissionnière sued Pierre Retou for payment of the

Table 3.2
Crops harvested in Batiscan, 1692–1831 (in *minots* unless indicated in livres [L])

Year	Wheat	Oats	Peas[1]	Maize	Flax	Tobacco	Hemp	Barley	Potatoes
1692	4,744	590	880	91					
1695	6,709	492	1,173	66					
1698	5,354	458	1,212	21					
1706	6,356	1,324	375	106	2		2		
1707	5,335	880	335	95	3		3		
1712	80,430	2,000	956	200	600L				
1713	7,827	4	4	242					
1714	4,800	520	300	62					
1716	5,000	500	300	122	2,000L				
1718	6,000	2,100	411	111	1,000L				
1719	4,000	650	600		1,000L				
1720	4,200	700	559	20	810L				
1721	4,300	800	570	30	850L	1,000L			
1722	5,200	900	580	45	830L	3,000L			
1723	5,000	800	1,000	40	900L	1,000L	300L	10	
1724	5,000	1,200	1,000	40	900L	1,000L	2,300L	110	
1726	6,500	1,250	1,100	500	1,200L	8,000L	800L	50	
1727	6,600	1,300	1,188	515	1,950L	10,000L	3,800L	60	
1730	5,250	960	800	20	1,000L	2,500L	3,000L	10	
1732	5,930	1,130	1,090	40	1,260L	2,840L	1,400L	20	
1736	11,430	3,100	600	20	2,000L	4,500L	2,800L		
1737	6,430	4,000	200	20	2,000L	2,000L			
1739	13,000	5,000	1,000	60	3,000L	3,500L			
1765[5]	(1,351	(822	(213						
1783	3,851	2,746	483						
1831[6]	18,671	23,657	6,722	120				684	41,747

Sources: Censuses of French and British regimes.
Note: The crop totals refer to Batiscan seigneury and represent the totals for the parishes of Saint-François-Xavier, Sainte-Geneviève, and Saint-Stanislas for the censuses of the British regime.
1 "Pois et menus grains" (during the French regime).
2 Flax and hemp combined, for 3,250 L.
3 Flax and hemp combined, for 1,700 L.
4 Oats and Peas added together, for 2,350 minots.
5 The amount sown only is indicated.
6 Also 3,283 minots of buckwheat and 263 minots of rye.

foodstuffs and other goods that he had supplied over the previous few years following a deed of gift (*donation entre vifs*). The largest single item in the inventory was brandy, but a number of different food items were listed. Of the 191 livres, value of food that La Bissionnière claimed to have provided, only 12 per cent consisted of game and fish: pigeons, ducks, Canada geese, bears, eels.[32] The geese, pigeons, and ducks were all birds that would have landed close to the shores

Table 3.3
Crops harvested in Sainte-Anne, 1692–1831 (in *minots* unless indicated in livres [L])

Year	Wheat	Oats	Peas[1]	Maize	Flax	Tobacco	Hemp	Barley	Potatoes
1692	1,583	250	438	81					
1695	1,643	333	595	47					
1698	1,967	229	596	9					
1712	3,000	855	339	94	739L				
1713	3,365	2	2	130					
1714	3,500	1,000	500	50					
1718	2,800	450	300	100	400L				
1720	1,916	254	265	117	435L				
1721[3]	2,500	300	350	300	600L	500L			
1722[3]	2,007	375	350	300	615L	510L			
1723[3]	4,084	2,200	700	100	3,285L	3,000L	49L	50	
1724[3]	4,084	2,200	700	100	3,285L	3,000L	249L	50	
1726[3]	5,000	2,200	700	110	3,100L	3,000L	250L	70	
1727[3]	5,500	2,300	760	125	3,400L	3,700L	500L	85	
1730[4]	8,660	2,724	1,126	90	3,225L	959L	4,337L		
1732[4]	8,835	2,840	1,194	115	3,460L	1,108L	1,800L		
1736[4]	11,845	3,777	630	160	3,072L	6,260L	1,952L		
1737[4]	5,970	3,249	301	95	1,183L	668L	1,584L		
1739[4]	14,550	4,382	906	257	3,414L	4,039L	1,785L	50	
1765[5]	7,385	944	112						
1783[6]	4,879	4,370	408	247					
1784	3,477								
1831[7]	17,681	28,961	2,933	152				406	35,032

Sources: Censuses of the French and British regimes.
Note: The crop totals refer to the parish of Sainte-Anne, not just the seigneury of the Lanaudière family. Therefore, to the extent to which boundaries can be ascertained for the censuses of the French regime, the totals also include the small seigneuries of Sainte-Marie and Dorvilliers.
1 "Pois et menus grains" (during the French regime).
2 Oats and peas added together, for 1,620 *minots*.
3 Sainte-Anne et Sainte-Marie totals together.
4 Sum of "Sainte-Anne pour moitié" and "Sainte-Anne pour moitié et Sainte-Marie."
5 Only the amount sown is indicated.
6 Also 280 *minots* of flour reported.
7 Also 2,771 *minots* of buckwheat.

and fields of the habitants. With the exception of the bears, these were not animals of the deep forest, and even bears scavenged near human settlements. If this proportion of indigenous animals was typical, the habitants made relatively little use of the possibilities offered by the North American forests, at least insofar as personal consumption was concerned. However, their use of the rivers was another issue. Habitants caught both eels and, in January, the tommy cod, which were common in the area.

The agrarian landscape of the region created an inhospitable environment for many North American species. The German officer reported in 1777 that the habitants had exterminated all the wild game in the proximity of the settlements. As a consequence, hunting was almost impossible, except at a great distance.[33] Much more important for the settlers' diet were the crops they cultivated, the livestock they raised on their farms, and the by-products that resulted. "The whole summer, the Canadian lives on bread, which is as white as snow, on milk, on vegetables, on flour: his cattle, fowl etc he saves for the rather long winter, and at that time does he live very well."[34] Thus without forgetting the importance of fishing and hunting for small animals (hares and pigeons particularly) and for fur-bearing animals, the German officer drew a portrait of a European peasant economy, one which relied on the mainstays of a typical western European agriculture.

DOMESTIC PRODUCTION

Except during the very early stages of the fur trade, agriculture represented the centrifugal force for other economic activities of the non-aboriginal population in the two seigneuries. Agriculture provided the basis from which other productive activities could be pursued. This agriculture remained primarily, but not exclusively, oriented towards local consumption. There was no "take-off" into a heavily capitalized agriculture based upon wage labour. Nonetheless, agricultural decisions did respond to market conditions.

The censuses of the French regime provide a partial portrait of agricultural activity.[35] Throughout that period, wheat remained the predominant food crop in the area, followed in importance by oats, peas, maize, and barley. The distribution of crops remained stable during the whole period (tables 3.2 and 3.3). The censuses indicate that certain non-comestible crops were grown as well: flax, tobacco, and hemp. The census takers were by no means interested in all agricultural production: there was no place for questions concerning garden crops, for instance. As it is likely that this production was carried out by women and children and was destined principally for domestic consumption, the censuses focused on field crops, which were the basis of traditional western European agriculture and were potentially marketable elsewhere.

Grain production permitted only small and occasional surpluses, especially since seigneurial and clerical dues reduced the size of any surpluses. Most households raised a small number of horses, cattle, sheep, and pigs (table 3.4). The average numbers of livestock per household remained small in absolute terms during this period;

Table 3.4
Number of livestock per household (or family), Sainte-Anne and Batiscan, 1685–1784

Year	Cattle (bêtes à corne)		Sheep	
	Sainte-Anne	Batiscan	Sainte-Anne	Batiscan
1685	3.3	3.7	—	—
1692	5.0	5.2	—	.1
1695	5.8	4.6	—	.1
1698	5.2	5.0	.3	—
1707	—	5.0	—	1.7
1712	23.9	5.2	.2	.4
1713	5.3	5.5	3.8	2.4
1714	17.4	5.0	3.6	3.0
1716	—	6.1	—	3.2
1719	—	3.3	—	2.3
1720	4.6	3.2	6.4	3.2
1721	3.6	3.5	5.4	3.4
1722	4.2	3.6	2.3	3.7
1723	7.4	3.7	7.3	1.6
1724	7.4	3.8	7.3	1.6
1726	6.7	4.2	6.6	3.9
1727	6.6	4.5	6.5	4.0
1730	6.5	3.3	5.3	1.9
1732	6.6	3.5	6.0	2.6
1736	9.3	4.0	6.4	2.5
1737	6.1	3.8	6.7	2.3
1739	6.1	3.8	6.7	2.3
1765	5.5	4.4	3.6	2.0
1783	4.4	3.3	7.3	3.9
1784	—	3.6	—	4.6

Sources: French regime censuses; 1765 census (includes in totals "boeufs, vaches, taureaux"); 1783 "état des grains etc." (includes "boeufs, vaches, taureaux"); 1784 census for Batiscan (includes "cows, heifers").

nonetheless, some of this production exceeded domestic needs and was sent to the urban markets of either Trois-Rivières or Quebec.[36]

Despite the limited agricultural surpluses, contemporary officials saw the area as being relatively prosperous. Intendant Gilles Hocquart considered the agrarian economy in Batiscan well enough advanced in 1735 to suggest the establishment of an ironworks: "One would have the advantage of finding in the area, all the wheat, peas, lard, and other staples necessary for the subsistence of all the workers who would be employed at the ironworks."[37] Other elements of local agricultural production also imply that the area's farmers not only filled local needs but also produced for external markets.

NON-COMESTIBLE CROPS

Without fundamentally altering their focus on grains, in one important case, habitants in the area shifted their production during the French regime. This change occurred because of a government-sponsored attempt to encourage hemp growing in the colony. Linked to French mercantilist designs to find a cash crop, in this case one which supplied rope for commercial and military needs, this policy experienced a number of vicissitudes. In 1713, for the first time, the colonial censuses listed hemp separately from flax. At that moment both Batiscan and Sainte-Anne produced small amounts of hemp. After the colonial government introduced guaranteed prices, however, local production increased.[38]

In 1720 Intendant Michel Bégon announced that the king's stores would purchase hemp at a rate of 60 livres per quintal.[39] This decision influenced the habitants' agricultural production in Batiscan and Sainte-Anne. By the late 1720s, according to Intendant Claude-Thomas Dupuy, the seigneuries of Champlain and Batiscan had become the centre of production. In 1727 he commented, "The habitants of Champlain and Batiscan have boasted of bringing in 150 thousand next year."[40]

But this production increased too rapidly for the paternalistic government officials. Dupuy suggested that habitants in this area had increased their attention to hemp at the expense of grain: "The parish of Batiscan barely grows anything else but hemp."[41] In fact, the change was not so drastic. Although according to the census, 3,800 livres, worth of hemp was grown in Batiscan in 1727, the seigneury's grain production still increased over the previous census. However, the amount of grain produced did drop in the early 1730s. That this emphasis on a commercial crop altered the nature of local agriculture was illustrated in the parish priest's complaints concerning his tithe revenue. By 1731 Bishop Pierre-Herman Dosquet informed the minister that the encouragement of hemp had had a negative impact on the subsistence of certain local priests: "There are even some parishes which in other times did not have a supplement [for the priest], and which really need one today, such as Lachine, Batiscan, Champlain, etc. The reason for this is either because the land is worthless and has been overworked, or because instead of wheat the settlers grow hemp and tobacco."[42] The intendants lowered the price for hemp to 40 livres in 1728 and to 25 in two years later. After 1734 the colony stopped exporting the product.[43] Part of the reason for the reduction in subsidies lay in the quality: French officials claimed that Canadian hemp was not prepared according to the proper methods.[44]

As a result of the declining fixed prices, production dropped in the 1730s in the two seigneuries. But in 1733 Intendant Hocquart informed the minister that, although the price reductions had discouraged many farmers, some habitants of Sainte-Anne had maintained their crops.[45] The censuses of 1737 and 1739 report no hemp in Batiscan, but the intendant noted that in that seigneury and its neighbours, "The cultivation of hemp is maintained as usual."[46]

In the 1740s, a period for which there are no censuses, production continued in Batiscan, thanks to the attention that the intendant focused on the area. By 1743 he could report that a local agent's encouragements had led the habitants of Champlain and the neighbouring seigneuries to produce high-quality hemp. But this activity was short-lived. In 1746 the intendant commented that hemp production had diminished because of high wheat prices.[47] Three years later Intendant François Bigot explained that the habitants had been discouraged by the reduction in subsidies. He added that they found tobacco a more attractive crop because of labour considerations: "this crop does not require as much attention."[48]

In this way, the habitants of Batiscan and Sainte-Anne responded to government subsidies for hemp production between the 1720s and the 1740s. They participated in a market-oriented economy not defined merely by local use values. Unlike flax and tobacco, which could also represent cash crops, hemp had few local uses outside its commercial value. The experience of these seigneuries demonstrates both the importance of state policies and the integration of the local economies into the colonial sphere.

This experiment with the cultivation of hemp is also interesting because the crop is a relatively labour-intensive one. Like flax, it requires much extended treatment before it is delivered to market: it must be retted and dressed. Government officials were pessimistic about the possibility of increasing the production of hemp because so much labour was required. Some suggested that African slaves be introduced into the colony for that purpose: "this crop cannot be strongly enough established in Canada for export to France unless Negroes are introduced."[49] When production did increase, a shift in domestic labour patterns was probably involved. Men undoubtedly contributed in the harvesting, but it is likely that women and children performed much of the preparation. This was the view of Intendant Dupuy, who explained the advantages of hemp in 1727: "The habitants can grow it in many types of inferior soil and occupy their wives and children in the work."[50] It was also Governor James Murray's assumption in the 1760s. He recommended an emphasis on hemp and flax production because "This will be one means of employing the

Women and Children during the long winters." Further, these crops would encourage the consumption of larger amounts of British manufactured goods since preparing the products for export would "divert them from manufacturing coarse things for their own use."[51]

However, after the Conquest, British officials had little success in promoting hemp production, and the habitants of the area continued to wear their homemade clothes. The German officer noted with some exaggeration, "The Canadian makes almost everything that he wears."[52] Nonetheless, various government officials and supporters attempted to encourage hemp growing again.[53] On behalf of the government to which he was so close, Charles-Louis de Lanaudière was particularly active in this regard in his seigneuries of Sainte-Anne and Lac-Maskinongé. In 1802 he appealed to his tenants to grow the crop. Praising Lanaudière's "public spirit," the editor of the *Gazette de Québec* published his address two months later. Lanaudière predicted that the price of wheat would fall in the wake of the expected peace treaty with France, and he encouraged his tenants to grow hemp on a half arpent of land, or even an eighth or a sixteenth. He offered to show them his hemp farms and to purchase the farmers' crops "at the highest price which will be offered to you ... knowing that many of you cannot leave to carry this trade item to the cities." Lanaudière was careful not to preclude the habitants' focus on grain production. He stated clearly that he did not wish them to sow less wheat than they usually did: "continue to cultivate a crop so necessary for subsistence."[54]

In his encouragements, Lanaudière was not alone. The government purchased farms at Bécancour and near Trois-Rivières on which it tried to encourage hemp farming; the commissioners for the Jesuit estates sent one of their agents to visit the farms in 1821, to investigate the possibility of encouraging hemp cultivation in their seigneuries.[55] Nonetheless, such attempts to promote hemp production met with little success. Despite the earlier interest in the crop in Batiscan and Sainte-Anne, agricultural production was changing in a different way.

Hemp was not the only non-comestible crop grown in the area; flax and tobacco were also important. The censuses of the French regime suggest that for most years these crops were even more valuable in Sainte-Anne than hemp. In Batiscan, tobacco production surpassed that of hemp, while flax assumed a lesser significance. The markets for these products are not known, and they may have been grown mostly for local use.[56] In 1762 tobacco was still listed as one of the main crops in the two Batiscan parishes.[57] Women and children probably played significant roles in the care and preparation of these two crops as well.

In the early nineteenth century John Lambert claimed that women and children were in charge of growing tobacco.[58] Flax was processed in a similar way to hemp. Women's productive activity was therefore linked at certain times to external markets.[59] Nonetheless, women's market-oriented work remained on the farm, unlike that of men, some of whom travelled great distances with the fur trade.

In general, the evidence portrays a mixed agricultural economy during the French regime, dominated by grains, livestock, and non-food crops, all of which probably moved through colonial exchange circuits at various times. As crop production shifted in the late eighteenth century, the habitants of Batiscan and Sainte-Anne apparently entered a difficult period.

CHANGES IN AGRICULTURE

At the beginning of British domination of the St Lawrence valley, agriculture in the Batiscan and Sainte-Anne seigneuries still concentrated on grains. The farmers in the well-established parishes along the St Lawrence sowed more wheat, oats, and peas than did their counterparts in the newer inland parishes (table 3.5). The detailed census of 1765 allows a clearer view of the distribution of production within the seigneuries.[60] A small number of habitants distinguished themselves from the rest; four households sowed 30 or more *minots* of wheat. In contrast, the majority of habitants grew amounts that did not permit a great deal of surplus production.[61]

Of course, censuses do not reveal the breadth of agricultural activity. A detailed, if perhaps over-optimistic, description of local agrarian practices for this specific region during the period comes from the German officer who spent the winter of 1776–77 in Batiscan and Sainte-Anne:

The fallow produces the most beautiful pasture for the livestock, and this in its turn yields the best wheat fields ... The field, which is to be sown in the coming year, is plowed in the late autumn, and is left so over the winter. In the spring the wheat is sown, and the field is drawn with three good harrows.

Very good wheat grows in Canada, as well as fair barley and oats. Rye – both summer and winter rye – is barely grown. Peas, vetch, and field beans are likewise cultivated; and in the garden one can find white cabbage, turnips, potatoes, carrots, pumpkins, cucumbers, leeks, onions, parsley, and not so infrequently asparagus and melons.[62]

While emphasizing grains, the officer did mention one relatively new addition to the habitants' fields: potatoes. Towards the end of the eighteenth and in the early nineteenth century, potatoes, for which

Table 3.5
Grains sown per household, Sainte-Anne and Batiscan, 1765

	Sainte-Anne		Grande Côte		Rivière Batiscan	
	Number	%	Number	%	Number	% (households)
WHEAT						
0	5	4.4	0	—	4	3.9
1–9	39	34.5	5	16.7	53	52.0
10–19	60	53.1	17	56.7	38	37.3
20–29	5	4.4	7	23.3	7	6.9
30–40	4	3.5	1	3.3	0	—
OATS						
0	20	17.7	1	3.3	38	37.3
1–9	41	36.3	8	26.7	44	43.1
10–19	45	39.8	15	50.0	19	18.6
20–29	4	3.5	5	16.9	1	1.0
30–40	3	2.7	1	3.3	0	—
PEAS						
0	54	47.8	2	6.7	35	34.3
1–2	49	43.4	7	23.3	57	55.9
3–4	9	8.0	18	60.0	10	9.8
5–6	1	0.9	3	10.0	0	—

Source: 1765 census.

the commercial opportunities are not apparent,[63] assumed a larger proportion of total production. Even though growing the crop may have permitted the increased commercial sale of grains, the shift in agriculture is more likely an index of increasing impoverishment in the area. An undated document from Frederick Haldimand's governance lists the contributors to the £79 collected for the habitants of Sainte-Anne, "to enable them to purchase Wheat to sow their land to be distributed to them by Cap. Louis Guion [Gouin] according to his discretion and knowledge of their distresses."[64]

Such difficulties may have encouraged changes in crop distribution; they may also be linked to the process of local accumulation, whereby particular families where able to amass marketable surpluses and acquire greater wealth than their neighbours. Although fewer censuses were conducted during the British regime than previously, two household-level listings in the 1780s and 1790s provide more detailed evidence concerning agriculture in the area. During the winter of 1783 the militia captains conducted an agricultural census for the parishes of Batiscan (Saint-François-Xavier), Rivière Batiscan

Table 3.6
Amount of grains possessed by individual households, Sainte-Anne and Batiscan, 1783

Minots	Sainte-Anne		St-Fr-Xavier		Ste-Geneviève	
	No. of households	% of households	No. of households	% of households	No. of households	% of households
WHEAT						
0	4	3.7	12	15.8	24	27.0
1–39	44	41.1	43	56.6	50	56.2
40–79	40	37.4	15	19.7	11	12.4
80–119	17	15.9	4	5.3	3	3.4
120–150	2	1.9	2	2.6	1	1.1
OATS						
0	8	7.5	27	35.5	42	47.2
1–49	60	56.1	39	51.3	36	40.4
50–99	27	25.2	7	9.2	9	10.1
100–149	10	9.3	3	3.9	1	1.1
150–200	2	1.9	0	—	1	1.1
PEAS						
0	19	17.8	40	52.6	58	65.2
1–9	80	74.8	29	38.2	25	28.1
10–19	6	5.6	5	6.6	6	6.7
20–29	1	.9	0	—	0	—
30–40	1	.9	2	2.6	0	—
MAIZE						
0	26	24.3				
1–8	77	72.0				
9–16	2	1.9				
17–24	1	.9				
25–34	1	.9				
FLOUR						
0	49	45.8				
1–2	14	13.1				
3–4	17	15.9				
5–6	14	13.1				
7–8	11	10.3				
9–10	2	1.9				

Source: UM-Baby, État des grains, 1783.

(Sainte-Geneviève), and Sainte-Anne in which they listed the amounts of wheat, peas, and oats the habitants possessed. In the case of Sainte-Anne the militia captain listed maize and flour as well (table 3.6).[65]

Although the specific purposes of these censuses are not recorded, they probably relate to the agricultural depression that had lasted since 1779 and had led to importations of flour from Britain.[66] Given the time of year in which the lists were compiled, these data do not provide production statistics. The habitants and their livestock would have already consumed a portion of the crops, and part of the herd would have been slaughtered for the winter. Also, some redistribution of crops in payment of commercial debts and seigneurial dues would have taken place. Thus the listings indicate the remaining agricultural products held by households in early 1783, allowing certain conclusions about potential marketable surpluses.

Holdings were highest in the older parishes of Sainte-Anne and Saint-François-Xavier. In Sainte-Anne over half the households possessed more than 40 *minots* of wheat. The households of Saint-François-Xavier owned generally lesser amounts of grains. Sainte-Geneviève was poorest in this regard: relatively large numbers of households had no wheat (27 per cent), oats (47 per cent), and peas (65 per cent). In each of the parishes a small number of habitants held a sizable amount of wheat, ranging from 120 to 200 *minots*.[67] Given the nature of the document, these figures do not necessarily reflect the amount of grain these people grew, but they indicate the individuals who were able to acquire grain by other means.

In comparison, the 1784 census, for which a copy of the schedule for Batiscan exists, lists the amount of grain sown per household.[68] Here again, a small number of habitants produced a much larger surplus than the rest. However, these censuses reveal little about the changes in crop proportions that were occurring in the late eighteenth century.

Tithe estimates provide an indirect measure of these changes. During the bishop's occasional pastoral visits, each parish provided figures for the annual tithe of various crops and for the number of communicants. As these are not precise calculations, it is not a question of drawing direct comparisons to census figures. Rather, if we assume a certain degree of internal coherence in tithe information,[69] a comparison of the amounts from different years can be made (table 3.7). Obviously, the conclusions we can draw from this analysis are limited by the products that were subject to the tithe: for example, no evidence of flax or hemp production is indicated in the records. The tithe fell chiefly on wheat, oats, and peas, though some minor crops were also recorded: maize, barley, rye, buckwheat, and *gaudriole* (a mixture of peas, oats and buckwheat). Some priests tried to tithe potato crops as well. Given the limitations of the source, it is nonetheless possible to discern some elements in the evolution of agricultural production.

Table 3.7
Tithe estimates for various crops, Sainte-Anne and Batiscan, 1767–1824 (in *minots*)

Year	Wheat	Oats	Peas	Potatoes	Gaudriole	Buckwheat	Barley
PARISH SAINTE-ANNE							
1767	390[1]						
1784	350	100	50				
1789	300	350	10	150			
1798	330	250	30				
1807	380	400	50		10	20	
1818	380	400	50		10	20	
1824	450	750	50			50	12
PARISH SAINT-FRANÇOIS-XAVIER							
1768	98[1]						
1784	90	60	30				
1789	100	35	12				
1798	120	80	40				
1807	200	100	20		3		
1818	200	100	20		3		
1824[2]	100	150	30			30	2
PARISH SAINTE-GENEVIÈVE							
1768	110[1]						
1772	<100[1]						
1784	110	90	20				
1789	250	200	15				
1798	150	100	25				
1807	200	200	40	190	15		
1818	200	200	40	190	15		
1824[3]	350	300	26		4	12	10
PARISH SAINT-STANISLAS							
1807	120	100	12	70	3-4		
1818	120	100	12	70	4		
1824[3]	50	100	70		10	25	15

Sources: 1784 tithe reports in Caron, *La colonisation de la province de Québec*, 279, app. 7; others in AAQ, Cahiers des visites pastorales, 69CD.
1 Total amount of tithe given without particular crops specified.
2 Also one *minot* of maize and three *minots* of rye.
3 Also three *minots* of rye.

Potatoes represented a key element in these changes, though the tithe data for this crop are far from reliable. A court case from 1798 provides evidence concerning the practice of tithing potatoes. Priest Pierre Gallet summoned Benony Marchand to court in order to force him to pay the potato tithe for the previous two years, pointing out that "the potatoes for which the tithes are requested have not been planted in the vegetable garden but in a field where he used to sow wheat, oats, and other grains five years ago."[70] The principle was thus based on the scope of production, that is, whether the crop was grown in one's garden or one's fields. The court agreed with the priest's request.

The priests of Sainte-Geneviève and Saint-Stanislas acknowledged receiving the potato tithe in 1789, 1807, and 1818,[71] but none was indicated in the returns for 1798 (despite the judicial decision) or in 1824. In Sainte-Geneviève in 1789, 220 *minots* of potatoes were delivered compared to 250 *minots* of wheat. The same evidence reports a potato tithe in Sainte-Anne only for 1789, a year of bad crops, and none at all in Saint-François-Xavier. Although in 1817 Priest Hot of Sainte-Geneviève wanted to require that his parishioners contribute fully one-twenty-sixth of their potatoes, the bishop reminded him, "You know very well that the potato tithe is not a requirement. The extreme meagreness of your revenues allows you this supplement, and I consent to your asking for it, not as a legal or moral requirement, but as alms that good parishioners would not refuse to their pastor. As far as the quantity of this tithe, do not determine it: receive happily and thankfully that which each person brings to you, without counting or measuring and without reproaching those who bring you nothing."[72] Thus the amount of potatoes indicated in the pastoral visits is clearly a minimum. Still, for the years in which the crop was tithed, the records suggest that it took up an increasingly large part of the farmland.[73] As early as 1789 the habitants of Batiscan in particular, and perhaps Sainte-Anne to a lesser extent, began to shift their agricultural production towards potatoes. By 1831 the crop dominated agricultural production in all the local parishes.

The declining importance of wheat in the composition of habitants' crops continued in the first quarter of the nineteenth century (table 3.8). With the exception of Sainte-Geneviève in 1824, the wheat tithe per communicant declined over time. The tithe in peas also decreased; however, the proportion of oats either stayed stable or increased between 1784 and 1824. By the 1820s the priests were receiving tithes for a larger variety of crops: in addition to the traditional grains, in 1824 the priests of Batiscan seigneury were given maize, barley, *gaudriole*, rye, and buckwheat. In Sainte-Anne the priest received only barley, *gaudriole*, and buckwheat. This information suggests an increasing agricultural diversification by this time, probably linked to the exploitation of marginal lands.[74]

Thus, despite the problems with tithe and census data, it nonetheless seems clear that agricultural practices shifted over time: from the heavy emphasis on wheat during the French regime, habitants in-

Table 3.8
Tithe estimates per communicant, Sainte-Anne and Batiscan, 1767–1824 (in *minots*)

Year	Ste-Anne	St-F-Xavier	Ste-Gen.	St-Stan.
WHEAT				
1767[1]	.65	.45	.29	
1772[1]			.28	
1784	.58	.45	.29	
1789	.40	.71	.36	
1798	.41	.50	.18	
1807	.45	.67	.29	.60
1818	.40	.59	.25	.40
1824	.35	.28	.50	14
OATS				
1784	.17	.30	.24	
1789	.47	.25	.29	
1798	.31	.33	.12	
1807	.47	.34	.29	.50
1818	.42	.29	.25	.33
1824	.58	.42	.43	.29
PEAS				
1784	.08	.15	.05	
1789	.01	.09	.02	
1798	.04	.17	.13	
1807	.06	.07	.06	.06
1818	.05	.06	.05	.04
1824	.04	.08	.04	.02

Sources: 1784 tithe reports in Caron, *La colonisation de la province de Québec*, 279, app. 7; others in AAQ, Cahiers des visites pastorales, 69CD.
1 For these two years, the pastoral visit report indicates only the total tithe.

creasingly turned to less-marketable crops under British rule. The clearest example of these changes is the introduction of the potato. Certain families addressed commercial possibilities at the same time as others became more and more marginalized.

While crop production changed, the nature of livestock raising remained similar to what it had been previously. The 1765 census shows that very few habitants raised sizable herds of cattle or sheep. The German officer again provides an optimistic description of the habitant's livestock: "Stockbreeding is very good in Canada. Each habitant has his horses, oxen, cows, pigs, and sheep; also now and then on rare occasions goats. The oxen weigh between 300 and 600 pounds, are very stout, and have uncommonly good-tasting meat ... Milk and butter are as good as one could wish; however, very little cheese is made. Each habitant has numerous chickens, turkeys, geese etc."[75] In contrast to the generally small numbers of livestock owned by most habitants were the herds of a few individuals. Most distinct was the seigneur of Sainte-Anne. Having abandoned a year-round presence in the seigneury, Charles-Louis de Lanaudière's demesne farming concentrated on growing oats and raising livestock. In 1783 he had some thirty-six sheep, twelve cows, and six steers on his land.[76] Even his herds remained small in absolute terms, though they were much larger than any others in the parish.

It is of course difficult to ascertain the overall domestic distribution of agricultural roles. The head of the household was assumed to be male. However, some evidence suggests that women and children were important in agriculture. This would have been true if they only performed domestic labour and therefore freed men from these tasks, allowing them to concentrate on farming. But there is further sparse evidence on this topic. John Lambert commented that women "are also fully employed in the other parts of husbandry."[77] Isaac Weld, who expressed concern that Canadian women exercised too much control over their husbands, blamed the men for allowing them this power, because of "the indolent men suffering them to take a very active part in the management of the farms."[78] Considering that men had economic opportunities which drew them away from their farms at various points, women and children probably played larger roles in agricultural production than is usually acknowledged.

In the context of changing agricultural practices, British "improvers" turned their attention to Canadian farmers here as elsewhere. The statements of agrarian reformers suggest that these seigneuries were similar to others in the colony. Throughout the British regime, various members of the colonial elite attempted to improve the practices of Lower Canadian agriculture, and not just by encouraging hemp cultivation.

For instance, when the British gentry family the Hales arrived in Sainte-Anne in the late 1810s, they demonstrated a disdain for French-Canadian practices. Elizabeth Hale claimed, "Farming is at present very little understood here."[79] John Hale devoted himself to showing the habitants English techniques: "I am very busy here Hay making, & upon a small scale showing the Canadians the advantages of Drill Husbandry for Turnips, and of Summer Fallows. I have likewise astonished them with a Hay Stack, which was never seen here before.[80] The establishment of an agricultural society in Trois-Rivières in 1819 was intended to encourage better husbandry and crop tending. The society held agricultural fairs and competitions in the region, noting that "a few wealthy individuals are sure to carry off every premium." Only twice in the period under study did habitants from either seigneury win prizes, one for particularly fertile ewes and the other during a ploughing match held at Batiscan.[81] In 1828 the new commissioner for the Jesuit estates proposed establishing an "experimental farm" on the seigneurial demesne.[82] Agricultural improvers wanted to reform the practices of the habitants in the two seigneuries. Though not evidently worse than practices elsewhere in the colony, techniques in Batiscan and Sainte-Anne did not measure up to the reformers' high standards.

CONCLUSION

Throughout the period the agricultural economy of the two seigneuries focused largely on domestic production and consumption. This did not preclude selling products in extra-local markets: the experiment with hemp production is the most obvious example of such activity. In the British regime, farmers shifted crop production away from wheat towards oats and potatoes.[83] This choice seems to have been linked to a growing level of impoverishment in the area. Increasingly, marginal farmers and their offspring provided a necessary workforce for the nascent local industries: small-scale forestry and, for a brief time, the Batiscan ironworks.

But agriculture remained the primary focus of the economy, without ever being the only market-oriented activity for most of the local population. It was the laborious work of generations of habitant farmers that transformed the landscape into one recognizable as European. This metamorphosis should not mask the fact that within the broad rubric of western European agriculture, many different combinations were possible. And in this region, important agricultural changes occurred: a brief shift into non-comestible crops between the 1720s and the 1740s and a larger move away from wheat at the turn of the nineteenth century. By then there was a clear hierarchy of opportunity within the farming community.

4 Ties of Blood and Marriage

A num'rous issue bless'd the royal pair,
And grandsons, pledges of their tend'rest care,
Gave hopes of joy; but man by Nature's doom,
Must seek for bliss in realms beyond the tomb.

Ovid, *Metamorphoses*, 100

Around the time of the British conquest, the number of people buried in the churchyards of Batiscan and Saint-Anne surpassed that of the living, and this ratio would never be reversed. Despite the promises of a farm on the "frontier," the limitations appeared early.

In agrarian societies the contours of experience are defined by demographic growth. In spite of the French authorities' earlier beliefs that immigration would shape the future of the St Lawrence valley, beyond the initial wave of settlers, natural increase largely determined growth. Early in the French regime, there are already indications of outward migration from the area, of a surplus of people leaving the region over those arriving. All the sons and daughters could not expect to die in the same location as their parents.

Those who remained found that their growing numbers placed them in increasingly convoluted and restricted family networks. The church and the state played a role in controlling some of the complications involved in this process. Family ties provided the bonds that strengthened local society. For people of all classes, the family represented the principal idiom of their existence. Yet despite the consensus on the importance of family, problems could arise within; family obligations involved arguments over rights and privileges. These arguments did not necessarily reduce the importance of family ties, but they do point to the limitations that legal and popular norms placed on individuals.

DEMOGRAPHIC REPRODUCTION

The Components of Local Population

The greatest single influence on the way that local society developed was the continuous growth of the population. That growth was mostly self-sustaining; immigration was only important in the first few decades of European settlement in the colony, and during that time few of the newcomers reached Batiscan and Sainte-Anne. In the first decades after the initial granting of the seigneury of Batiscan, wars with the Iroquois rendered settlement impossible. The intendant justified the slow progress of settlement in Batiscan and Champlain seigneuries thus: "the country being troubled then by the continual attacks and massacres that the Iroquois inflicted upon the habitants."[1] Finally, in the late 1660s a wave of Europeans began to clear land in Batiscan and Sainte-Anne. This immigration came largely from nearby Trois-Rivières and Cap-de-la-Madeleine seigneury.[2] In this way, initial settlement occurred in step with the general tendency of the European population of the St Lawrence valley to become more and more concentrated in rural areas.[3] Later, the people of the two seigneuries participated in the gradual, colony-wide movement of population westward. In the eighteenth century, immigrants to Batiscan came from the Quebec area, while emigrants left for the Montreal region.[4]

Of course, the vast majority of permanent residents of the two seigneuries were of French origin. After the initial immigration movements of the late seventeenth century, most of the locals were born in the colony. Nevertheless, some individual migrants from France and other parts of Europe married and settled in the seigneuries. These people were not necessarily marginalized in society: the merchant and seigneurial agent Dalbert de St-Agnian, from France, was a prominent example of a later arrival. A few displaced Acadians appeared in the area in the 1760s. As well, in that and the preceding decade a number of French soldiers married local women.

The occasional foreigner also put down roots in the area. A few naturalized English men and women, brought to the colony as prisoners, integrated in the local population. Marguerite Drue, Étienne Lafond's wife, was originally from England.[5] So were the master weaver Louis Black and his son in Sainte-Anne. Some British immigrants settled in the area after the Conquest. More appeared at the beginning of the nineteenth century, when a number of English speakers were employed by the Batiscan ironworks. The Reverend R. Short of Trois-Rivières reported in 1816 that there were a few Protestant families in Batiscan, "whom I visit occasionally."[6]

Outside this small minority of English-speaking people, there were other daily reminders to the local inhabitants that theirs was not a strictly homogeneous society. Many Amerindians were baptized, married, and buried in the local churches. It is doubtful that their presence implied integration with the local European population. The parish registers indicate only a few marriages between Amerindians and European settlers.

The clearest instance of racial diversity was the local slave population. Over fifty Amerindian and black slaves lived in the area at some point. The richest local inhabitants owned the slaves, the La Pérade/Lanaudière family having by far the largest number.[7] The economic role of slaves is not clear, but most likely served as domestic servants. Many of them had been enslaved at a very young age, and their mortality rate was high. Overall, the average age of the slave population at death has been calculated at 19.3 years.[8] Mistreatment was probably part of the cause; for example, the Pawnee Jacques ran away from La Pérade to escape beatings.[9] At least two of the Amerindian slaves married Europeans. Jean-Baptiste Courchaîne, *dit* Pichoux, married Marguerite Lafond, *dit* Mongrain, in 1710.[10] Pierre Chauvet, *dit* Lagerne, eloped with La Pérade's slave Madeleine in 1726.[11] A number of other slaves bore children to unnamed fathers.

Thus, although the population was by a wide margin of French origin, there was a small Amerindian and British presence in this French-Canadian heartland. At no time was it an entirely ethnically homogeneous population.

Population Growth

Despite occasional migrations into the seigneuries, "natural" demographic movements alone can account for the entire increase in population. The population curves for Batiscan and Sainte-Anne, drawn from the various censuses of the French and British regimes, show rather steady growth throughout the period (figure 4.1). Census figures provide evidence of a high level of net out-migration during the French regime from these relatively prosperous rural seigneuries (table 4.1).[12] During the period of economic change between 1790 and 1825, both seigneuries again experienced a net loss in population, though at a lower rate than during the French regime.

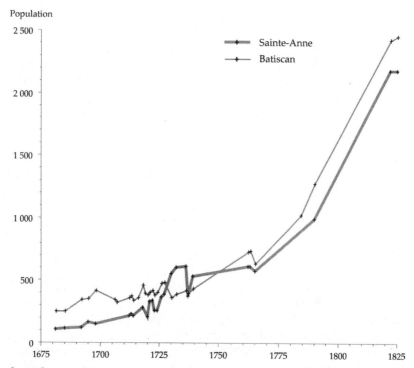

Population

Source: Censuses of the French and British regimes. For a detailed list, see Coates, "The Boundaries of Rural Society," 440.

Figure 4.1   Population in Sainte-Anne and Batiscan, 1681–1825

External events impinged upon local conditions. Even though the region was not the site of any battles during the Seven Years War, the demographic impact is unmistakable. A noticeable rise in the number of burials in the parishes demonstrates the dire local experience of the war.

Population growth resumed after the end of the conflict. If natural population growth outstripped the economic capacity of the two seigneuries, we would expect to see signs of impoverishment and demographic difficulties. The data provide some confirmation for this hypothesis, as the numbers of burials fluctuated in step with crop failures or epidemics. But the economic difficulties illustrated by the changes in crop composition in the early nineteenth century did not lead to absolute destitution. Still, locals commented negatively on the changes they were experiencing. By the late eighteenth century, in the two seigneuries as elsewhere, habitants experienced greater difficulty in establishing their children on new lands.

Table 4.1
Natural growth (births minus deaths) between censuses and estimated net migration, Sainte-Anne and Batiscan, 1681–1825

	Sainte-Anne			Batiscan		
Year	Census	Total growth[1]	Net migration[2]	Census	Total growth[1]	Net migration[2]
1681	108			261		
		945			1,083	
1765	578		−475	642		−702
		—			269	
1784	—			1,027		+116
		441			159	
1790	991		−28	1,281		+95
		1,333			1,665	
1825	2,175		−149	2,454		−492

Sources: Manuscript censuses and parish registers.
1 Total baptisms minus total burials between census dates.
2 Total growth plus first census total minus end census total.

Household Size

Testifying before a committee of the House of Assembly in 1823, habitants spoke of the prospect of impoverishment. François Ayotte of Saint-Stanislas warned of the consequences of restricting new land grants: "Fathers of families are often under the necessity of dividing their Lands, whereby they were [sic] reduced to poverty." Joseph Trepanier of the same parish suggested another outcome: "many young persons remain at home with their father and mother, and do not venture to marry because they have no Lands."[13] These community representatives defined increasing household size as an indication of economic difficulties.

Although the largest households were often evidence not of poverty but of wealth, in general, we can hypothesize that an increase in the average number of people per household suggests a corresponding difficulty in establishing one's offspring. As table 4.2 shows, the average number of people per household increased from census to census. For the two censuses where comparisons between the Batiscan parishes are possible, the younger parishes had smaller average households than the older ones.

In this way, the 1825 census returns provide corroboration for the habitants' arguments. The average number of people per household was 5.6 in Sainte-Anne, 6.4 in Saint-François-Xavier, 6.0 in

Table 4.2
Average size of household, Sainte-Anne and Batiscan, 1681, 1765, 1784, and 1825

Year	Sainte-Anne	Batiscan	Batiscan parishes		
			St-F.-X.	Ste-Gen.	St-Stan.
1681	4.9	4.9			
1765	5.2	4.9	5.3	4.7	
1784		5.3			
1825	5.6	6.1	6.4	6.0	5.7

Source: Nominative censuses.

Sainte-Geneviève, and 5.7 in Saint-Stanislas. The habitants of Saint-François-Xavier and Sainte-Geneviève were experiencing difficulty establishing their young on new concessions. Saint-Stanislas and the northern part of Sainte-Anne seigneury (actually part of Saint-Stanislas parish) were still in relatively early stages of development, and the situation was not as critical there. It was becoming more difficult for the habitants of the region to reproduce their way of life. As households grew larger and young men and women remained dependent on their parents for longer periods, hierarchical relations within the family were strengthened.

SOCIAL REPRODUCTION

The Family Idiom

Thus, by the beginning of the nineteenth century, demographic expansion had outstripped local abilities to absorb growth. However, in a different sense the people of Batiscan and Sainte-Anne were more successful in reproducing their society. Before the opening of schools in the late 1820s provided a place for extra-familial socialization, the family remained the primary institution.[14] At all levels, it provided the framework within which people composed their economic and social strategies and attempted to ensure stability from one generation to the next. However, the consensus on the importance of family ties did not preclude a number of arguments within and between families, as well as conflicts with the church over legitimate conjugal relations.

The belief in family bonds is a key element in explaining why insults were taken so seriously in this society. The court case that followed the public defamations of Madeleine de Verchères and Priest Gervais Lefebvre of Saint-François-Xavier parish illustrates that the image of the family and, in particular, of female sexuality could serve as a metaphor for local politics.[15] Insults were also at issue in a number of other cases. The wife of François Baribault appealed to the intendant after being accused of witchcraft, since the charge injured her family's reputation and impeded her son's marriage.[16] Michel-Ignace, Pierre, and Marguerite Dizy sued Charles Dutaux, *dit* Tourville, because "he spoke badly of their family." The case seemed to come to a conclusion when Dutaux declared before the Conseil Supérieur in 1721 that he recognized them "as people of integrity and of honour."[17] However, two years later an ordinance was issued which may have been related to this affair. Intendant Michel Bégon prohibited the singing of insulting songs in Sainte-Anne, Batiscan, and Champlain: "Forbidden to all people of whatever condition and quality to compose, spread, or sing defamatory songs."[18] At a lower level of the social hierarchy, insults were still taken seriously, although they did not necessarily reach the same courts. Martin Lefebvre from Sainte-Geneviève summoned Prisque Trépanier to the seigneurial court in 1742 claiming that the latter had accused his daughter of theft and had called her a *friponne* (rascal).[19] By insulting one member, a person insulted the whole family.

Although family honour was an important issue to be defended, relatives also fought among themselves. Nonetheless, the evidence suggests that ultimately family ties tended to prevail. In 1720 the widow La Bissionnière complained to the *chirurgienne* (surgeon) Marguerite Dizy that Dizy's cousins M. and Mme Levrault de Langis had beaten and bruised her with a stick and a bull horn. They then stole the cow that she had taken on an earlier occasion.[20] Ten years later the affair still rankled. Priest Lefebvre suggested that one of the reasons Daniel Portail had joined up with Madeleine de Verchères against him was to avenge the insult done to his father-in-law, M. de Langis: in 1720 the latter had been forced to make amends with Mme La Bissionnière for the incident.[21] In this way, defending family honour was a justification for holding grudges and for pursuing lengthy and costly court cases.

Ties within families also provided a key element in economic decisions. In a period before the firm reliance on contractual relations,[22] family considerations were vital in determining investments. Joachim Gouin lent his brother Claude 285 *livres tournois*, worth of wheat and lard for a fur-trading expedition.[23] Charles-Louis de Lanaudière invested in fur-trading enterprises with his cousin Verchères and brother-in-law Luc de Corne St-Luc.[24] Likewise, most of the participants in the Batiscan ironworks were related: Thomas Coffin was John Craigie's brother-in-law; Benjamin Joseph Frobisher married

Craigie's stepdaughter. Joseph Frobisher expressly purchased a one-twelfth share in the company for his son Benjamin Joseph.[25] Craigie justified his interest in the Batiscan ironworks as an attempt to provide for his children. He commented in 1807 that he participated "with a view of forming some provision for my growing family."[26] Similarly, the Hales purchased Sainte-Anne seigneury in large part to provide landed property for their offspring: "I cannot but consider America as the rising Country & thus our Children or GrandChildren will be very glad to have property here."[27] The family supplied the acceptable idiom within which to engage in enterprises and to justify investments.

Fighting over Property

In this sense, the extended family network could function more or less as an economic unit. This did not mean that individuals could not make claims on family wealth. In a number of cases, family members appealed to the authority of the seigneurial or superior courts for help in determining their just dues, revealing some of the logic upon which family claims could be adjudicated.

The devolution of property within families took place at different stages in the life cycle. When couples married, property was turned over to them through dowries and other legal transfers of wealth. After parents' deaths, the stipulations of legal custom led in theory to the division of property among the children. But pre-mortem devolutions of property became increasingly important during the eighteenth century, when parents made deeds of gift surrendering property in exchange for their maintenance.[28]

In the early years in Batiscan and Sainte-Anne, habitants sometimes made deeds of gift to unrelated parties. These cases illustrate both the family imagery at play and the donors' tenacity in claiming consideration for the transfer of their wealth. Pierre Retou (or Retor), who apparently never married, made at least three different contracts, all of which he later renounced. In 1688, at the age of about fifty-one, he transferred his land to Charles LeSieur de la Pierre in exchange for food and lodging. The following year he revoked the agreement, promising to repay LeSieur 400 livres.[29] In 1690 he made a second deed of gift to Pierre de Lafond, stipulating that the Lafond family would "house the said Pierre Retor with them and as them, regarding him as one of their own children."[30] This alliance with a powerful family was intended to provide security for Retou.

But apparently this contract also came into difficulties. In 1702 Retou promised Noël Trottier La Bissionnière to turn over his grain and, upon his death, his land in exchange for necessities during his lifetime. For five years of this verbal agreement, La Bissonnière took the precaution of writing down the amounts of grain that he received and the goods that he had given Retou, especially since the latter did not transfer title to the land "by a legal deed of gift which he always promised me, without carrying out his promise." But Retou was unhappy with the amounts he received, and in 1707 he complained to the intendant. Although the decision in the case is not known, La Bissonnière produced witnesses who testified that he had indeed delivered goods on numerous occasions to Retou.[31]

Michel Rivard made a similar agreement with the militia lieutenant Joseph Lefebvre, *dit* Villemure, in 1746, surrendering his belongings in exchange for maintenance in health and in sickness. Only one year later Rivard took Villemure to court to demand that the lieutenant provide clothes for him according to their pact. Villemure claimed that he was willing to follow their contract, but that he would only provide for Rivard "according to his quality and condition," arguing that Rivard should not receive the white shirts and other vestments he demanded. Rather, he would have to accept one good set of Sunday clothes and a short cloak (*mantelet*) of homespun for the rest of the week, "like all the other habitants." The judge agreed with Villemure's position.[32]

Family members also disputed the conditions of deeds of gift. In 1743 Catherine Baril, represented by her son François Massicot, summoned her other son, Jacques, to the seigneurial court. She demanded the annual payment of six flagons of brandy according to the contract of 1736. Jacques agreed to deliver three of the six flagons per year, explaining that the death of his father removed the necessity of providing the whole amount.[33]

Contracts and family ties (metaphorical ones in the case of Retou) did not resolve all future tensions. The reason for making plans "in case they [the parties] are temperamentally incompatible" was apparent in at least one dispute over a deed of gift. In January 1770 Antoine Lefebvre and Marie-Anne Morant of Batiscan sued their son for having neglected the terms of their contract made six years previously. They complained about his ingratitude, charging that he "even used violence towards them." They asked the judge to summon their son to court in order to establish an annual payment in lieu of the property transfer.[34] These last two conflicts over deeds of gift suggest some of the tensions which could exist within families. The donors' beliefs that they represented the source of wealth and that they were owed respect for that reason underlay these disputes.[35]

The death of a family member occasioned numerous quarrels over property and debts. As in the conflicts over deeds of gift, people made individual claims on property; it was passed down through the lineage, and individuals defended their rights to their inheritances, even when these may not have amounted to much. It is interesting that the only explicit statement of normative values made by a habitant before the seigneurial court concerned the sanctity of property: "according to the law, one should not take anything away from another without his permission. It is contrary to all customs to act in this way and take without permission."[36]

In inheritance disputes one issue was the prevalence of the immediate family over the extended family. Madeleine Choquette had left her immediate family to live with her grandfather. After she died, her mother, represented by her son, François Dupont, asked for Choquette's belongings. Choquette's uncle, who had taken over the grandfather's house after his death in 1731, refused to deliver them up to her mother, claiming that "her said mother never gave her anything." The uncle asked that her belongings be used to pay for her funeral and for future masses for her soul, as the woman had requested. When Choquette's aunt claimed expenses for caring for the dying woman, Dupont argued that the woman's grandfather should have been able to look after her, as she had lived with him since she was ten years old. In the end, the judge turned over the property to the woman's mother.[37]

The protection of inheritances, even small ones, was also at issue. In 1742 François Thomas purchased the wood of a decrepit barn from the heirs of Jean Baril. He proposed to dismantle the barn and move it to his property, but was impeded in doing so by Antoine Trottier, who had inherited a small part of the structure.[38] Claude Lepellé, *dit* Lahaye, tried to maintain his rights to his parents' pew after their death. He opposed the auction of the pew, hoping to pay the same amount for it as his parents had.[39] A logic based on the inalterable rights of the inheritor justified these actions.

In contrast to this clinging to rights, surviving relatives sometimes tried to avoid their obligations to the deceased, such as paying for funerals. The warden of Saint-François-Xavier parish sued Marie-Anne Adam for the funeral expenses of her husband and son. Adam replied that she was not obliged to pay her late husband's debts and funeral expenses. But in the absence of another heir willing to assume the debts, she was condemned to turn over the sum.[40]

Not surprisingly, inheritance disputes could occur at all levels in society. In the cases of two noble families, the issue revolved around the rights of the second wife. In 1740 Marguerite Jarret de Verchères, widow of Léon Levrault de Langis, complained to the seigneurial court that Levrault's children from his first marriage had made a hasty division of his property without taking her claims into account. Joseph Levrault and Daniel Portail contended that their stepmother "asks for everything and adopts all the qualities." The local judge accorded her 1,300 livres in recompense for what she had brought into the marriage, but the issue was appealed to the Trois-Rivières court and to the Conseil Supérieur.[41]

After his father's death in 1775, Charles-Louis de Lanaudière renounced the agreement that he and his father had reached three years previously. He had received Sainte-Anne seigneury as a way of ending their disagreements over finances. But based on his understanding of the legal implications of the recently promulgated Quebec Act, he argued that their agreement had been worthless: "against the Spirit and the true intention of the Laws of this province ... which very expressly prohibit dealing with the inheritance of a living man."[42] Lanaudière explained why his stepmother would have difficulty understanding his legal rights: "It is not at all surprising that a lady will not have reflected on the real meaning of the Quebec Act. Ladies are not educated to become jurisconsults."[43] Writing to his stepmother himself, Lanaudière explained his actions as an attempt to maintain his rights as eldest son: "besides Madame, I do not wish to lose my rights as the oldest son, being the only one in that position."[44] For her part, his stepmother sighed, "Crosses rise up on the footsteps of widows."[45] Although women did exercise their claims to inheritances, male privilege often upstaged their rights. At all levels of society, the attempts to maintain one's property and lay claim to one's inheritance represented the limits of family unity.

Forging Families: Conjugal Relations

Family relations thus involved a certain amount of economic conflict and strategy. Outside the sentimental ties in conjugal relations, which are almost impossible to gauge from the historical documents, marriage also represented the strategic formation of family alliances. The seigneurs and the local elite seem to have practised a high degree of endogamy. The marriage market for the colonial nobility extended throughout the St Lawrence valley in order that nobles could find spouses of similar social status.[46] The Lanaudière family provided a typical example of this practice. Until the early nineteenth century the clan always established ties with other members of the colonial nobility. Thomas-Xavier Lanouguère wedded Marguerite-Renée Denys de La Ronde, who when widowed married Jacques-Alexis de Fleury

Deschambault. Pierre-Thomas La Pérade espoused Madeleine de Verchères. Their daughter married successively three nobles, their son, Charles-François-Xavier, two noble women. All of Charles-François-Xavier's children either married into noble families or remained single. Marie-Anne, the only surviving child of Charles-Louis de Lanaudière and Geneviève-Élisabeth de La Corne, who ultimately inherited the seigneury of Sainte-Anne on the death of her parents, remained unmarried. In the 1810s and 1820s her Lanaudière cousins were the first in the lineage to marry outside the French-Canadian nobility, but they joined prominent families nonetheless: Gordon, Joliette, and Loedel. In all, the clan's marital choices were rather typical of the colonial nobility, both in the high level of endogamy in the eighteenth century and in the increasing connections to the upper bourgeoisie in the nineteenth.

The local elite also practised a high degree of endogamy, but under different circumstances. Since its members were more linked to the region, after only a few generations their alliances ran afoul of church regulations about intermarriage. The elite and other local families created problems for church and state officials.

Priests and government officials applied the laws regulating marriage practices. They faced two main problems: bigamous marriages (the arrival of potentially married men from abroad made these possible) and unions between cousins (church regulations governing marriages between relatives made vigilance necessary). Authorities were occupied with both matters throughout the period, but forbidding bigamous marriages to outsiders of dubious background became less important with time than preventing intermarriages among the locals.

Initially, conflicts over marriages arose when local women married men recently arrived in the colony. For example, in 1728 Marie-Anne Levrault de Langis and Daniel Portail, Sieur de Gevron, married *à la gaumine*; that is, they exchanged vows publicly but without authorization when the parish priest Lefebvre was saying mass. Their unorthodox wedding was not a rejection of church authority but an appropriation of it according to their own principles. It was apparently carried out because the priest had refused to marry them until Portail could prove his marital status. Given the uncertainty surrounding the recent death of the bishop, who normally provided the proper certificate, the couple probably faced a considerable delay in receiving permission. By forcing the matter, they achieved legal, if grudging, recognition of their union. To avoid such situations, the priest required a certificate of liberty of marriage for recently arrived men. In 1742, for instance, in Sainte-Anne, Claude Devaux Retor married Marie Madeleine Gendro. The groom provided assurance from Commissioner Jean-Victor Varin that "the said Claude Devaux came as a bachelor (and free to marry) from France to Canada, being listed as a bachelor with the salt thieves and smugglers."[47]

In the early 1760s, during the British military occupation of the area, the priest of Sainte-Anne warned local women not to become debauched by British soldiers. In fact, one illegitimate child had been born in the parish in 1761, and two soldiers married women in Batiscan in 1762 and 1764.[48] In addition to the temporary presence of Americans in 1775 and later of German soldiers, another influx of foreigners occurred in the early nineteenth century with the opening of the Batiscan ironworks. Some employees married local women: John Slicer wedded Véronique Elie, *dite* Breton, in 1803; his brother Thomas married Margaret Barribo two years later. The couples were married at the Protestant church in Trois-Rivières, thus avoiding potential difficulties with the local Catholic priest.[49]

But other foreigners posed problems for the priest. In 1821 the proposed marriage of a certain McKay with a woman of Sainte-Geneviève parish led to two problems. The bishop told the priest to ascertain that McKay had not been married outside the country since "his name indicates that he is a foreigner." More important, he had to put a stop to McKay's illicit behaviour with his fiancée, whether or not she was in her second pregnancy.[50] But in itself a marriage with a foreigner was not at issue.[51]

The second matter, intermarriage, especially between first cousins, caused problems because of canonical restrictions. By the 1740s and 1750s, couples were already beginning to need dispensations from the bishop for their unions. The registers for the two Batiscan parishes and for Sainte-Anne provide thirty-three cases of marriages requiring dispensation from the bishop or the vicar-general before 1765. In addition to that of the noble Gatineau, seigneur of Sainte-Marie, the other incidents almost all involved families of the local elite. A certain marital strategy seems at play in many of the marriages. Thus three Germain brothers from Cap Santé all married Biguer Norbert sisters. Other families also had recourse to this type of marriage: the Gouins (three times), the Guillets (four times), the Rivards (seven times), and the Mongrains (twice). Of course, the financial requirements to receive the dispensation may have limited this form of marriage to an elite group.[52] But there also seems to have been an attempt to reproduce the local elite through a large degree of endogamy.

The relatively high mortality levels at the time and the uncertainty of war and occupation may have played a role in these choices.

Fifteen of the marriages occurred during the 1750s and twelve in the 1760s. Furthermore, most of the dispensations for very close relatives were given in the latter decade: four sets of first cousins married in either 1760 or 1765. In one case, the woman had already borne their child a year and a half earlier.

By the early nineteenth century, the bishop's correspondence with the local priests was concerned with more difficult cases of intermarriages. When second or third cousins wanted to marry, as long as they obtained the proper dispensations, their alliances went unquestioned. In one case, a couple later claimed that they did not know they were related "du troisième au troisième degré," an assertion that did not impress the bishop.[53]

More serious for the church were the marriages between first cousins, of which a number occurred in this period.[54] A certain Massicot asked the priest of Batiscan in 1801 for permission to marry his cousin (*dispenses au second degré*). The coadjutor, Joseph-Octave Plessis, noted that the priest did not provide any good justification for the marriage, and he reserved judgment.[55] In some cases, the bishop consented to the marriages. In 1806 he unwillingly agreed to the wedding of first cousins Antoine and Mariane Frigon, while decrying the fact that Mariane was only twenty-two years old. "Finally," the bishop sighed, "I could no longer resist the insistences and the tears of a young man nor his pious sentiments towards his infirm parents and his young brothers and sisters."[56] In this case, family considerations determined the decision, though the bishop insisted that the wedding be conducted in secret.

A couple could influence the result by engaging in sexual relations. In 1811 the cousins Louis and Madeleine Normandin were given permission to marry, but only after they agreed to a formal and humiliating public penitence. After separating for three months, they were to attend mass for three weeks in a row, kneeling and holding a lighted candle in the middle of the main aisle of the church. On the last of the three Sundays the priest was to declare: "Louis Normandin and Madeleine Normandin his cousin, whom you have seen in penitence in the middle of this church for the last three Sundays, ask for God's and the parish's pardon for the great scandal that they have inflicted by their criminal relationship."[57] But even if members of a family had once received a dispensation, their wishes were not necessarily granted a second time. In 1815 Augustin Frigon asked for permission to marry his cousin. The bishop replied that he would pass the request on to Rome.[58] A year later Frigon importuned the bishop with the same request, to the latter's consternation:"It is useless to send your Aug. Frigon to me. Neither his insistence nor his folly will convince me to exercise a power that I do not enjoy. It is not to accommodate a particular family that the Church grants dispensations in the degree involved in this case."[59] Although these cases were clearly peculiar, they hint at two possible developments: a shrinkage in the choices for marriage partners and the necessity for certain less-affluent families to keep their alliances within a small network.[60]

In addition to controlling official marriages, the church and the state also played a role in regulating non-marital relations. Demographers have pointed out that non-marital and premarital pregnancies were less common among the French population in the St Lawrence valley than in the home country.[61] Up to 1765 there were twenty-seven cases of illegitimate births among the non-aboriginal population in Batiscan and Sainte-Anne. Only in one case did the mother declare the identity of the father during the baptism ceremony: the soldier Michel Bausac de Grillemont.[62] At least three cases involved female slaves; another two, servants. These women's silences were undoubtedly linked to their lack of power.[63]

The first record in the two seigneuries of an infant being abandoned is from 1747. At 12:30 a.m. on 2 September a man shouted from outside the presbytery of Saint-François-Xavier that he was leaving a child at the door.[64] This practice became more common between 1755 and 1765, as sixteen infants were abandoned in this decade. The demographic and economic difficulties of that period undoubtedly played a role in this higher rate of abandonment; the increased number of soldiers in the area may also have been a cause.

If indeed the unknown fathers were military men, imbalances of class and power were probably involved in these non-marital relations. Charles-Louis de Lanaudière later confided to his cousin what were probably a typical nobleman's sentiments: "I suppose that you have not lost the ordinary custom when one is not with one's wife, one finds another."[65] But the problems of non-marital sexual relations and concubinage that the church addressed in the late eighteenth and early nineteenth centuries occurred farther down the social scale. The problem in these cases was not only the circumstances themselves but the degree to which they were publicly known.

In 1820 Ignace Grimard, who had been living with his partner, wanted their union blessed by the church. The priest was told to refuse to marry them until they proved that they had ceased to live in concubinage and that they were willing to make a public apology.[66] Fifteen months later the bishop learned that Grimard had not ceased the practice: "He had pretended to stop living in concubinage, even while continuing to do so." Again, the priest was told to demand two months of separation and a public apology.[67] When a man "abducted" a woman, apparently with her consent, the couple was required to apologize publicly for the scandal before a wedding could take place.[68]

Even the appearance of unseemly relations had to be avoided. A widower was supposed to cease living with a girl, even though their relationship was innocent: "he should send her away as soon as the public is offended."[69] Likewise, a man and his live-in domestic servant could not be married unless they separated for a decent interval after the publication of the bans.[70] The overt nature of these unorthodox relationships made them unacceptable.

When circumstances were less widely publicized, the issues could be handled more discretely. A woman in Sainte-Geneviève parish "who secretly committed fornication a number of times" was permitted to receive communion "on the understanding that she has entirely given up the practice and will not be tempted again."[71] A man who had slept with a certain woman and subsequently married her sister was obliged to have the marriage rehabilitated. But what to do about the bride, who might not know of her sister's fornication? If she did know, the priest was to rehabilitate the marriage in private; if not, in order to avoid scandalizing her, the groom would have to obtain her marriage commitment surreptitiously: "he will skillfully obtain her consent anew, without allowing her to suspect his sin."[72] Although these incidents obviously frustrated the priests, it is more telling that, regardless of the relationships they maintained, these people wanted the church to legitimize their unions. They all eventually aspired to the public recognition of their family ties.

The courts undoubtedly also played a role in controlling conjugal relations. In 1808 Angélique Deveau of Sainte-Anne sued François Nobert of Sainte-Geneviève for support of their child. The court ordered Nobert to pay ten pounds to the plaintiff.[73] In 1823 the seigneur of Sainte-Marie sued P. St-Arnault for having eloped with his daughter.[74] Judicial records, like priests' correspondence, illustrate the attempt to enforce the boundaries of family relations. In general, the local inhabitants did not reject officially sanctioned unions; rather, despite the problems their relationships might pose, they generally attempted to acquire the blessings of the church.

Forging Ties: Godparentage

If marriages represented strategic links between families, so did the choice of godparents. On the basis of anthropological findings,[75] historians are turning to the examination of the institution of "fictive" (or spiritual) kinship. A study of village life in early modern

Württemberg points out the usefulness of these alliances in forging vertical relationships.[76] One historian of colonial New York sums up the possibilities of this analysis: "The ties between the natural parents and the godparents can be structured vertically, thereby linking together individuals of differing status and power or horizontally, binding members of the same group or class."[77] In other words, by studying godparentage, we can analyze the types of alliances that families wanted to make, whether they were primarily inter-class or intra-class connections. The advantage of this analysis, over even the study of marriage partners, is the relatively unrestricted choices that people could make. While wealth differences may have restricted marriage options to a great degree, if not absolutely, the same cannot be said for the godparents. They might be related or unrelated, superior or inferior in the social scale, older or even of the same generation as the child being baptized.

Contemporary ecclesiastical and judicial authorities in France and New France recognized the social importance of the institution. According to Bishop Saint-Vallier, ties rendered future marriage between the godparent and the child impossible. Moreover, the links were not only with the child: "they [the godparents] will contract a spiritual alliance with the child and his father and mother."[78] In law, this alliance was considered important enough to provide grounds for challenging the judge if he were the godparent to the opposing party; likewise, parties could not use as a witness the godparent to their children.[79] The records show that children tended to be given the names of their godparents. More than half of boys and more than 40 per cent of girls were given the Christian names of their godparents.[80] Thus, for reasons imbedded in French legal and religious culture and social practices, godparentage was a significant institution in New France.

To begin at the lowest level of the social hierarchy, the baptisms of slaves provide evidence of the use of godparentage to forge vertical links. When the fifteen-year-old Hyppolyte, an Amerindian slave belonging to Fleury de la Gorgendière, was baptized in Sainte-Anne in 1733, his godparents were Gatineau, seigneur of Sainte-Marie, and Gatineau's mother.[81] Similar links were made in cases involving free Amerindians. In Batiscan the local elite assumed the role: Charles LeSieur, the Jesuits' agent, and Marguerite Legardeur, widow of a militia captain, served as godparents to the Amerindian Charles Pierre in 1702.[82] The noble and non-noble elite desired to reinforce local hierarchy through this expression of paternalism.

At the highest level of local society, the practice of choosing godparents was very similar, although the connotations were clearly different. Here the spiritual kin were other nobles, very close relations, or members of the local elite. When Marguerite-Marie-Anne de La Pérade was baptized in 1707, her godparents were the Chevalier de Ramezay and her grandmother, Marguerite Denys.[83] Marie-Madeleine de La Pérade's godparents were her brother and sister.[84] In 1733 Joseph Portail's uncle Alexis de Langis and the seigneurial court judge's widow served as his godparents.[85] The possibility of acting as godparent to a local noble was thus restricted to a small number of families.

Taking two of the Batiscan seigneurial court judges as examples,[86] we can see the complexity in the choices they made, given the legal rules involved. Nicolas Duclos served as godfather sixteen times in Saint-François-Xavier and Sainte-Geneviève parishes. The families with which he thus contracted alliances represented different social strata: Levrault de Langis; his Duclos relatives; his wife's family, Lafond; other official families such as Rouillard, Rivard, and Lefebvre Villemure, as well as Couturier, Perot, Adam, Leculier, and Baril. His wife, Marie Madeleine Lafond Mongrain, was godmother to essentially the same families: Lafond, Moreau (a grandson), Rivard, Gouin, Lefebvre, and Perot. Not surprisingly, these selections were largely reciprocal. The families that the Duclos chose as spiritual kin for their children were Duclos Carignan, Rivard, Perot, Lafond-Mongrain, Duto, and Marchand.

However, the judge's successor, Jacques Rouillard St-Cire, showed a different pattern. He served as godfather only to his Rouillard relatives (his wife also was godmother to Bertrand St-Arnould and Millet). Rouillard did not serve as godfather after he became judge, perhaps because of the legal difficulties that the relationship might cause. The couple's choices for their own children demonstrate a larger spreading of their alliances: Desbroyeux, Rivard, Guillet St-Marc, Dessuraux, the curé Lefebvre, Lecuyer, Larioux Lafontaine, and Lafrance. Still, his family and hers (Trottain) predominated. The presence of many of the local elite families among the Rouillard and Duclos alliances provides evidence of the forging of close ties within this group.[87]

For the habitants in general, godparentage provided a way of reinforcing family ties or making alliances with social superiors. In the latter case, it involved looking for the "protection" of the superior or represented greater social aspirations. For the elite, it served as recognition of their own superiority.

When we look at the population as a whole, there is an evolution in the choice of godparents over the period.[88] Table 4.3 shows an increase in the percentage of times close family members were chosen

Table 4.3
Proportion of baptisms with at least one related godparent[1], Sainte-Anne and Batiscan
(all parishes combined), 1700–03, 1750–51, and 1800–04

Years	Total baptisms	No. with related godparent
1700–03	108	41.7%
1750–51	108	49.1%
1800–04	72	62.5%

Source: Parish registers.
1 Baptisms in which at least one godparent had the same family name as one of the parents.

to assume this role: from about 42 per cent in 1700–03 to 49 per cent in
1750–51 to about 63 per cent in 1800–04.[89] This pattern suggests that
the institution of godparentage declined over time as a means of linking unrelated families. In turn, it bolsters the conclusions concerning
the shrinking of economic horizons by this period and the consequent
increase in the importance of family ties. Over time, the institution of
godparentage shifted towards more intra-family, and therefore intra-
class, alliances. Consequently, family networks were reinforced and
became more and more localized.

CONCLUSION

In this way, family boundaries became ever more restricted over time.
Just as the habitants found their economic activities increasingly focused on the local area in the late eighteenth and early nineteenth
centuries, their social ties were more confined within their family cir-
cles.

Throughout the period, the image of the family represented the
principal method for expressing values. Nevertheless, there were disagreements over the proper roles for individuals within families and
over the ways of establishing conjugal unions. Individuals contested
elements of family ties with church and government officials and
with other relatives, but they did not reject the image of the family.

There was, then, a consensus concerning the value of family ties.
Still, class differences within local society came into play. The significance of hierarchical relations was apparent, particularly in the
French regime, when the marital and godparentage choices of the
seigneurs and non-noble elite distinguished them from the rest of the
population.

Although the seigneuries under study were not among the poorest
ones in the St Lawrence valley, they were seldom able to absorb the
natural population increases. In the French regime, this problem

implied a relatively high rate of emigration from the area. During the period of difficulties in local agriculture in the late eighteenth and early nineteenth centuries, the rate of emigration slackened, leading to an increased dependence of children upon their parents. As a result, the families of Batiscan and Sainte-Anne made sense of their world by drawing smaller and smaller boundaries around it.

5 Lines of Authority

E'en as before the led the leader goes,
E'en as the steersman ranks o'er him who rows.

Ovid, *Metamorphoses*, 491

In 1737 most of the men of Sainte-Anne sent a petition to the intendant. They asked that the local surgeon, Yves Phlem, be permitted to continue practising his art. The order in which the names were affixed to the document illustrates the local ideal of the male social order: first the seigneur, La Pérade, and then the priest, the militia captains, the lieutenants, the ensign, a tanner, a tailor, and numerous habitants.[1] Hierarchy determined one's place in this world.

This vision of local society largely persisted throughout the period under study, though important changes had occurred by the early nineteenth century. Hierarchical assumptions operated on different levels, from land ownership to social relations. Like family ties, the image of hierarchy represented one important way in which the local people made sense of their world.

Hierarchy provided particular roles for seigneurs and other members of the local elite. The seigneurs supplied a link with the colonial government. Other members of the elite (other nobles, priests, and militia captains) were also important in the chain of power. In fact, this elite, and not the mass of habitants, created many of the incidents that attracted the attention of external ecclesiastical and state authorities.

The composition of the elite changed over time. Fully involved in defining local issues during the French regime, seigneurs had become more distant from those concerns by the early nineteenth century. Meanwhile, the local clergy broadened their influence, as did militia captains. Over time, the process of economic differentiation in the countryside created a petty bourgeoisie of merchants and larger-scale farmers. The introduction of parliamentary elections in 1792 provided a potential public forum for this non-noble lay elite.

MADELEINE DE VERCHÈRES VERSUS CURÉ LEFEBVRE

The Court Cases

Struggles for local pre-eminence elucidate the character of social relations. By their nature, the court cases in 1730 involving Madeleine de Verchères and the priest of Batiscan pitted two local authority figures against each other. They provide a glimpse into the arguments over local hierarchy and power.

On 22 March 1730 Madeleine de Verchères wrote to the new bishop's coadjutor, Mgr Pierre-Herman Dosquet, complaining of the actions of two local priests. She charged that priest Gervais Lefebvre of Batiscan and priest Joseph Voyer of Sainte-Anne, together with another man in a canoe on the Rivière Sainte-Anne, had chanted a lewd and insulting litany:

Sancte Sacrebleu, ora pro nobis
Sancte tout au monde, ora
Sancte voyes bien ça, ora
Sancte la grande vache rouge, ora
Sancte Mme avec ses petites citrouilles, ora
Sancte niandier [(La) Naudière?], ora
Sancte mon fils aîné, ora
Sancte Lolotte, ora
Sancte Sacrebleu, ora
Sancte Sacrebleu, iras-tu panser les vaches, ora
Sancte Touranyeux [Tarrieu?] foutu bougre ira tu voir
   si le moulin tourne, ora
Sancte le bonnet a Boilleu soubs le chevet a Mde la
   Pérade, ora
Sancte sa naissance, ora
Sancte sa nature, ora
Sancte la femme à Portail, ora.[2]

Saint Sacrebleu, pray for us
Saint everyone
Saint do you see that
Saint big red cow
Saint Madame with her little pumpkins

Saint Niandier [(La) Naudière?]
Saint my eldest son
Saint Lolotte
Saint Sacrebleu
Saint Sacrebleu, will you go groom the cows
Saint Touranyeux blasted bugger will you go see if the mill is working
Saint Boilleu's bonnet under Madame la Pérade's bed
Saint her (his) birth
Saint her (his) nature
Saint Portail's wife

Verchères requested that the acting bishop put an end to such calumnious activity and that he ensure "an exemplary justice."[3]

This was no minor, hotheaded accusation. Insults were taken seriously in New France, as in other early-modern societies. In the eighteenth century, 44 per cent of the individuals brought before the royal courts of the colony were accused of verbal or physical violence, the one often connected to the other.[4] Furthermore, insults not only reflected cultural norms;[5] they also often represented a means of bringing more protracted disputes to a head.[6] For this reason, one could not easily ignore an insult.

But Verchères had not merely accused Lefebvre of defaming her; she implied that he had committed the worst type of insult, blasphemy, because he had profaned the litany.[7] Furthermore, she claimed that he had convinced a parishioner to make a false deposition.[8] Mgr Dosquet ordered the dean of the cathedral chapter to write to Lefebvre, compelling him to clear his name or make reparations. Lefebvre arraigned Verchères before the provost court in Quebec. The case would drag through, first, the provost court and then on appeal to the Conseil Supérieur, before Verchères sailed to France to plead her case before the king. In the meantime, calumny would pile upon calumny, as each party and his or her supporters criticized the other.

Although much of the litany is difficult to decipher (and was so even for contemporaries), many lines appear to be attacks on Verchères, her family, and her social circle. Naudière and Tarrieu, for example, were surnames of the La Pérade family. Mme Portail was her friend. The litany also cast aspersions on the local priests. In addition to its blasphemous character, it questioned Lefebvre's own celibacy. Furthermore, in some versions, such as the one proposed by the notary Arnould-Balthazar Pollet, homonyms for the name of Voyer appear in almost every line.

At the trial, Lefebvre denied having sung the litany. But he found that he had even more accusations of impurity to answer for.

Verchères's five witnesses, all residents of Batiscan and a number of them nobles, told stories of the priest's unrestrained misconduct. Two of them, Daniel Portail, Sieur de Gevron, and his wife, Marie-Anne Levrault de Langis, added to the testimony about the litany that the priest had called Verchères a whore and Mme Portail a slut (*gueuse*). Furthermore, Lefebvre had threatened that he would "screw" (*baiserais entre les deux jambes*) Mme Portail. Finally, the priest had nicknames for his religious brothers and superiors, and he called himself "Big Codpiece" ("Grande Brague") and would lift up his cassock, saying, "See my big codpiece."[9]

The military officer Joachim Sacquespée informed the court that Lefebvre had told him that if he (the priest) had a child, he should not worry about being punished. This was a possibility, he suggested, since Lefebvre believed that Verchères and Mmes de Langis, de Bellecourt, and de Champlain were all in love with him. According to the witness, the priest had nonetheless criticized Langis's son's illicit involvement with the de Brieux's daughter. Worse, La Bissionnière's son had facilitated the liaison by acting as pimp (*maquereau*).[10] Louis La Bissionnière had also heard the latter allegation from Lefebvre, except that he claimed that the priest had called Mme Brieux the pimp (*maquerelle*), not himself.[11]

Undoubtedly, in such a trial, where the only evidence possible is hearsay, Lefebvre would have found it difficult to prove that he had not insulted Verchères. First, he demonstrated that she had accused him of slandering her. He summoned three witnesses connected with the church. All three testified that they had heard Verchères make public statements about Lefebvre's alleged insults. A few days later two habitants of Batiscan and a goldsmith from Quebec, who had been visiting Lefebvre, declared that the litanies were false. They agreed that Pollet had admitted that Verchères had forced him to write the litanies. Furthermore, one of them added, Pollet admitted having been bribed: "I don't give a damn about that. I still got 25 *minots* of wheat."[12] Over the next three weeks, Lefebvre and Verchères both submitted their reproaches against the witnesses, a process that will be examined later. When the provost court delivered its sentence on 29 August 1730, Lefebvre had lost. He was ordered to pay 200 livres in damages as well as the costs of the trial; he was also to submit to canonical punishment for his crimes.[13] Lefebvre immediately appealed to the Conseil Supérieur.

For the new trial, the priest requested eight witnesses and Verchères three. Lefebvre's witnesses, most of them residents of Quebec, claimed to have overheard Verchères's first witnesses reneging on their testimony. Four of them testified that Pollet and Sacquespée had tried to convince the third man in the canoe, Beaussac, to speak. "If you don't support the certificate I gave," Sacquespée allegedly threatened him, "I'll pass for a damned liar."[14] Beaussac nonetheless refused to discuss the matter with Verchères. Other witnesses argued that Mme Portail regretted her involvement and had warned Lefebvre previously about her husband's "bad tongue."[15] Furthermore, one habitant of Batiscan said that his wife and Mme Portail had nicknamed Lefebvre "Big Codpiece."[16] Finally, one witness submitted that Verchères's son had questioned the wisdom of the judges and the coadjutor in not restricting Lefebvre from celebrating mass. Obviously, through his witnesses, the priest succeeded in questioning the reliability of the original witnesses, while at the same time placing in doubt the integrity of Verchères's family.

Her witnesses tried to reaffirm the testimony about the litany while casting new aspersions on Lefebvre's morality. Pollet repeated a shortened version of Lefebvre's litany, placing the event, not in a canoe on the Rivière Sainte-Anne, but rather in the vestry when Pollet was attempting to steal the chalice.[17] Another witness, Pierre de La Croix de Villeneuve, corroborated this evidence, while Augustin Trottier made new accusations. Lefebvre did not always follow proper liturgy, he affirmed. Worse, he once touched a women "up to her naked knees."[18] Lefebvre had also bragged to him that he had fathered two illegitimate children.

Of course, there is no way for us to be certain whether any of the individuals actually said what they were accused of saying. The most we can do is assume some degree of verisimilitude for these accusations. In other words, we can examine why this particular rhetoric was considered unacceptable by the other side.

The Themes

Illegitimate sexuality was one major theme in the accusations. The gossip focused on women as well as on the priest Lefebvre. He had impugned Verchères's and Mme Portail's sexuality, accusing them of being whores. In the context of the period, to question a woman's sexuality was to cast doubt on her husband's control over her and the legitimacy of her family bonds and alliances. Even if the alleged insults had never occurred, at the trial itself Lefebvre used an analogy which attacked Verchères's sexuality. When she complained to the coadjutor, the priest affirmed, Verchères was "similar to that woman who, holding in her hand the innocent Joseph's coat, demanded that he be punished for a crime he had not committed."[19] This reference to Genesis 39:7 compared Verchères to the Egyptian lord's wife who had tried to seduce the slave Joseph and, when she failed, had publicly accused him of attempting to rape her. In other words, Verchères was not only a liar but a whore as well.

The ability to attack the wife stemmed from cultural precepts. It was at the point of creating family ties that women's power seemed dangerous to men. In other words, their sexuality, if it were exercised illegitimately, could weaken authority. If women engaged in illegitimate sexual relations, their family's whole clientage nexus might crumble, for their alliances would have been false ones.[20] In an eighteenth-century text on jurisprudence, François Dareau discussed the consequences of suspected adultery: "If the husband … has reason to suspect the virtue of his companion, dark worries will obsess him, everything will worry him, everything will displease him. He will no longer enjoy those tender feelings that an unquestionable paternity inspires. His children, formerly so dear to him, will not have the same charms in his eyes."[21] The male fear of being a cuckold represented a weak point at which to attack authority. This interpretation explains why so much of the invective concerning male figures of authority in the eighteenth century actually focused on the wife.[22]

Given his particular position as a necessarily celibate male, the slander directed at Father Lefebvre could also stress illegitimate sexuality. From his virile nickname to his threats against Mme Portail and his alleged fathering of two illegitimate children, the gossip about Lefebvre threw his own networks of support into disarray. Could parishioners still trust their priest in their day-to-day dealings with him?

In themselves, these accusations of illegitimate sexuality threatened the supporters of the two individuals. But Lefebvre and Verchères attacked their opponents' supporters in other ways too. In part, the nature of the legal system encouraged denunciations of one's opponent's witnesses. According to legal custom, before delivering testimony, each witness had to swear to not being a relative, ally, servant, or employee of the parties. The opposing party had the right in each instance to contest the impartiality of the witness. In this trial the challenges seemed endless. Not only did Lefebvre and Verchères oppose the other's witnesses, but each replied to the charges, and in some cases the challenger responded to this reply. These reproaches provided numerous occasions for attacking the other's supporters.

For example, Verchères claimed that Rivard and Herbec *fils* were inadmissable as witnesses because they worked for Lefebvre.[23] The priest had promised Joseph Gaillou money in his will, and Herbec *père* was an intimate friend.[24] Furthermore, Herbec was not worthy of attention, as Verchères had indicated to him herself when she told him that "she did not waste time with scum like him."[25]

Lefebvre made similar charges concerning Verchères's economic power over her clientage. Pollet, in his position as notary and bailiff (*huissier*), was "consequently in their pay."[26] In fact, shortly after the first trial, he had received a commission as royal notary for Batiscan, Champlain, Sainte-Anne, and Grondines seigneuries.[27] Furthermore, another witness, Pierre de La Croix de Villeneuve, lodged with the La Pérade family and acted as a private tutor to the children.[28] Both therefore had economic ties to the seigneurs.

But the most revealing accusations were based on family ties. In such a battle over alliances, the priest's knowledge of parish records afforded him a great advantage. Daniel Portail was the son-in-law of Verchères's brother-in-law. Louis La Bissionnière was the son of her brother-in-law's father-in-law's nephew. Joachim Sacquespée had married Verchères's brother-in-law's father-in-law's niece. Augustin Trottier was related to everyone, being first cousin to Verchères's brother-in-law.[29] And as if marriage bonds were not capable of creating enough alliances, Verchères also used spiritual (or fictive) kinship. Not long before the trial, she had acted as godmother to Arnould-Balthazar Pollet's child.[30] Because of her control over her clientage of relatives and lackeys, Lefebvre suggested, their testimony was invalid.

It is important to note the true nature of the allies of the two parties. Verchères's witnesses came from her extended family and from local military personnel and royal officials. Parish registers indicate that in the ten years previous to the trial, the La Pérade family signed the registers at the baptisms, marriages, and burials of only a restricted circle in Batiscan and Sainte-Anne.[31] This circle also almost exclusively comprised family members and officials, especially militia officers. On this point, Lefebvre was correct. This clientage, of which the witnesses were part, seemed to be very much composed of local nobles and officials. On the other hand, Lefebvre's witnesses from Batiscan were all habitants and were his immediate neighbours in the parish.[32]

As the priest saw the accusation and the trial, it was very much a question of Verchères's social network combining against him. "There has not been a week since the beginning of these proceedings," he claimed, "when one has not seen them meeting in each other's houses to plan Lefebvre's downfall."[33] Moreover, a local cabal was at work, trying to destroy the priest: "The Court is too shrewd not to see the cabal organized between relatives, allies, and friends to ruin Lefebvre."[34]

But he would not make any detailed attempt to explain why so many people wanted to cause his downfall. He claimed merely that Verchères's "passion" and "fury" hindered her from dealing with the issue in a more reasonable, quiet manner. Lefebvre claimed that her problem was that "her passion has taken her far beyond reason."[35] Speaking of Verchères and her husband, Lefebvre suggested, "Religion should have imposed silence on them, but fury and passion have carried them away and have blinded them."[36]

Loyalty to superiors was an important issue, and passion could threaten proper social hierarchies. If Verchères had indeed united a cabal against Lefebvre, she would be opposing royal justice. Thus he accused her and her husband of placing themselves higher than they should: "[they] claim that they are as noble as the king."[37] They "believe themselves better than everyone and act like sovereigns."[38] Unlike them, Father Lefebvre knew his place in the social hierarchy exactly, and he took pains to make this clear:

Lefebvre recognizes as his superior in this country Mr le Marquis de Beauharnois, who represents the person of our invincible monarch. He also recognizes as superior Monsignor de Samos, coadjutor of Quebec, who represents the sacred person of his bishop, Monsignor du Mornay, bishop of Quebec. He has as a superior Mr Hocquart, intendant of New France at the head of the Conseil Supérieur in Quebec; he has as superior Mr La Tour, senior vicar of this diocese; he has as superior Mr de Lotbiniere, archdeacon in his visits; he has as superior Mr the Governor of Trois Rivieres, in whose government his parish is situated.[39]

Despite Lefebvre's acknowledgment of the proper chains of hierarchy, both he and Verchères were quick to accuse the other of rebelliousness, of opposing their superiors. For example, Verchères argued that Chapter Dean La Tour's testimony should not be permitted since she had spoken to him in confidence. Lefebvre saw in this reproach an attack on La Tour's sincerity. Since the dean was "a person as honourable as the leader of this country, M. le marquis de Beauharnois," Verchères had sullied his reputation in suggesting that he had invented his testimony.[40] Similarly, when Lefebvre criticized her for having given twenty-five *minots* of wheat to Daniel Portail, she riposted that she was only following the orders of Governor Beauharnois.[41] Furthermore, she pointed out, in questioning the means by which Portail and Sacquespée had come to Canada, Lefebvre insulted the governor's judgment: "Lefebvre attacks if he thinks it useful my sire the governor-general."[42] Each party thus accused the other of disrespect for superiors. Hierarchy, along with alliances and sexuality, provided the imagery for the arguments.

The notion of a "public" also entered into the debate. It was not merely the insults which had bothered Verchères. Rather, it was the fact that they were so widespread. When she came to complain to the acting bishop, the litany was already well known, being "public throughout the city."[43] Likewise, because Verchères's accusations against Lefebvre were so well known, he had to defend himself: "Mr Portail and the lady La Pérade make so many outrageous remarks in the countryside and in the city."[44] Consequently, with the struggle so widely discussed, Lefebvre could not see it as merely involving himself. His rank was in danger of losing respect. This was especially true for a priest, since a scandal was even more threatening when one held that position: "A pastor or a priest, whose life should be a model for his people, and whose bad examples could cause a universal scandal throughout the Church."[45] In fact, several of the clergy had asked Lefebvre to defend himself in order to protect the status of churchmen.[46] Lefebvre went so far as to term the La Pérades "enemies of priests."[47] For him, the accusations threatened the legitimacy of the clergy.

Clearly, what had begun as a suit for slander committed against Madeleine de Verchères ended with Lefebvre himself being the victim of slander. It was a difficult case, and the solution was even harder to reach. On 23 December 1730 the case was thrown out of court and Verchères condemned to pay expenses.

Madeleine de Verchères had reason to be dissatisfied with the result. Not only was she required to pay the expenses of the trial, but her integrity was in question. Consequently, she appealed to the only place left, the king's court. Her voyage to France was not entirely successful. She managed to interest the secretary of state for the navy, the king's minister responsible for New France, in this rather peculiar judgment, but in the end he refused to reopen the matter. Instead, judging the case already "too well-known" (*trop eclatté*), he requested that Governor Beauharnois and Intendant Hocquart try to conciliate Verchères and Lefebvre.[48] On 21 October 1733 the two parties reached an agreement. Verchères would not have to pay the expenses of the trial, and Lefebvre agreed to keep silent, "in order that no one may speak of it nor enter into disagreement over it."[49]

In the trial Lefebvre had succeeded in casting doubt on many of Verchères's accusations against him. In fact, there was little to corroborate the litany that had launched the whole affair. Lefebvre agreed in the end that someone had indeed chanted bawdy litanies, but he claimed that that person had died in the course of the trial.[50] It is not clear from the evidence just what the priest himself had done. Moreover, Verchères and her husband had attempted to head off the trial on 26 June 1730 by presenting a certificate to Lefebvre indicating that they did not believe that he had composed the litany.[51]

Nonetheless, it would appear that Lefebvre had done something, for despite the finding of the Conseil Supérieur, church authorities were less generous with him. Summoning the priest, the coadjutor "shared with him his knowledge of his crimes of impurity, drunkenness, and impiety." He asked Lefebvre to resign his post, on the condition that he be allowed to return to his church for three months "in order that the people suspect nothing." Although Lefebvre carried out his duties in Batiscan from at least 3 February to 25 June 1731, the coadjutor added that "he could not keep the secret."[52]

Perhaps the origins of the struggle are a bit more obscure that a mere response to name-calling. Let us not forget that Joseph Voyer, Verchères's parish priest, was supposed to be in the canoe with Lefebvre the day that they chanted the rude litany. If we examine Voyer's and Lefebvre's earlier problems, perhaps we can come closer to the origins of the conflict.

Origins

Since 1726 Lefebvre had battled with his civil and ecclesiastical superiors over the splitting of Batiscan parish.[53] The proposed division would have drastically reduced his tithe revenues as well as his payments for services. The priest later claimed that he spent 500 livres fighting for his parish.[54] He had signed the final agreement in the dispute just as Verchères launched her attack on him.[55]

For his part, Voyer's struggles in the 1720s primarily involved the local seigneurs. He had cut down trees on Île du Sable for firewood, maintaining that the island had traditionally served as a common.[56] In 1728 Voyer and some of the habitants had refused to grind their grain at the seigneurial mill, thus contravening their obligations. When taken to court, the habitants claimed that La Pérade's mill was dilapidated, that the miller was a knave, and that he gave preferential treatment to other customers. They also requested that some kind of scale be available at the mill. Verchères, who represented her husband in court, took this case very seriously. She accused the habitants "of a spirit of rebellion and of disobedience."[57] She argued that the mill was in fine condition, that she had already replaced the miller fourteen times in the previous eighteen years, and that an earlier experiment with scales at the mill had led to innumerable disputes. As a result of the tenants' refusal to follow their duty, Verchères had seized the grain from the mill that they visited at Saint-Pierre, across the St Lawrence River. The intendant ruled in favour of the seigneurs.

This case was not the only occasion in these years when the La Pérades attempted to acquire the colonial rulers' affirmation of their rights. On 10 July 1728, the same day the previous ruling came down, Intendant Dupuy rendered a second favourable judgment. He condemned the co-seigneur of Sainte-Anne, François Dorvilliers, to pay dues to La Pérade for eight arpents on Île Saint-Ignace, following a long-standing disagreement concerning ownership of the island.[58]

At the same time as the La Pérades were seeking favour and were fighting with their parish priest, the latter received tenure in an unorthodox manner. After Bishop Jean-Baptiste de Saint-Vallier's death in 1727, when the chapter canons claimed his powers, they named six *cures inamovibles*, that is, posts from which it would be very difficult to remove the priest. Traditionally in New France, unlike in the home country, the bishop had the right to withdraw a priest from his position. Only in a few parishes, one of which was Batiscan,[59] did the priest have secure tenure. The colonial bishops generally tried to retain their power over priests. Coadjutor Dosquet later described the problems that tenured positions involved for his authority: "A title serves often only to make the pastor independent and more disobedient, and to make the parishioners gossip, when it is necessary to discipline the priest."[60]

One of the six that the chapter had offered titles to was Joseph Voyer. After his arrival in the colony, the bishop's coadjutor, Mgr Dosquet, demanded that the priests relinquish their titles. Voyer refused; he contested the coadjutor's right to annul the chapter's decision. In early 1730 Archdeacon Eustache Chartier de Lotbinière visited the priest to discuss the matter with him. Lotbinière also involved the seigneur of Sainte-Anne, who signed the monition against Voyer.[61] Refusing to relinquish his titles, Voyer appealed against the coadjutor's orders to the Conseil Supérieur, which refused to hear the case. On 22 March, the same day that Verchères launched her accusation against Lefebvre, Voyer relinquished his titles, still protesting against the coadjutor's decision and promising to continue his search for legal recourse.[62] Did he give up his titles because Verchères's complaint implicated him as much as it did Lefebvre? The coincidence in timing suggests as much. In the end, Voyer did not pursue any further action. But he would continue to experience problems with the local seigneurs.

There are a number of different issues which the court cases elucidate. First, they demonstrate the link between local politics and larger colonial issues.[63] Secondly, they reveal how power was associated closely with the individual; otherwise, direct attacks on the person, such as the insinuations concerning Verchères's and Lefebvre's sexuality, would not have been taken so seriously. The cases also illustrate the images of power, hierarchy, and clientages that were shared by the participants. Ultimately, both parties argued over local allegiances: both were firmly rooted in their hierarchical positions in the community and in the colonial world at large. These elements can be seen in other local disputes during the French regime as well.

LOCAL ARGUMENTS

Appeals to Hierarchy

Arguments over local hierarchical relations were not unique to the conflict between Verchères and Lefebvre, although they were seldom expressed with such vehemence and recorded in such detail. In a number of other cases, the concept of hierarchy and the respect due to superiors surfaced in arguments which made reference, at least by implication, to some ideological understanding of society. Although the appeals were often raised when a social superior confronted someone of lower status, individuals of similar status also used the same imagery.

According to both lay and ecclesiastical seigneurs, habitants were not entitled to criticize their actions. The Jesuits' representatives followed this line of attack in the early years of settlement in Batiscan. When the habitants complained in 1669 about the surveying of their property lines, a seigneurial official riposted that their leader, Nicolas Rivard, "attacks the Reverend Fathers and taxes their patience with petty squabbles. This man should only have respect for them; he knows what obligations he has towards them."[64] Likewise, the Jesuits' representative in 1745, in appropriating land that Antoine Trottier claimed for himself, scolded him for pursuing a trial against "these seigneurs for whom he should have all respect and honour."[65] It was not only that the habitants were following the wrong legal path; by their very resistance, they were subverting the social order.

As we have seen, when their tenants refused to have their grain ground at the banal mill, the seigneurs of Sainte-Anne used similar inflammatory language. They did so on other occasions too, the accusation taking on a symbolic appearance. In 1715 the family of Jean Ricard walked to the La Pérades' house to take up the job of cutting their wheat. As the Ricards waited to begin their work, the seigneur's son began to beat some dogs that had followed them. The Ricards tried to stop him, but he would not listen. Mme Ricard commented, "What a malicious boy." Hearing this, La Pérade senior began to hit and kick the pregnant Mme Ricard and threw her to the ground. He assaulted others in the family with a walking stick and even grabbed a rifle from his house. Madeleine de Verchères herself entered the fray, hitting various members of the family. Ignace Quyon, a habitant of Saint-Charles des Roches who was passing through the parish, stepped into the argument and took the gun away. This physical assault, which Ricard reported to the provost court in Quebec,[66] was an imposition of class privilege: the La Pérades would not countenance being directed by mere peasants. Moreover, in turning the violence away from the dog towards the Ricard family, the La Pérades symbolically put them in what they considered their proper social place: alongside stray dogs.

Struggles against other members of the local elite could take on large proportions as well. When in 1737 La Pérade tried for a second time to stop Voyer from felling trees on disputed land, the priest evoked his clerical ascendancy at the same time as he appealed to La Pérade's sense of social importance: "the said priest recognizes Monsieur de la Pérade as the first among the faithful of the parish, and he respects him as such, not only loving him as the most dear sheep in the eyes of the Lord." La Pérade responded by accusing Voyer of treason: "He was not at all surprised by the kiss of Judas that the said priest gave him."[67] These disputes reveal the rivalry that inspired the priests and seigneurs in disputing local prominence.

Other members of the local elite, particularly state officials, also openly appealed to respect for hierarchy, even when they were in a subordinate position. To justify his own claim to the land on the seigneurial boundary of Batiscan from which cedar posts had been taken, Alexis Raux, dit Morinville, second militia captain for Champlain, claimed that he "had only worked as a good ensign."[68] Similarly, in trying to defend the outcome of a lottery held at Batiscan in 1740, the defendant Dontigny, along with François Chorel d'Orvilliers, co-seigneur of Sainte-Anne and militia captain for Champlain, accused the plaintiff of being disrespectful towards the judge who had presided over the lottery.[69] To discredit others, it was easy to claim that they were not respectful of the proper hierarchy of authority. In themselves, hierarchy and one's position in it were proper means of arguing.

Problems with the Local Elite

But hierarchical relations were at issue in another sense as well. One of the most interesting facets of the disputes during the French regime is that members of the local elite caused many of the problems which attracted the attention of external authorities. As the conflict between Verchères and Lefebvre illustrates, these disputes often involved the seigneurs and noble military officials confronting priests (who in many cases tried to get support from the habitants).

For example, in 1694 priest Nicolas Foucault of Batiscan openly fought with the noble military captain François Desjordy Moreau de Cabanac. Foucault claimed that Desjordy was having an illicit affair with Marguerite Dizy, wife of Jean Desbrieux. The bishop forbade Desjordy to attend the churches of Batiscan and Champlain. The captain appealed to the Conseil Souverain (later the Conseil Supérieur) to have the interdict lifted, with little success.[70] About the same time a conflict between civil and ecclesiastical authorities concerning payment to soldiers led the priest of Sainte-Anne to refuse to hear Governor Philippe de Rigaud de Vaudreuil's confession.[71] Such local scenes were echoes of broader disagreements between church and state officials.

In exercising their duties regarding the moral conduct of their congregations, priests confronted local nobles. In 1719 Lefebvre was given permission to excommunicate the parishioners who refused to fulfill their Easter obligations, in this case the noble Levrault brothers and Jacques Tessier.[72] As we have already seen, in 1727 Daniel Portail, Sieur de Gevron, and Marie-Anne Levrault de Langis, married *à la gaumine* while Lefebvre was celebrating mass. The rehabilitation of the marriage the following year illustrates the social prominence of the couple: the La Pérade family, the Levrault de Langis family, ensign Alexis Lahaye, and military officer Joachim Sacquespée were all in attendance.[73]

Following their disagreements with the La Pérades, both Lefebvre and Voyer were forced to resign their charges. From Lefebvre's point of view, his trials with Madeleine de Verchères led to his downfall: the bishop demanded his resignation, "providing no more allegations than that following the court case that I just finished with the sire and lady La Pérade I could do no good in my parish."[74] The rupture between the civil and religious authority in the area was too great to permit Lefebvre's continued ministry. For his part, although he obeyed his ecclesiastical superiors' wishes in surrendering his fixed title in 1730, Voyer would also eventually lose their confidence. In 1742 Bishop Henri-Marie Dubreuil de Pontbriand summoned him to Quebec to be disciplined for his drunken excesses. "He is a subject lacking in sense, little intent on learning," Pontbriand complained, "against whom there have been many complaints before this."[75] At least one of these complaints came from the La Pérades; it is likely that others did also.

Lefebvre's successor in Saint-François-Xavier was no more fortunate in his relations with the local lay elite. François Richard had to leave his parish in October 1735 for a short trip to Quebec. During that time, in a type of charivari, his horse was stolen. He believed that

Pierre and Joseph La Bissionnière and De Montégrand *fils* de Langis had taken it, ridden it up and down the royal road, and cut off its tail and mane. The seigneurial court judge of Batiscan oversaw an interrogation of witnesses to discover the perpetrators. The inquiry was entirely inconclusive since all witnesses denied that they knew anything about the issue.[76] However, the detailed nature of the questioning suggests strongly that the witnesses were suppressing knowledge, presumably to save the well-placed young men from punishment.

Thus social relations during the French regime present two apparently contradictory, but ultimately mutually reinforcing, tendencies. First, authority figures relied strongly on a concept of hierarchy. Secondly, some of these same authority figures caused much of the disorder that occurred in the region. In their dealings with each other and with external authorities, members of the local elite were content to compete for the scraps of power that they felt they could wield. In the end, external authorities generally sided with the seigneurs.

While common people were not credited with much ability to initiate actions on their own, it is possible that the authorities blamed the local elite for creating problems for which it was not always responsible. In 1760, when seven militiamen from Batiscan deserted at Pointe-aux-Trembles, officer Jean-Daniel Dumas blamed Jean Trépanier, the *aide-major*. He also recommended the dismissal of Captain Villeneuve for having abetted the deserters.[77] It is by no means clear that Trépanier had caused the incident, but on this and other occasions, external authorities tended to assume that the local elite was behind whatever difficulties occurred.

There was consequently little room for habitants to record their perspectives on social relations. They do not seem to have openly challenged the social position of their superiors;[78] rather, they were content to demand that the latter fulfill their social obligations, for instance, concerning the maintenance of the gristmill in working order or the correct surveying of property lines. In that way, they too appealed to a sense of hierarchy. Thus the debate over hierarchical positions was a shared argument concerning the boundaries of local behaviour.

AUBRY VERSUS HIS PARISHIONERS

In the decades following the Conquest, rural social relations in the two seigneuries, despite their outward stability, underwent an evolution. The gradual suppression of the Jesuit order and the Lanaudière family's tendency to remain in Quebec reduced their local importance. Priests assumed aspects of the seigneurs' role. After the initial suppression of the institution and its substitution by bailiffs, militia captains too enhanced their position over time. The struggle between Laurent Aubry of Sainte-Geneviève parish and his parishioners is indicative of some of these shifts.

In September 1789, five years after Aubry became priest of Sainte-Geneviève parish and its mission church, Saint-Stanislas, the bishop acknowledged to him that "the major part of this parish is entirely opposed to you."[79] A series of complaints developed concerning the priest's role in the parish and the way in which he acquitted his duties. Although the initial issues are not clear, they apparently involved "a secular matter" (une affaire temporelle), possibly the question of church land which arose later. The militia captain was the leader of the revolt, Aubry claimed. Unhappy with the result of their dispute, the captain expressed his disgust with the priest. When Aubry extended his hand to receive the kiss of peace, the captain stated that "he had too much of a grudge against me to act in that way." He left the presbytery, threatening to make sure that Aubry would lose his parish. Aubry complained that the captain did nothing but stir up trouble: "he has no other vocation than to run from morning to night and from night to morning, from house to house, to read a paper to one person and to write one to someone else, to counsel this one and whisper to that one, everything tending towards court cases, which are his only occupation ... As he is astute and wily and the habitants are simple and crude, he leads them as he wishes." The priest concluded by asking to be removed from "this place of disorder and of affliction."[80] Nonetheless, Aubry did not take up the bishop's offer to change parishes.

Other conflicts between the irascible Aubry and his parishioners continued to fester. On a variety of pretexts, he delayed the publication of marriage bans for the children of Prisque Trépanier and Laurent Foucault in January 1790. This incident was also reported to the bishop.[81] But many of Aubry's problems were more general ones. The habitants of Saint-Stanislas, who lived at some distance from the church of Sainte-Geneviève, asked Aubry to support their wish to make Saint-Stanislas into a parish, presumably because they might thus acquire a full-time priest and escape Aubry. He forwarded the request without taking a position on it.[82] The bishop refused the appeal and shortly afterwards commanded Aubry to provide more services for the people near the chapel. He was to bury all those who died in Saint-Stanislas in their local cemetery, instead of at Sainte-Geneviève. As a result, Aubry would have to make the trip to Saint-Stanislas more often.

The bishop came to this decision after listening to two representatives of the habitants; they complained that the priest had implied that the bishop wanted them to ornament the church and had encouraged them to overspend on decorations. The bishop reproved Aubry: "You have very incorrectly used the name of the bishop to engage the habitants to build their presbytery. After I demonstrated the uselessness of this building, you told me that the habitants had convinced you. Today it appears that you have been the only motor and entrepreneur of the whole affair. All this, if you are not careful, will finish badly for you."[83] In a less than submissive reaction to the bishop's comments, Aubry held a public assembly to discuss the affair. According to the priest, after the two representatives had explained their position, the other habitants contended that they had willingly built the church.[84]

A few months later the conflicts between Aubry and his parishioners shifted back to Sainte-Geneviève parish. The habitant Michel Veillet disputed the church's right to a plot of land. At a parish assembly on 5 March 1790, an agreement was reached to take Veillet to court. On 27 June that year Aubry called a second assembly to consider the matter. Only a small number showed up, and nothing was resolved.[85] A third meeting a week later, held without the priest, decided the issue, making an exchange with Veillet for the land and thus avoiding the court case.[86] Aubry rejected this agreement because it had been reached without him.

The following January fifty-nine habitants signed a petition requesting the bishop to remove Aubry from his post. Their representatives alleged that he insulted his parishioners publicly, that he hit some of them, and that he spent too much time at the house of one Michel Hurteau.[87] Despite the bishop's admonitions, Aubry continued to create problems by leaving his parish for periods of time.[88] He also came into conflict again with his parishioners in Saint-Stanislas concerning a piece of land. Aubry claimed proprietorial rights over the land but had let the local habitants use it for the profit of their chapel. When he tried to reclaim the land, the large majority of habitants at Saint-Stanislas refused to turn it over to him.[89]

In March 1792 four habitants of Saint-Stanislas presented the bishop with a petition signed by twenty others which agreed with the tenor of the complaints made by the parishioners of Sainte-Geneviève: he arrived at the chapel too late to hear confessions, he refused the sacraments to habitants who disagreed with him, and he spent time outside his parish.[90] Aubry responded by denying all the complaints and added, "Which public man can avoid all criticism?"[91] His defences were not enough for the bishop, who finally made him change parishes. The priest Jean of Contrecœur, who was facing his own parish revolt, was told to exchange positions with Aubry.[92]

Meanwhile, the seigneur of Sainte-Anne, Charles-Louis de Lanaudière, had attempted to intervene in the affair. He wrote to the bishop on behalf of Aubry, "who is my friend," requesting that the priest be allowed to take the church in his seigneury of Lac-Maskinongé. He added that the tithe revenues would not be particularly high at that parish, but he thought Aubry might still be interested: "I conceive that self-interest is not the only issue."[93]

Aubry's tribulations, some elements of which were not at all unique to him (though the frequency may have been rare), suggest some hypotheses about the similarities and the subtle shifts in the nature of authority some sixty years after Lefebvre's court case. First, as before, habitants continued to argue in a way that did not fundamentally challenge the position of authority figures, but rather, demanded that those individuals fulfill their duties as the habitants understood them. In other words, this was not evidence of popular anticlericalism.

However, what was different was the extent to which the priest appeared an outsider. Unlike the dispute involving Lefebvre, Aubry seemed unable to enlist leading members of the community in his defence and was overwhelmed by his parishioners' opposition. Moreover, the conflicts quickly expanded beyond the area. Both sides endlessly appealed for the intervention of an external authority, the bishop. In this way, the locals did not argue with Aubry; rather, they leagued up against him. The neighbouring seigneur, siding this time with the priest, was also a marginal figure. His intervention had little effect in resolving the dispute. Instead, it was the militia captain, now acting as an important local leader, who played a large role in bringing the issue to a head. Throughout the incidents the local community maintained a strong degree of integrity, unlike the situation in 1720s and 1730s, when the community had divided along lines of support for either the priest or the seigneur.

HIERARCHY IN THE BRITISH REGIME

Local Leadership

Other local priests experienced similar antagonistic relationships with their parishioners. Two of Aubry's successors were appointed after having faced strong opposition in their previous parishes.[94] Another priest of Sainte-Geneviève, Hot, was particularly interested in the revenues from his charge. He fought with Antoine Mongrain, whom he termed le coq de village," over the proceeds from hay growing around the church.[95] After the bishop had tried to control his behaviour many times – for instance, in forbidding him to practise medicine – the priest was ordered to change parishes in 1818.[96] Reliant on his representatives in the localities in this period of relative scarcity of priests, the bishop nonetheless demonstrated a certain degree of mistrust of them.

A similar attitude embodied the relationship between the British colonial government and its local representatives, the militia captains. During the military occupation, the British governors left the captains in their positions and made them responsible for the observance of army dictates.[97] The institution was later suppressed, only to be resurrected gradually over the next few decades.[98] Beginning in 1765, the appointments of bailiffs confirmed a return to the status quo ante, at least in the seigneuries of Batiscan and Sainte-Anne. A number of representatives of families that had traditionally held the positions of militia captains under the French were appointed bailiffs: in Batiscan, Marchand, Rivard, and Trépanier; in Sainte-Anne, Gouin and Lanouette. Other bailiffs were chosen from families which had served as seigneurial agents, such as the Mongrains.[99] In 1768 the bishop made clear his desire that the bailiff should be seen as the equivalent of the old militia captains. In a pastoral letter he enjoined local priests, "you will render him the same honours that militia captains previously received."[100]

Just before the American invasion of 1775, the institution of militia captains was reintroduced, with the confirmation of the same families in the positions. The captains took on some of the symbols previously bestowed upon the seigneurs. According to the German officer, the seigneurial privilege of the maypole was by 1776 given to the local militia officers, if only for the practical purpose of identifying the officers' abodes.[101]

The same German officer also observed that some local priests filled a social role functionally similar to that of the seigneur. He noted that Lanaudière's presence in his seigneury was typified by "visits" and that the priest of Batiscan was almost as important in entertaining the German officers billeted in the area as was Lanaudière. "But did we have many distractions this winter? I answer: absolutely! You see, there are a good number of 'seigniors' and 'curés' in our neighbourhood ... Thanks to this man [Lanaudière] we had many small 'fêtes' in his castle. The 'curés' are not negligeable either. They are good royalists, and having the ability to be 'bons vivants,' they are able to furnish supper for twenty people and to provide them with good wine."[102] It is not surprising that the priests came to serve as functional equivalent of the seigneur in Batiscan, since the British government had restricted the Jesuits' ownership of their lands to the last, aging members of the order. In 1790 Aubry wished to help the colonial government, answering a request for statistical information and complaining that the Jesuits had not themselves responded. "Nothing, Sire," he assured the postmaster general, Hugh Finlay, "Nothing could have stopped me from completing your request except for the delays of the seigneurs up to today."[103] In the space partially vacated by the seigneurs, the priest's and the militia captain's local importance increased in the late eighteenth century.

Priests and militia captains also served as intermediaries between the local inhabitants and the external world. At least, they wished to assume this position. Their word, more than that of the habitants, counted with their superiors. As in the French regime, external authorities continued to rely on their representatives in the local area.

Thus habitants were not supposed to complain openly to the bishop about their priests. When the parishioners leagued up against Aubry in 1792, the bishop pretended to ignore their complaints. "I told them nothing," he informed the priest, "I even pretended to regard their complaints as the grousing of habitants."[104] Similarly, when a number of parishioners requested permission to use money from the church strongbox in Sainte-Anne, the bishop refused because the priest had not signed the letter.[105] Nevertheless, habitants continued to appeal directly to the bishop because, even if they did not get immediate satisfaction, the bishop would sometimes act on their complaints. In 1825, when the priest of Sainte-Geneviève demanded that the habitants help build the church, vestry, and presbytery, regardless of their means, the bishop wrote to him, "I do not like to criticize priests in front of habitants, even when the former are at fault."[106] But even if their wishes might eventually be granted, the habitants did not receive the satisfaction of being heard.

For their part, secular officials found themselves held responsible for the actions of the people of their area. After the American invasion, the militia officials almost to a man lost their commissions.[107] Likewise, during the War of 1812 the rumour spread that the local militiamen were to be sent to Germany. Colonel Thomas Coffin blamed this problem on the lack of vigilance and action of two captains, and he recommended that their commissions be revoked.[108] In a similar fashion, the habitants of Batiscan refused to pay their rents in 1824 because the local captain misread the proceedings of the House of Assembly: "Capt[ai]n Le fevre the man I have alluded to has hindered the censitaires of St Geneviève & St Stanislas to come to my call, saying that I had no papier terrier [land register], And that it was dangerous to put their money into my hands."[109] External government and church authorities chose to interpret local actions by attributing fault to members of the elite. Hierarchical understandings of society persisted into the early nineteenth century.

THE ADVENT OF POPULAR SUFFRAGE

The introduction of electoral politics after 1791 presented a potential challenge to that hierarchical ideology. However, this new outlet did not signal a fundamental shift; rather, it only confirmed the gradual decline of the seigneurs' prestige and the rise of a lay elite. An early brush with the effects of popular will had occurred during the invasion of the American rebel army in 1775. Under popular pressure, many local officials abandoned their loyalty to the British government. Louis Gouin was an exception, since he recruited twenty-two militiamen from his parish to march against the rebels at Montreal that autumn. Gouin's loyalty earned him the enmity of some of his neighbours: "he attracted the indignation of the majority of his parish ... He has been robbed, disarmed, and insulted on many occasions."

However, when the Americans established control of the Trois-Rivières district, he bent to their domination and agreed to serve as militia captain under their authority. In both Sainte-Anne and Batiscan the Americans used local assemblies to choose militia captains. In most cases, the royally appointed captains maintained their positions. In Sainte-Geneviève, for example, Captain Antoine Lacourcière turned over his commission to the Americans in Trois-Rivières and returned to his parish in order to hold an assembly at his house to elect new militia officers, "which assembly maintained them all in their respective positions." However, in Saint-François-Xavier parish, Lieutenant Pierre Frigon was rejected because of his partisanship for the British government: "It seems that Pierre Frigon lost his position only because he executed the King's orders with too much firmness."[110] With certain exceptions, this brief experience of popular choice largely confirmed the existing social hierarchy.

However, the advent of legislative elections in 1792 was not expected to have such a subtle impact. The British government was concerned about the large suffrage that the imposition of English property qualifications would imply in the colony. As Solicitor General Alexander Wedderburn had written in 1772, "To admit every Canadian proprietor of land would be disgusting and injurious to all the men of condition in the Province, who are accustomed to feel a very considerable difference between the seignior and the censier [*censitaire*], though both are alike proprietors of land."[111] The introduction of an elective assembly, even with its restricted powers, could occasion, in theory at least, a recasting of hierarchical social relations.[112]

Word was quick to spread that old loyalties had broken down. In 1792 Louis Gouin felt compelled to spell out in a letter to the *Gazette de Québec* that his deference to his seigneur was still intact: "It has been reported to me that there is a rumour circulating among our compatriots that Monsieur de Lanaudière and I have had an disagreement occasioned by the upcoming election. I declare on my honour which no one can take from me, especially spiteful people, that I – and many other notables of the county – do not disagree with him at all on this matter; and that for more than a hundred and thirty years, my ancestors have continually been in the service of his family, and for almost fifty years I have done so myself."[113]

Beyond this admittedly rare public pronouncement reaffirming deference, it is difficult to evaluate the local impact of this new outlet of expression. The constituencies extended far beyond the borders of each seigneury: Batiscan lay within Saint-Maurice county and Sainte-Anne within Hampshire county. The only inhabitants of either seigneury to win election in the period were Thomas Coffin (Saint-Maurice, 1792–1804, 1808–09) and Pierre Bureau (Saint-Maurice, 1819–36).[114] Many of the elected members lived outside the ridings. Still, electoral politics provided a public outlet for a rising bourgeoisie.

The membership of the Constitutional Committee of 1822, established to work against the union of Upper and Lower Canada, revealed the composition of local political leadership. Of the fifteen members from Batiscan and Sainte-Anne seigneuries, five were militia captains, two were notaries, and at least four were merchants.[115] In the face of the major constitutional challenge, the petty bourgeoisie assumed political leadership in the area.

The Relative Decline of Seigneurs

In parallel with the rise of a local lay leadership in the early nineteenth century, the influence of the seigneurs, the government in Batiscan, and the noble Lanaudière family in Sainte-Anne, declined.[116] Lord Selkirk concluded, after having spoken with Lanaudière, that the seigneur's authority among his tenants was rather weak: "The Seigneurs who still remain have not much influence with the country people – the Habitant has no intercourse with his Seigneur, but what is of an unpleasant nature – holding his land in perpetuity he is under no dependance & has no favors to ask – but he is called upon annually for his Rent – for his multure – & occasionally for his Lods & Ventes, which appear to him unreasonable taxes & burdens on his industry."[117] However, as Selkirk commented favourably, Lanaudière maintained a noble and paternalistic attitude towards his social inferiors: "The Lower Canadians seem to have a good example in the behaviour of some at least of their superiors – Lanaudiere when we were going out to Montmorency speaking to a young lad his servant always used the appellation 'mon fils' & his manner was equally kind."[118] The noble's absence from his seigneury reduced his local influence, but in theory his agents could have filled the gap somewhat. Louis Gouin, an important merchant and a militia captain, remained the seigneurial agent in Sainte-Anne for many years. As his public announcement concerning the 1792 election made clear, he wanted to preserve traditional social relations.

In Batiscan the seigneurs' influence was weaker. The change from Jesuit ownership to state control led to the appointment of agents from other areas. From 1792 to 1800 F.-X. Larue from Pointe-aux-Trembles was the Jesuits' agent, although he had local representatives: Mme Moreau on the Grande-Côte and Jean Trépanier on the Rivière Batiscan.[119] Larue tried to keep his position when the estates reverted to the Crown, appealing to both Governor Robert Shore Milnes and the commissioners and noting that "some favoured people had anticipated him in this process."[120] His fears were justified when Joseph Badeaux, a resident of Trois-Rivières, was chosen. Perhaps because of his non-residence or because of the change in seigneur, Badeaux had difficulty imposing his authority. He reported that he could not always convince recalcitrant habitants to pay their arrears: "one person told me that I was authorized only to receive, not to request."[121] One of Badeaux's successors, A.G. Douglass, noted in 1824 that he had to spend ten extra days in Batiscan, "being detained by the most part of the Inhabitants not comming [sic] to my call."[122]

Finally, in 1825 the commission appointed the first local agent in over two decades. In applying to Mathew Bell for his assistance in obtaining the position, the notary Louis Guillet commented that the appointment was highly desired by the locals: "The habitants have requested for a long time that an agent be resident in each seigneury, under the control of the attorney of the commission. This agent would be required to visit the seigneuries from time to time, and to listen to the complaints of the habitants."[123] With the exception of refusals to pay seigneurial dues, the Batiscan habitants' relations to their seigneurs were not much different from what they had been during the French regime. They requested the repair of the seigneurial gristmills, asked for concessions, and complained about survey lines.[124] As before, these were all appeals to seigneurial authority, not rejections of it.

Also as before, the seigneur was valued locally for his connections to external authorities. When parishioners wanted permission to cut wood for a church at Rivière des Envies, they applied to John Hale, the colonial government official who had purchased Sainte-Anne seigneury from Lanaudière's heir. Hale wrote on their behalf to the commissioner of Jesuit estates, John Stewart.[125] As seigneur and as a member of the colonial bureaucracy, Hale still acted as a liaison between the local community and the government.

If anything, the imagery of hierarchy was even stronger now than previously. The habitants would show a deference towards Hale that Madeleine de Verchères could only have dreamed of. When the government official John Bigsby visited Hale in 1825, the seigneur accompanied him on a symbolic walk around the village of Sainte-Anne. Bigsby remembered the progress fondly: "a walk through the village with him was a very agreeable thing. It was a promenade of unconstrained greetings and pleasant looks. Red worsted caps and uncouth hats were doffed at every turn."[126] Yet this deference also reflected the exclusion of the English seigneur from local social relations; unlike Verchères, Hale would never be personally integrated into the arguments of everyday social life.

Thus deference was a public performance in which both habitants and seigneurs played their parts. Hale was at least a little insecure in his position as seigneur. He felt it important to ask Lieutenant-Colonel François Vassal de Monviel to announce clearly that Joseph Lanouette's promotion over Nicolas Dury was not on Hale's recommendation: "Captain Dury is much mortified at this circumstance, of which he naturally considers me to be the Author, and I think it necessary to remove such an Impression."[127] In this case, Hale felt obliged to clarify the hierarchical understanding that generally underpinned such decisions. As a colonel in the militia and as the local seigneur, he was concerned about earning and maintaining his respect in the community.

In the early nineteenth century, the seigneurs and the priests maintained the strongest links to external authorities. In contrast, the militia captains and other members of the local elite appeared much more tied to local concerns. A certain community feeling had emerged by the 1820s which excluded seigneurs and priests from social relations in the community.

CONCLUSION

Throughout the period under study, hierarchy provided the imagery for local social organization: all members assumed certain roles and expected others to fill theirs. At the top of the hierarchy, seigneurs, priests, and militia officers were powerful local figures. They struggled among themselves for ascendancy.

As seigneurs partially withdrew from social relations in the area, the priests, militia captains, and local petty bourgeois elite gradually assumed a larger importance. Consequently, the seigneurs were less integrated into the community by the early nineteenth century. This was the period when the local habitants were able to act most cohesively as a community.

A 1830 petition in favour of a bridge over the Rivière Sainte-Anne is a good example of the subtle changes that had occurred in social relations. Unlike the petition of the previous century, which had captured the social hierarchy of the parish so well, this one was not so obviously a mirror of status. Neither the seigneur's nor the local priest's name appears on the roll. Joseph Barabé and Michel Paré, two illiterate habitants, were the first names affixed to the petition, although it is likely that they added their crosses after the initial signatories: the militia captains and notaries.[128] In the social hierarchy, the local elite had to a large extent assumed the pre-eminence that seigneurs had previously enjoyed. This change would have profound consequences on the politics of nineteenth-century Quebec.

6 Lines of Community

Let age, in right and wrong, experienc'd, draw
Its frigid dogmas from the web of law.

Ovid, *Metamorphoses*, 355

In 1740 the merchant Jean LeRoux, *dit* Provençal, held a lottery in the seigneurial manor at Batiscan to dispose of some merchandise. Despite the presence of the local judge and the seigneurial agent, it ran into serious difficulties. The press of people was so great that LeRoux was unable to ascertain whether the tickets had been properly distributed; a table was overturned and tickets were lost. Various people did not pay for their tickets, and the commotion did not subside. "They continued this disorder," the bailiff recorded, "till the end as if it was plunder." A habitant from Champlain village, the apparent winner, subsequently brought LeRoux to the seigneurial court in an effort to uphold the validity of the lottery. The judge adjudicating the case ordered that the lottery be redrawn.[1]

Given the historical distance, it is difficult to ascertain the rights and wrongs of specific arguments among locals. However, it is possible to gauge the tenor and the focus of the arguments. While the mere act of fighting over a lottery, a debt, or a road may appear meaningless at this distance, it is still possible to extract deeper significance from the most mundane disputes.

The unsuccessful lottery of 1740 illustrates a pattern evident elsewhere: in our rare glimpses of the moments when members of the local society entered their public realm, they tended to do so in an "individualistic" and somewhat disorderly fashion. The difficulty of pursuing a public enterprise is apparent in this episode, as is the appeal to state officials. Such incidents illustrate the complexity of social relations in the region and the difficulty of enforcing community

standards. Although the concept of hierarchy implied a certain vertical ordering of society, horizontal relations were less well structured.

There are few detailed studies to illustrate the ways in which all the
inhabitants of particular areas of the St Lawrence valley constituted
(or did not constitute) functional communities, bound in a symbolic
sense to one another in the space they shared.[2] In contrast, in the
American colonies to the south in the seventeenth and eighteenth
centuries, functional communities were apparently common. Many
historians argue that communal sentiments predominated in small-
scale, homogeneous villages, only to disappear under the onslaught
of various "modernizing" forces. For example, William E. Nelson argues that a sense of cohesive community disappeared from Plymouth
County, Massachusetts, by the end of the eighteenth century as the
possibilities for self-regulation were negated by "the spread of commerce, religious dissent, and political conflict."[3] Bruce H. Mann and
Kenneth A. Lockridge, among others, have proposed similar declines
in community sentiment.[4] But the meaning and measure of "community" vary in many of these works. Darrett B. Rutman argues that historians of colonial America often ground their interpretations on their
ability to quantify what they believe should constitute a community.[5]
However, as anthropologist Anthony P. Cohen points out, "community" is a symbolic construction,[6] a boundary of the mind that locals
can utilize for specific purposes. This approach stresses a dynamic
understanding of "community," one which does not either assume or
idealize homogeneous communal sentiment. In a society with significant socio-economic divisions, like the seigneuries of the St Lawrence
valley, a perpetual state of unity would serve to mask differences. For
this reason, moments of unity require as much analysis as moments
of disunity.

Therefore it is important to examine the ways in which the local inhabitants defined their own relationships. Of course, locating evidence on how people understood the organization of their society is a
difficult endeavour. The historian must often rely on documents produced at the behest of external figures, documents themselves aimed
at the control of local society. Public disputes and judicial activity, in
particular that of the seigneurial court of Batiscan, reveal how the local
inhabitants themselves defined their horizontal relationships. But we
must be careful not to assume that the society was defined only by its
conflicts. Rather than arguing that meaning *only* arises out of such
confrontations, I contend merely that they allow glimpses of the members of a society in action, adopting different roles in a play of which
no one could be entirely sure of the conclusion.[7] The local understanding of "community" emerges out of the disputes; it is a shared

discourse concerning local issues. As the historian of early-modern Germany David Sabean states, "What is common in community is not shared values or common understanding so much as the fact that members of a community are engaged in the same argument, the same *raisonnement*, the same *Rede*, the same discourse, in which alternative strategies, misunderstandings, conflicting goals and values are threshed out."[8] Thus "parish pump" issues provide evidence for reflections on the nature of local community.[9] Church construction, ditch digging, and road building represent topics directed at public purposes. Such seemingly petty concerns provided the occasion for addressing larger issues of local control. In this way, the arguments can not always be read in a literal fashion: the larger nexus of power relations and the social content of disputes must also be considered.

PUBLIC SPACE

Public space, necessary for the development of sentiments of community, remained limited in these two seigneuries up to 1825. Unlike their counterparts in the British colonies to the south, the people of Batiscan and Sainte-Anne did not have access to permanent local institutions based on popular expression. Nonetheless, public space did exist, as revealed by the places where arguments developed. A few areas constituted proper settings for fighting: the common, churches, and courts.

By its nature, the common implied mutual obligations and therefore constituted a symbolic terrain for public disagreements. Likewise, in other spaces, people met as members of a community. Taverns undoubtedly served as one such place. But the principal public spaces seem to have been the church and the local court. The shared religious devotions of the vast majority of the inhabitants of the seigneuries made the parish churches places where community relations flourished. There locals met as members of a congregation and were expected to contribute their share of expenses.

The church was one of the main sites where arguments dealing with status developed. It was a place to establish one's social preeminence. The seigneurs of Sainte-Anne and Sainte-Marie had fought over the location of the parish church in the late seventeenth century. In 1725 the co-seigneurs of Sainte-Anne disputed physical precedence in the church by arguing over the placement of their pews.[10] Militia captain Loranger of Sainte-Anne had a similar argument concerning pews with Jean Baril Duchesny.[11]

Other members of the community used the church as a place to fight one another. In 1733 François Rivard and François Massicot came to blows in front of the church of Sainte-Geneviève.[12] In 1744 Étienne Prade complained that Jean-Baptiste Baribault, who had just returned from a fur-trading expedition, assaulted him in front of the church door of Sainte-Anne. Baribault gave Prade "a punch in the head and then hit him on the head with a cane" and was only stopped from worse actions by the militia captain. Baribault was drawn away, threatening Prade that he would find him elsewhere.[13]

The church was a place where individuals introduced external issues. The arguments sometimes represented the priests' confrontations with parishioners, but individuals also pursued their own arguments in the church. Thus in 1794 personal disagreements between the Mongrain and Lefebvre families created a crisis for the priest of Sainte-Geneviève when it became necessary to make a decision concerning cantors.[14] When a later priest made the vestry into "a room for the men," he quickly came to regret his decision. Not only did the men smoke in the room, but women used it also: "women enter into it and ... small indiscretions occur."[15] In this way, habitants were willing to perceive church space as a public area.

To a large extent, men dominated the public realm. Nonetheless, as the women's presence in the vestry suggests, they too occupied this space at certain times. Before turning to an analysis of the seigneurial court at Batiscan, it is instructive to raise the issue of women's participation in the court. Although subordinate to their husbands in legal terms, women nonetheless did appear. For instance, Madeleine de Verchères often represented her husband and family in legal issues before the Conseil Supérieur and the intendant in Quebec. An examination of the women who came before the local court suggests the same phenomenon. Ten women acted as plaintiffs, six as defendants. Fourteen were widows; seven of the women represented themselves in court. Two other women represented their husbands. Charlotte Trottain even represented the Jesuit seigneurs in her husband's absence.[16]

However, some women had difficulty making themselves heard in court. Françoise Mercerot appeared for her husband when the merchant St-Agnian demanded payment of their account. St-Agnian requested that proceedings be delayed until the husband himself appeared.[17] The merchant's mother-in-law later faced similar problems, even though she did not appear personally in court. In 1746, acting as the Jesuits' agent for the seigneurial mills, she summoned the miller, François Baril, to court to force him to give proper accounts to her. Baril responded that he did not recognize Mme St-Onge's right to act as agent, but rather, he would listen only to her son-in-law. The miller accused her of wanting to "wrap herself up in a deceitful quarrel only intended to confuse the innocent mind of the said defendant."[18] Two years later, when St-Agnian represented his mother-in-law in court to receive payment for a loan, the defendant, priest Charles Poquelot, had some difficulty distinguishing between St-Onge and her son-in-law: he attacked the latter for having forgotten the services which the priest had provided him. St-Agnian was forced to remind Poquelot that "he [the merchant] had not appeared with the ability to discuss a possession that did not belong to him, but rather to his mother-in-law."[19]

In these cases, women's presence in the court was accepted rather grudgingly. In general, their appearance in this public realm was determined by class. Women of high status appeared most frequently as plaintiffs. At least seven of the sixteen women were seigneurs, notables, or merchants. Thus women, especially powerful widows, were able to appeal to the normative powers of the court. Nonetheless, in this space, as others, men made the decisions and appeared most frequently.

If we keep the under-representation of women in mind, the seigneurial court of Batiscan provided an important location for disputes. But an examination of the activity of the court shows the limitations of this space as an outlet for public disagreements.

THE SEIGNEURIAL COURT OF BATISCAN

Scope

During the French regime the seigneurial court at Batiscan provided a relatively accessible place for settling local legal disputes. The deed that granted the seigneury to the Jesuit order in 1639 had provided the right to "haulte Moyenne et Basse Justice."[20] But although a court functioned at least intermittently in Batiscan in the late seventeenth and early eighteenth centuries, no records survive for the period before 1726.[21]

It seems likely that the Batiscan court only began to function in a more formal fashion in the 1720s. The death occurred in 1723 of the seigneurial judge of Champlain, Michel-Ignace Dizy, *dit* Montplaisir.[22] His brother, Pierre, received a commission as his successor, but he did not actually exercise the charge until the 1750s.[23] Rather, Nicolas Duclos, a prominent local resident, assumed alone the role of seigneurial judge for Batiscan in 1725 and also served in that capacity for the surrounding seigneuries.[24] Jacques Rouillard St-Cire was appointed judge on Duclos's death in 1738.[25] He in turn was replaced by Pierre Dizy de Montplaisir, who served as seigneurial judge for the neighbouring seigneury of Champlain until at least 1758, during which time he also exercised the charge at Batiscan.[26]

Thus after 1726 the inhabitants of Batiscan and the neighbouring seigneuries had access to a local court. The records it produced provide examples of the conflicts in the day-to-day life of a rural community in New France. A close examination of the activities of the seigneurial court of Batiscan permits an evaluation of the role of state-sanctioned authority in the countryside.[27] We can determine what issues were brought to the court, who confronted whom, and how they were able to define the issues at stake. We can also see how they presented their cases and how their arguments were received by the judge. Given the problems that the external authorities had with the local elite, it is important to note how the court system propped up the established hierarchy. Despite its theoretical powers, the court was generally restricted to cases of *basse and moyenne justice*: that is, relatively small-scale disputes and debts.[28] On occasion, the judge functioned as a representative of the intendant (*subdélégué de M. l'intendant*), acquiring evidence on the spot which would apparently be used at a later trial. Sometimes the intendant referred the parties to the local court, as in one case involving two habitants of the seigneury of Saint-Pierre across the St Lawrence River. The judge also seems to have played a role in contributing to the general maintenance of public order, overseeing the lottery in 1740, for example, and helping the Jesuits' agent in ordering and taking a census of the inhabitants in 1753.[29]

The judge was not an entirely impartial official. He was a member of the community, with social and kinship ties to many of the people who came before him in court. In a seigneury owned by a religious order, he was one of the most prestigious individuals, being among the few members of the community who had any direct connection with the intendant.

The judge was aided in his tasks by the clerk (*greffier*) and bailiff (*huissier*). The clerk drew up laconic summaries of the cases, transcribing evidence in the third person. Despite this rhetorical distance, we can discern elements of the individual's argument. In any case, these sparse notings are as close as we come to hearing members of the local community define their view of what was important to them.

The cases brought before the court at Batiscan were similar in nature to those before the court at Notre-Dame-des-Anges, near Quebec (table 6.1). As a study of the latter court notes, this branch of the justice system functioned chiefly as a venue for settling financial disputes.[30] Commercial cases were even more common in Batiscan

Table 6.1

Comparison of cases before the seigneurial courts at Batiscan, 1726–58, and at Notre-Dame-des-Anges, 1754, 1755, and 1758

Nature of case	Batiscan	Notre-Dame-des-Anges
Commerce	49 (55%)	23 (28%)
Inheritance	6 (7%)	17 (21%)
Property	7 (8%)	17 (21%)
Seigneurial rights	8 (9%)	7 (8%)
Other	11 (12%)	4 (5%)
Unknown	8 (9%)	15 (18%)
Total	89	83

Sources: See note 27. For Notre-Dame-des-Anges, see Dickinson, "La justice seigneuriale," 335. Dickinson's definition of commercial cases is rather broad, since it includes "les réclamations pour des ... services non-fournis." Therefore disputes over leases are included in this category for the purposes of comparison, while they might easily be placed in the category of "property."

than in Notre-Dame-des-Anges: 55 per cent compared to 28 per cent. Cases involving "inheritances" and "property," however, were more common in Notre-Dame-des-Anges: 7 per cent to 21 per cent and 8 per cent to 21 per cent. Both courts had a similar proportion of cases involving seigneurial rights. The higher number of "other" cases in Batiscan is probably imputable to the judge's role in ensuring the policing of the local community, a task which would have been handled differently in the larger Jesuit seigneury near the capital of the colony.

A comparison of the status of the plaintiffs and the defendants reveals the power relations which were played out through the court (table 6.2). Habitants represented the largest single group of plaintiffs, though less than a third of the total number. Merchants were responsible for bringing 21 cases before the court. Clearly, given their numerical preponderance in the seigneury, the habitants were greatly under-represented and merchants, seigneurs, church people, and notables over-represented. This difference in power relations becomes even clearer with the study of the defendants: the vast majority were habitants, 65 out of 89. Even though almost three-quarters of the defendants were habitants, they still were relatively under-represented.

Rarely did a person of a lower rank take a superior to court. In one of these few cases, which involved a militia captain against a seigneur, the officer lost. The habitants did not address complaints against seigneurs to this court. Clearly, it supported the local social hierarchy.[31]

Table 6.2
Social interaction of plaintiffs and defendants at the Batiscan court, 1726–58

Social group Plaintiffs	Defendants						
	Habitant	Artisan	Merchant	Church official	Notable	Seigneur noble	Total
Habitant	20	4			3		27
Artisan	4				1		5
Merchant	16	3	1		1		21
Church official	10				1		11
Notable[1]	6	3		1	2	2	14
Seigneur/ noble	9		1		1		11
Total	65	10	2	1	9	2	89

Sources: See note 27.
1 "Notable" includes state officials (e.g., notaries), *fermiers* for seigneurs, and military officers.

The Logic of Dispute

An examination of the construction of arguments before the court supports the emphasis on status. The Batiscan court provides an interesting historical case study for the theories of legal anthropologists. An analysis of the logic of dispute among rural people in Botswana suggests: "The dispute process ... represents the main forum in which Tswana converse daily among themselves about the organization of their society, the nature and content of their normative repertoire, and the attributes of their culture."[32] Likewise, in Batiscan the seigneurial court involved local discourses on social organization.

Much historical and anthropological work on legal systems assumes that people appeal to courts in order to maintain community, that is, to avoid the escalation of disputes.[33] Indeed, in a few cases the judge at Batiscan filled the role of conciliator. In 1740, for example, Antoine Fouché, a schoolmaster from Champlain, summoned the tailor Jacques Lizée of Batiscan to court in order to ascertain the price for a specific piece of work, Lizée having previously refused to commit himself to a figure.[34] In one dispute over payment for land, the opposing parties agreed in court over the resolution of the conflict.[35] Two habitants appeared before the judge and the seigneurial agent in 1752 in order to reach agreement concerning a verbal lease of land

and "to end all the difficulties."[36] In this small number of cases the court functioned as a formalized and officially recognized arbitrator.

If more cases had been like this one, it might be possible to conclude that the court's purpose was solely to maintain social peace in the community, and that individuals used it rather than letting disputes get out of hand. However, most cases involved disagreements of some importance. And only a few were ever resolved by formal arbitration instead of judicial decision. Thus we can only come to a different, and on first glance hardly surprising, conclusion: people who used the Batiscan court disagreed. Or further, those who came before the court did so not merely to maintain social peace but to win their cases. In order to discern the logic behind the court-centred disputing process, we must look at the way in which people disagreed, whether over the definition of the issue at hand, the facts of the case, or the norms to which the facts were applied.

The plaintiff was generally able to establish the issue upon which the dispute would be adjudicated. The defendant very seldom attempted to redefine the issue that the judge should examine. An exception to this rule is illustrative. The militia commander of Champlain (and future judge of the court), Pierre Dizy de Montplaisir, summoned the seigneur of Champlain to court to make restitution for the damages that her pigs had caused in his cornfields. She, or rather her son, was able to shift the debate to the issue of proper consultation: his mother had not been confronted with the complaint, she had not agreed to an estimation of the damage, and Dizy had chosen to raise the issue while Mme Champlain was not home. The judge took the seigneur's side in the case, adopting her definition of the issue at hand over the militia commander's.[37] This was a rare exception.

Instead, without expressly agreeing to the plaintiff's frame of reference, defendants sometimes challenged the other parties to prove their contentions or to ask for a delay. When a guardian of minors was required to pay some of the deceased parents' debts, the request for proof may have only been to provide official recognition of the necessity to pay, so that the guardian would not later be held liable.[38] In some cases the assumption may have been that proof would be difficult to find. When Pierre Gouin summoned Michel Stanislas Lapellé, *dit* Lahaye, to court to account for his cutting of trees on Gouin's land in the dead of winter, Lahaye may have asked for witnesses in the hope that Gouin would be unable to convince anyone to come forward to prove the case.[39] As it turned out, a witness was forthcoming: the man who had cut down the trees for Lahaye.[40]

In cases of commercial debts, defendants requested delays in order to have time to raise the necessary sums. When Marie-Magdeleine Lafond, a merchant and widow of the judge Duclos, took Marie-Anne Adam to court for a debt owed by her late husband, the since-remarried and pregnant Adam asked for a delay until she was able to give birth. Lafond replied that she could not wait, not knowing when Adam was due. The judge agreed with Lafond, condemning Adam to pay the note within eight days or pay with interest.[41] Ten days after the court met, Adam did in fact give birth.

In this way most defendants did not openly disagree with the plaintiffs on the social norms under dispute. Instead, they pursued the arguments in two ways: contesting the conclusion reached by providing more information or offering alternative and irreconcilable facts. These are variations on the same strategy (the first approach challenging the plaintiff's implicit contention that she or he had provided all the appropriate information to the judge). We shall look first at cases where the facts were contradictory and irreconcilable.

In September 1735 the seigneur of Sainte-Anne de la Pérade accused a number of habitants of illegally harvesting hay on the common. The response of all concerned was to deny that they had ever cut or taken hay from the common. Grimard *père* claimed that he had been sick and at home since 20 July.[42] In another instance, priest François Richard of Saint-François-Xavier parish sued Jean Lafont for not fulfilling the terms of his lease. The defendant replied that he had not been present when the lease was signed.[43]

A variation on this kind of disagreement occurred when the defendant provided extenuating information which would reverse the likely conclusion. Many such cases involved debts, the most common issues before the court. As these debts were generally recorded on paper, it presumably should have been difficult simply to deny that they existed. Instead, the defendants claimed that they had already paid back part or all of the debt, or had provided supplies in return. For example, André Rotereau asked the court to help him collect 30 sols from Étienne Langevin in exchange for a half *minot* of wheat lent to him. Langevin contended that he had had a third party repay Rotereau for the wheat.[44] When the merchant St-Agnian tried to force Pierre Périgny to pay seventeen livres he owed, Périgny claimed that he had furnished forty-six livres, worth of supplies to St-Agnian. However, he could only produce an undated and unsigned statement to that effect.[45] The noble Joseph Levrault de Langis was summoned to court by the tailor Lizée to pay eight livres for the suit and trousers made for him. Levrault agreed that Lizée had indeed made the clothes at his behest, but claimed that the tailor had made a most ugly suit, and he therefore refused to pay him.[46]

As this last case suggests, elements of pride and class privilege could enter into the debate. Sometimes the response seems calculated only to avoid admitting guilt in front of the judge. Louis Chayé and Joseph Magny complained that Jean Baptiste Germain, *dit* Magny, and Charles Tiffaut had killed a seal or beluga whale (*loup marin*) which the first two had chased for about three hours, and that they had refused to surrender it. The latter pair claimed that the first two had agreed to accept half the seal in recompense, which they offered to prove by witnesses and oaths.[47] Pierre Gagnon, when accused of stealing 250 sheaves of hay from the barn of the *fermier* (estate manager) of the seigneur of Sainte-Anne, claimed that the hay was being spoiled in the barn.[48]

It is, of course, not surprising that almost all the people who came before the seigneurial court of Batiscan should disagree. Of more interest is the way that defendants adopted the frame of reference imposed by the plaintiffs and subsequently denied guilt before the judge. For example, in the case concerning the removal of hay from the common, the defendants did not claim that the common was by right accessible to all. There was little attempt to appeal to the appropriateness of other norms. Given the recentness of European settlement in the colony, communal traditions had not developed to the extent that they existed in France. This circumstance worked in the favour of the elites, who had written titles and precedents to back up their claims. Thus, in light of the social biases evident in court participation, it is clear that the elite was more successful in defining issues before the court than were the habitants. In this public realm the horizontal communal ties linking litigants were given little acknowledgment.

The court thus reinforced the local social hierarchy. It was clearly a place where personal honour came into play. Status was important to the judicial process not only in New France but in other early-modern societies too; a review of the legal historiography of colonial America argues, "Honor makes the disputants irreconcilable."[49] The method by which the judge made his decisions confirms this point.

Resolutions

The importance of being able to define the nature of the dispute becomes apparent when we examine the ways in which the cases were brought to a conclusion. Not only did the "popular classes" have less ability to define their disputes; they also had different levels of success as far as judicial outcomes were concerned. To comprehend fully the nature and possibilities of these types of negotiation, it is important to consider who won the decisions, even though the outcome cannot be ascertained in all cases. Whose arguments did the state-sanctioned authority favour? And how did the judge reach his verdict?

For some seventy-four cases, we can determine how the judge reacted to the arguments before him (tables 6.3 and 6.4). In eight cases he presided over the process of reaching an agreement or compromise between the two parties. In ten cases the definitive sentence was delayed as the parties waited for further evidence, usually until account books or witnesses could be produced or until experts made a ruling. No other records indicated whether this evidence was forthcoming or whether the parties reached some kind of agreement on their own (or indeed, whether the documents have since disappeared). In eight cases the judge decided in the favour of the defendant. But in the majority of cases – forty-eight – he decided in favour of the plaintiff. Habitants were particularly likely to lose their disputes.

As was the practice in metropolitan France, there was often little indication how the judge reached his decision. In a few cases he referred to intendants' ordinances. But generally he did not give detailed reasoning for his verdict. The assumption seems to be that his judgment followed directly from the evidence given. Yet from the documents alone, a number of cases lacked clear proof. In those instances with no reference to witnesses or to written agreements or contracts, the judge had, from the evidence of the case report, little to base his judgment on, except his knowledge of the individual or of general human nature.

Nonetheless, he was usually able to come to a decision. The determining factor in at least thirteen cases seems to have been the oath sworn by one of the parties on his evidence.[50] When the warden of Saint-François-Xavier parish summoned Michel Rivard, *dit* Fisette, to court to pay the rent for his pew, Fisette claimed that the warden had refused to accept his offer of money in exchange for a contract of concession. To disprove this claim, the warden swore that Fisette had never asked for a contract.[51] In a dispute over the title to land from which cedar posts were taken, the judge accepted an oath from one of the parties about the proper title.[52]

Swearing an oath was more than an empty ritual. Accused of stealing hay from the estate manager of the seigneur of Sainte-Anne, Pierre Gagnon refused to swear an oath on his counterclaim that the hay was in danger of being spoiled when he took it.[53] The widow St-Onge's representative left the judge's office before the miller, François Baril, was able to swear on his statement.[54] The value of an oath varied with one's

Table 6.3
Judicial decisions according to the status of the *plaintiffs* at the Batiscan court, 1726–58

Social group Plaintiffs	Win	Lose	Agree	Delay	Unknown	Total
Habitant	10	5	4	3	5	27
Artisan	2			2	1	5
Merchant	14		2	3	2	21
Church official	7	1			3	11
Notable	9	2	1		2	14
Seigneur/noble	6		1	2	2	11
Total	48	8	8	10	15	89

Sources: See note 27.

Table 6.4
Judicial decisions according to the status of the *defendants* at the Batiscan court, 1726–58

Social group Plaintiffs	Win	Lose	Agree	Delay	Unknown	Total
Habitant	4	36	5	8	12	65
Artisan	2	4	2		2	10
Merchant		2				2
Church official		1				1
Notable	1	4	1	2	1	9
Seigneur/noble	1	1				2
Total	8	48	8	10	15	89

Sources: See note 27.

social status: while struggling over the question of the suit made by tailor Lizée, the military officer Joseph Levrault de Langis not only claimed that he was not interested in Lizée swearing an oath on his testimony, but he deigned not to swear on his own.[55] The question remains of whether oaths were used to break a judicial deadlock, or whether the judge asked the party whom he believed anyway to make an oath in order to justify his verdict. In either case, personal reputation was asserted through the experience in court. As one legal anthropologist points out in a different context, "it is the man who makes the oath believable rather than the oath the man."[56] Some people's words counted for more than did others' in eighteenth-century Batiscan, and the court offered the force of its legitimation to those people.

In this way the sense of "community" that emerges from this analysis of the seigneurial court at Batiscan favoured the local social elite in normative issues. This conclusion is not in itself all that surprising, but it does indicate the problems in identifying a homogeneous rural community in New France. The court did not serve to smooth over social divisions between hierarchical levels, and thus maintain harmony, but rather, it imposed the views of the elite on lower levels.

Alternative Messages

In general, then, the public realm of the court allowed for a top-down definition of local relations. And yet in a small number of cases, and in certain public issues during both the French and the British regimes, we can see a minority, alternative message concerning the nature of social organization. For instance, some court cases over debts provide hints of a different way of viewing social relations.

Defendants sometimes claimed that they had paid back debts to the plaintiff with supplies or with payments to third parties. Antoine Trottier summoned the master cobbler François Thomas to demand payment of a debt of nineteen livres. Thomas replied that he had paid eight livres to François Massicot. He offered eleven livres to Trottier and stated that the latter would have to receive the rest from Massicot. The judge told Trottier to accept Thomas's offer of eleven livres.[57] On the one hand, this defence probably relates to the cash poverty endemic to the colony.[58] On the other, it implies a view of a complex web of economic relations which extended beyond the two who had negotiated the original debt. Without contesting the initial social norms which the plaintiff raised, defendants sometimes invoked the complexity of their horizontal social relations in their attempt to win the judge over to their side.[59]

Likewise, in property relations some defendants attempted to appeal (though unsuccessfully) to different norms. In this region of recent European settlement, written records had greater legal standing than "traditional" rights.[60] When challenged by seigneurs to give up their pretensions to certain pieces of property, François Massicot and Antoine Trottier both made general appeals to what we might term "traditional" rights. Massicot claimed that he had not been told that the land he worked did not belong to him; in fact, he had used the land for the last fifty years and should have been informed earlier if that had not been the case.[61] Trottier's tenure had been shorter, only five years, but he made the same claim that he should be able to exercise rights on the land in question.[62] Both habitants invoked the seigneur's alleged acquiescence to justify their actions.

In a similar fashion, despite lacking a written title, Jean Massicot claimed ownership of property in Sainte-Anne for which the seigneur wanted to demand *lods et ventes*. Massicot justified his use of the land by noting that he had paid the dues.[63] Two years previously he, along with Jacques Massicot and Joseph Jouinot Latulippe, had refused to show their contracts and survey certificates to the seigneurs of Batiscan. The three men argued that their land had been surveyed fifty years earlier and that the seigneurs could locate their contracts themselves. "If the land had not been surveyed," they added, "they would never have paid rent for it."[64] In these ways, habitants appealed to prescriptive rights to property.

But in all these cases the judges agreed with the seigneurs. The latter contended that the habitants' lack of written confirmation of their rights rendered their claims invalid. In this way, seigneurs, like merchants, appealed to the authority of written documents against tradition. The habitants, in invoking the complexity of daily life and not the dry facts of contracts, invoked a different sense of social relations. Even if their arguments show them clutching at straws, these habitants still proposed a view of social relations which it was possible to present, one in which seigneurs owed certain responsibilities to their tenants and in which horizontal relations between habitants should be recognized for their interconnectedness.

PUBLIC WORKS IN THE FRENCH REGIME

Ditches and Roads

To stress the links between members of the locality did not necessarily imply that all expected equal treatment. Rather, habitants often invoked the particularities of their social position. This practice reflects the difficulty of pursuing public enterprises during the French regime. Disputes arose over how responsibilities were distributed for works of public utility. These projects were often defined by external authorities, such as the chief road officer or the bishop, and included new churches, public roads and bridges, and drainage ditches. State authorities intervened when habitants created problems concerning civil public works by refusing to contribute to the extent that they were expected. These cases provide other evidence of the ways in which individuals were symbolically able to state their position in the community.

The removal of forests and the use of land for agricultural purposes made drainage ditches vital. As property lines were laid out according to principles that did not necessarily respect topographical realities, ditches had to cross many habitants' lots to be effective. By their very nature, these ditches required some cooperation on the part of habitants, not only for the initial digging but also for their maintenance. The history of the drainage ditch on the Grande-Côte of Batiscan illustrates the habitants' uncooperative nature and the necessity of appealing to external authorities to manage internal difficulties.

Originally ordered in 1707 by Intendant Jacques Raudot, the ditch was intended to drain the waters that flowed from the depths of the forest and flooded the habitants' lands each year. A number of habitants worked on the project that year, but it was not maintained. In 1728 the seigneurial agent of Batiscan appeared before the local court to complain that the late M. Chatelleroy and Magdelenne Quatresous had not respected the order. A ditch on their land was supposed to join up with the main one. Their heirs' representative stated to the court that he could not agree to pay for the ditch in light of the burden it would place on the children, contending that natural creeks took care of the problem. The judge ordered that the representative complete the ditch.[65]

In 1730 Intendant Hocquart confirmed the earlier ruling that habitants must complete the drainage system.[66] Nonetheless, the ditch was still not maintained. A number of habitants informed the intendant in 1744 that, since its construction, "no one wished to clean out the said ditch." Over the years, it had become level with the surrounding land. The land of Michel Pellé, *dit* Desrives, was particularly damaged by the runoff; his land was swamped in the spring and during harvest time. An embankment was required to redirect the water. An unspecified number of habitants requested that the intendant "condemn all the habitants to work communally on the said ditch, and also to work each on their own properties."[67] Local arbiters who examined the ditch recommended that it be widened and deepened, and that the land be cleared of trees on either side. The intendant's representative adopted their report and ordered that an allocation of the workload be drawn up.[68] Thus even such an issue of practical economic utility required the involvement of state authorities.

The construction of roads and bridges posed similar problems of harmonizing local efforts. In these cases also, the habitants were careful to defend their own, often individual, interests. Roads were of local utility, of course, but rivers also served as communication routes for the locals. Indeed, the primary purpose of roads was to permit others to pass through the area, not to enhance local communications. Moreover, they were one of the main examples of state power. It is no coincidence that the commissioners assessing the rebellious parishes after the American invasion in 1775 emphasized the importance of road maintenance: "Recommended to the officers to maintain the roads in good order."[69] From the point of view of the state, the roads constituted a precious military asset.

In Batiscan the problem of maintaining secure roads came into conflict with local attitudes concerning land usage. In 1716 the chief road commissioner surveyed a road through Batiscan seigneury some distance from the shore of the St Lawrence River and ordered the habitants to construct it according to his instructions. They protested that the road would be more appropriately built along the shore. In 1724, despite commenting that the habitants had lied about a lack of wood for bridges, the road commissioner accepted their proposal to clear the road where they wanted. He noted that their refusal to follow his orders "required us to submit to their wishes." However, he observed that, if the road were harmed by erosion caused by the river, the habitants would have to rebuild the route on the location originally proposed.[70] Eight years later, the chief road officer was summoned to the seigneury to certify that the road had indeed become impassable.[71] Jean-Eustache Lanouillier de Boisclerc, apparently a much more forceful figure than his predecessor, ordered that a new road be cleared behind the habitants' buildings. He drew up a detailed account of the work that each family should contribute to the project.[72] For successful public projects, individual responsibilities had to be made very clear.

Sometimes the opposition to an external order regarding local roads was restricted to a small number of individuals, concerned that they were contributing more than their share to the project. Intendant Hocquart ordered the militia captain of Sainte-Geneviève in 1730 to oversee the rebuilding of a bridge over the Rivière à Veillet, washed away in the spring breakup. The militia captain was supposed to divide the task according to people's abilities.[73] However, in 1734 officials reported that the bridge was still incomplete. The intendant promulgated two further ordinances on the same subject, and by 1737 these had had their effect. However, Fonville and Rouillard St Cire *fils*, members of the local elite, only provided two workdays of the required three. When the surveyor general tried to make them pay the workers' wages for the other workday, they refused.[74]

In Sainte-Anne seigneury in 1732, the road commissioner reported on the deficiencies in the roads. Not only were they often impassable, but the small bridges over the numerous creeks were unsafe: "all the bridges are so bad and so narrow that horses and even pedestrians cannot pass over them without running the risk of breaking their legs."[75] Ten years later La Pérade apprised the commissioner that the problems had not been solved. He requested that the habitants be forced to maintain the bridges and roads, "given the failings of the habitants and the respect that they should show for official orders."[76] The roads represented an occasion for La Pérade to vaunt his social superiority; for him they provided more evidence of the habitants' lack of appropriate respect for the social hierarchy. The consequent report of the road commissioner noted the poor quality of the roads and divided up the repairs. For the habitants, roads represented a tax burden, which had to be judiciously distributed if it were to be respected.

Churches

Local reactions to church-building projects were similar. A study of politics in the lower Richelieu region examines the arguments which pitted lay members of the community against the priests. The church represented a contested terrain between these two groups, particularly with regard to contributions to the construction of new chapels.[77] However, the church also symbolized a "contesting terrain." The disagreements over levies for church expenses did not always present a unified congregation against a spendthrift priest. Often the problems lay among the parishioners and revealed a variety of social divisions.

For instance, Bishop Saint-Vallier complained in 1690 that the habitants of Sainte-Anne refused to take their parish priest to the chapel in Grondines so that he could celebrate mass there, as the bishop had ordered.[78] Parish boundaries represented a limit to the social obligations that habitants were willing to fulfill. Even within parishes, difficulties arose respecting church works. The bishop also admonished the parishioners to complete the church and cemetery which they had begun, noting that "you have somewhat diminished in the zeal that you demonstrated at the beginning."[79] In order to ensure the completion of church buildings, it was necessary to weigh carefully the amount that each was supposed to contribute. In 1716 Intendant Bégon ordered seigneurial court judge Guillaume Larue to draw up a roll of the amount that each habitant was expected to furnish towards the construction of a church, the amount to be determined "according to his abilities" and voted on by an assembly of habitants.[80] In 1731 a similar process took place when Intendant Hocquart ordered that the habitants should provide their share to the building of the presbytery: forty habitants providing one-half *toise* of stone, thirty one-third *toise*, and thirteen one-quarter *toise*.[81] To envision building a new public structure, it was necessary to take account of the differing fortunes and capabilities of the habitants. Such determinations presumably reflected disparities in wealth and the local consensus on those differences. Nonetheless, parishioners sometimes contested the burdens placed upon them, and external authorities had to step in to legitimize the local decisions.

For the parishioners, the problems involved in the 1720s division of Saint-François-Xavier parish were caused as much by practical economic issues as by local loyalties. Following Attorney General Mathieu-Benoît Collet's inquiry into the convenience of parish church locations in 1721, civil and church authorities agreed on establishing a chapel along the Rivière Batiscan.[82] Initially, the priest at Batiscan was responsible for serving this chapel. In 1726 the habitants settled along the depths of the river complained that priest Gervais Lefebvre was ignoring them. He replied that his health did not permit him to serve the chapel once a month as he had promised to do, but he offered to spend eight days in the spring and in the fall, as well as the day of Sainte-Geneviève, at the chapel. When the habitants along the river refused this offer, Intendant Bégon ordered Lefebvre to resign from the Sainte-Geneviève charge and commissioned André Jorian of Champlain to take it up.[83]

Lefebvre opposed this drastic reduction in the size of his parish. The troubles continued for the next five months, and the new intendant, Dupuy, ordered that Jorian be confirmed in his post and that the habitants of Rivière Batiscan contribute to the construction of a presbytery for the priest.[84] About thirty habitants met to estimate the costs of the construction and determined that each house should furnish one *minot* of wheat or 40 sols. However, a number of habitants did not attend the meeting, and they refused to contribute their share of the costs.[85] While Lefebvre's opposition stemmed from his loss of the major part of his tithes, he was supported by some parishioners who did not want to contribute to the building of a new presbytery. Furthermore, a number of habitants refused to pay tithes to Jorian, leading the priest to appeal to the authority of the seigneurial court.[86]

Attempts to resolve the issue went far beyond the local community. Lefebvre and a majority of his parishioners addressed a request to the king. They claimed that the division of the parish had taken forty-two families from the seventy-five that had composed the old parish. The ability of Saint-François-Xavier to support a priest was therefore reduced. Furthermore, the habitants who had had to contribute to the expenses of the old church, presbytery, and cemetery now had to bear the burden of new costs. The minister in France ordered the governor and intendant to examine the case again,[87] and ultimately in 1730 Lefebvre signed an agreement to end the difficulties: nine families were added back to Saint-François-Xavier parish.[88]

This extended dispute over parish boundaries illustrates a number of points relative to the nature of local community. Under the leadership of the local priest, the community divided into camps over the changes in parish boundaries. Lefebvre, the parish priest since 1715, was able to secure support from a number of his parishioners in his fight with the colonial government. The habitants divided over the issue because of related expenses and the distance they would have to travel to attend church. In particular, they were greatly concerned about being taxed more than their share.

But the question also reveals some of the problems in the internal organization of local society. The difficulties of carrying out and maintaining public endeavours made themselves known to external authority. The community itself did not provide any mechanism for resolving such issues. A study of the construction of the first royal road between Montreal and Quebec concludes, "Authority was the only factor of unity."[89] The state and church officials were willing to allow local officials to take care of the difficult apportioning of the burden, but these local decisions too often came into dispute. The habitants made a calculated assessment of their situation and refused to contribute more than they deemed appropriate.[90]

COMMUNITY UNDER THE BRITISH REGIME

Churches and Roads

Under the British regime, church-related expenses remained a divisive issue. We have already seen the problems faced by the unpopular priest Aubry in the building and decorating of the chapel at Saint-Stanislas. His difficult personality did not cause all the problems. One of his successors faced similar issues. By 1813 the Saint-Stanislas chapel was no longer sufficient for the population and was falling into ruin. Forty-nine men signed a petition requesting that they be allowed to build a new one.[91] The following year, with the bishop's approval, the parishioners appealed to Thomas Coffin of the Court of Commissioners for his permission.[92] Having fulfilled the requirements, they petitioned again in 1817 for the authority to make estimates of the work and to draw up a roll of contributions.[93] The work was still not completed in 1822: "the habitants have not managed to begin building because of their bad harvests and the scarcity of money."[94] Three years later the priest Côté complained to the bishop that they had abandoned the project. He too was beginning to despair: "I, along with the elders, have also abandoned the project, because after all the trouble taken for the last two months by the workers to divide up the costs, to ascertain the prices of the different works required, etc., and to see such little goodwill, this has really discouraged me."[95] Economic difficulties and different opinions concerning the proper place for the church had led the parishioners to delay the project.

The fear of double taxation was also at issue, since a new parish was to be created for the habitants of Saint-Stanislas. A number of habitants in the remote areas of Sainte-Anne attended the chapel of Saint-Stanislas because the mountains cut them off from the church at Sainte-Anne. They were careful to make sure that their contributions to the chapel would not be doubled by a requirement to help with the village church.[96] At the same time, nineteen habitants of Champlain seigneury who were to be transferred to Saint-Stanislas protested that they were closer to Sainte-Geneviève and had already made contributions to the parish of Champlain.[97] Similarly, a group of habitants of Batiscan seigneury who lived on the south side of the Rivière des Chutes asked to be left in Sainte-Geneviève parish.[98] Indeed, the seigneurial agent reported that habitants were apprehensive of taking up new land in Batiscan seigneury because of the public costs involved. If they accepted land along the Rivière des Chutes and on the Côte Saint-Stanislas, they expected to be assessed for contributions to the church at Sainte-Geneviève.[99] Following all these hesitations, two trustees of Saint-Stanislas complained to the bishop in 1825 that Côté had demanded more from the habitants than they could afford.[100] Achieving consensus on the issue was clearly a complicated process.

In Sainte-Anne, priest Morin also had to wait many years for repairs to be made to his presbytery and the church. In 1809 the bishop addressed a pastoral letter to the habitants of Sainte-Anne, pointing out the decrepit state of the presbytery and calling for an end to their divisions. Over the years, he commented, the habitants had been divided over how to remedy the situation: "you have not been able to agree, some of you wishing to construct in wood, others in stone, and ... the project stopped there, partly because of the lack of agreement among you and partly because of the usual lack of zeal for public works."[101] The bishop concluded by threatening the parishioners that they would lose their priest if they failed to act. The following year the majority of the habitants requested permission to build a stone presbytery.[102] By 1814 the building was more or less habitable,[103] but two years later it still had not been completed: "by the bad faith of those who through poverty or otherwise did not furnish their share."[104] The construction of presbyteries revealed divisions within parishes concerning the degree to which each family could be expected to participate. The protracted nature of the problems illustrates the difficulties of achieving local agreement on such issues.

Even the parish cemetery was not exempt from such differences. When Moll, the new priest of Sainte-Anne, suggested digging a canal to drain the cemetery, the bishop replied: "you know how difficult it is for this parish to agree on public contributions. Some of the habitants will bring earth, the others not; part of the cemetery will be filled up, the rest will be neglected, and waters will stagnate there."[105] The bishop commiserated with Moll the following year when the priest proclaimed his disgust with the parish.[106]

These parochial disputes spread over a hundred years and more do not illustrate a perpetual hostility between priests and parishioners. Rather, they show a general reluctance to provide funds and energy for various public works. They also supply evidence of poverty within the community and of disputes between habitants jealous of their time and money and fearful of being overtaxed relative to other members of the community.

There is some evidence that a similar practical attitude towards public roads persisted into the British regime. The commissioners for the improvement of the internal communication of Saint-Maurice county proposed in 1818 that the government grant £200 for the construction of a bridge over the Rivière Champlain. The fact that the river formed the border of Champlain and Batiscan seigneuries and was therefore within neither made agreement on construction difficult to achieve. The poverty of the inhabitants was also a factor, they explained.[107] In another case, in 1824 the agent for the Board of Commissioners of the Jesuit Estates reported that the road leading to the mill at the Rivière des Envies was becoming impassable. The habitants, he learned, "were liable to the Servitude of the Road, and it was a difficult matter to get them to come forward, their indifference about the State of the Road appears to arise from the opinion they express of the Miller[']s want of knowledge in working the Mill."[108] The habitants' attitude was not determined so much by a general opposition to the required corvées as it was by utilitarian views. Their cooperation in any public endeavour was contingent on many factors, the principal one being the benefit that they as individuals, much more than as members of a community, would receive from it.

Local Leadership and Community Action

Some road and church-related expenses thus remained divisive public issues. However, as a consequence of the rise of a local lay elite by the early nineteenth century, there was a higher degree of willingness to organize public endeavours. For example, in 1812 an unspecified number of habitants petitioned the House of Assembly to allow a change in the management of the Sainte-Anne common; the "proprietors" wanted to be able to elect three or more trustees to regulate it.[109] In contrast to many of the disputes concerning other public works, in 1800 some habitants voluntarily repaired the dike at the seigneurial gristmill, although they were careful to submit a bill for the work to the agent of the commission for Jesuit estates.[110] We have already seen the actions of local entrepreneurs during the 1810s and 1820s in building mills to replace the decrepit banal mills.

The clearest examples of local initiatives occurred in the late 1820s. They represented responses to the policies of the Parti Patriote in the House of Assembly, and in this way they acknowledged an increased government intervention in local affairs. The assembly offered subsidies for schools and roads.[111] In 1829 it approved a bill funding primary schools. Later that year, three schoolrooms opened in Sainte-Anne. A local citizen provided part of his house for one of the classrooms until a proper building could be completed. The schoolmaster noted that this prospect was not imminent because of "the opposition that we have had from the priest as well as from some of his partisans who are against these schools."[112] The other two schoolrooms, one for boys and the other for girls, shared a house built under the trustees' supervision.[113] In 1830 and 1831, schools were opened in each of the parishes of Batiscan, the local priests serving as trustees.[114]

Similarly, after the assembly promised subsidies for highways, the habitants demonstrated that they could on occasion agree about a public project. In 1830 almost the entire male population of Sainte-Anne signed a petition requesting a government subsidy for the construction of a bridge over the Rivière Sainte-Anne.[115] This petition provides some evidence of an increasing ability to function as a unified community. To the extent that public projects supply confirmation of community sentiment, greater local unity developed in response to the initiatives of the assembly, even if relations with the local priest were not always smooth.

The clearest evidence of a united community is provided by poll books for Hampshire county from the 1820s. The poll books reveal the extent of public unity: every voter listed for Sainte-Anne in 1826 voted for Pierre-Antoine Dorion, an important local timber merchant.[116] The next year each of 401 electors voted for Dorion again. The vast majority of this number declared for a second candidate, F. Drolet, as well, although some 13 supported one of the winning candidates, F.-X. Larue.[117] It is impossible to know whether or not

everyone willingly agreed to vote for Dorion. Given the lack of a secret ballot, it is probably safer to assume that the voters had to be seen
publicly supporting the local candidate, a member of the petty bourgeois elite.[118] In this way, electoral politics permitted the establishment of strong community links with the developing new lay elites.

This unanimity on the political front leads to certain reflections on the
changes that occurred in social relations in the early nineteenth century.
With the exception of a few church and road projects, local leadership
achieved a large degree of consensus on certain issues. This petty bourgeoisie, which had developed through the process of economic differentiation, was able to shift the focus of local politics. Thus the people of
Batiscan and Sainte-Anne experienced their moments of unity in their
dealings with the state, at the same time that the government, through
the assembly, was beginning to play a more interventionist role. By offering funds for the construction of public works, the assembly resolved
some of the public divisions that had so often plagued local projects.

CONCLUSION

The early nineteenth century did not find the habitants of the two
seigneuries functioning as the unified rural communities that are so
celebrated in twentieth-century urban mythology. As the problems
over church construction illustrate, individuals could find occasions
to dispute and delay public enterprises. The evidence does not show
an entirely harmonious, self-regulating community.

This feature of local social relations was common throughout the
period. As the records of the seigneurial court during the French regime reveal, there was a locally felt class structure involving significant distinctions. The court served to legitimize hierarchical ties at the
expense of horizontal ones. The various public projects of both the
French and the British regimes also illustrate the divided character of
local society. Generally, individuals appealed to their special circumstances in disregard of communal aims. The local elite often had to
solicit external authorities for help in completing public works.

Nonetheless, the community did on some occasions speak with a
unified voice. As was true in the French regime, but more common in
the early nineteenth century, circumstances led the habitants of Batiscan and Sainte-Anne to form a communal front when they faced the
outside world. The case of the new schools suggests that in the 1820s
the colonial assembly began to intrude more and more into local affairs. This process occurred at a time of increasing social differentiation. The petty bourgeoisie, more than the seigneurs, was able to
channel local energies in favour of public enterprises.

A purposeful community emerged most clearly in relations with the external world; concerted action was much more difficult within the locality. If the concept of "community" implies a degree of unity, the people of Batiscan and Sainte-Anne behaved most like a community in their dealings with the state. The colonial state, as represented by British rule and a Canadian-dominated assembly, was thus an implicit presence in the development of local community.

7 An Industrial Landscape

Round roll the embers, shaping as they meet;
Wake while they roll, and glow with living heat.

Ovid, *Metamorphoses*, 502

By the early nineteenth century, the seigneuries of Batiscan and Sainte-Anne, like other parts of the St Lawrence valley, had entered a period of important political and socio-economic transition. Against the backdrop of modifications in the agricultural base and an increasingly influential local elite, British immigrants attempted to modify in a dramatic fashion the local society of the Batiscan and Sainte-Anne areas. From 1799 to 1813 the Batiscan Iron Works Company brought one of the colony's largest industrial endeavours to the outskirts of the village of Sainte-Geneviève.[1] In the 1820s the well-connected Hale family purchased the seigneury of Sainte-Anne with visions of creating an English idyll on the banks of the St Lawrence.

In the end, neither of these two projects would radically alter the focus of the region. The failures of these visions contrast with the success of the French-Canadian population in surviving British attempts at assimilation.

RESOURCES AND COMMERCE

An industrial focus on the region was slow to develop. Explorers of the sixteenth and seventeenth centuries did not fail to comment on the shields of forests that faced them as they sailed along the St Lawrence River, but commercial perspectives on the trees developed slowly. Well into the eighteenth century, timber still represented little more than an obstacle to the reshaping of this landscape. An anonymous critic wrote in 1706 that the land already cleared in Batiscan was the best available. With the rest, "it is impossible to do anything or to take anything from it."[2] No market existed to justify the removal of these forests solely for the sake of the timber.

Despite some efforts under the French regime to encourage forest-based industries and the presence of a sawmill in Batiscan as early as 1722 and one in Sainte-Anne from 1726, it does not appear that external markets greatly influenced the cutting of local timber.[3] However, proposals to establish an industry such as an iron foundry could have created a commercial purpose for local wood. In the 1730s a group of experts visited two sites on the Rivière Batiscan to ascertain if either was suitable for the construction of an ironworks. In the end, they decided on a site on the Rivière Saint-Maurice.[4] However, the presence of iron ore in Batiscan still attracted external interest. In 1748 the governor argued that Batiscan (and two other places) offered more promising conditions than did the ironworks already constructed on the Saint-Maurice: "there are places where one can much more easily place furnaces. For the availability of wood, the proximity of minerals, and the greater quantity of water, the seigneury of Mr de Tonnancour, the Rivière Batiscan and Terrebonne seemed to me to be better choices than the Saint-Maurice."[5] But the recommendation would come to nothing. Throughout the French regime the commercial possibilities of the forests of Batiscan and Sainte-Anne remained largely untouched.

By the late eighteenth century the forests offered more clearly the possibility of commercial profits. After the Conquest the British colonial leaders applied state prerogatives with flexibility, at least in this domain. Not until the 1820s did the colonial administration attempt to benefit from the Crown's timber rights.[6] The promise of untrammelled profits from timber influenced seigneurs' attitudes towards the local landscape. The German officer commented in 1776, "All the Seigneurs still have enough woodland, which they can sell."[7] However, until external demand for this wood increased, the profits remained only potential ones.[8]

Ultimately, the problems posed by the distances involved in timber cutting in these two seigneuries were overcome by the investment of capital and by the use of state privileges. Charles-Louis de Lanaudière used his position in 1778 as surveyor general of forests and rivers and his connections to the government to sell timber from the forests of the region to the army garrisons.

Lanaudière's land-granting policies implied a new attitude towards the forest resources of Sainte-Anne. His attempts to secure more "determinate" tenure by abolishing the seigneurial system were linked to his desire to obtain higher prices up front and to make more commercial use of the forests of Sainte-Anne. By the early nineteenth century he had raised rents for concessions beyond what habitants were willing or able to pay.[9] "I have made frequent application to Mr. Lanaudière our Seignior," Louis Gendron testified before a legislative committee in 1823, "but he never chose to concede at the same rate at which the old Lands along the River in his Seigniory were conceded."[10] Lanaudière similarly refused to open his seigneury of Lac-Maskinongé west of Trois-Rivières to settlers, in the belief, according to M. James McDouall, "that the land would become more valuable in the process of time, and that he preferred to sell them at 5s. per acre."[11] Although Lanaudière's actions did not imply an antipathy to agricultural land use, they did reveal his desire to profit from his seigneurial title, both by raising dues and by conserving timber while markets developed for it. The change in the perceived value of trees in the late eighteenth and early nineteenth centuries lay in the increase in their market value outside the seigneury.

The timber and mineral resources of Batiscan were finally put to large-scale use in the final years of the eighteenth century with the establishment of the Batiscan Iron Works Company. When Thomas Coffin and John Craigie decided to invest funds that the latter had borrowed from the colonial government in an enterprise established to compete with the Saint-Maurice forges, they were attracted by both the iron ore deposits and the expansive forests. Part of the appeal of this industrial endeavour was that it allowed the forests to be put to direct commercial profit.[12]

Coffin began employing locals in 1799 to cut and carry wood. In one of the final titles he granted, the last remaining Jesuit, Father Jean-Joseph Casot, gave Coffin exclusive rights to cut pine in all unconceded parts of the seigneury.[13] Despite the fact that he had received vast concessions, Coffin was somewhat indiscriminate about where trees were felled. In 1799 Jean Trépanier complained to the Jesuits' agent that wood was being cut on land belonging to the mill.[14] Although the colonial government was made aware of the company's use of the forest, it apparently did nothing to hinder the firm's access to the resources it needed.

The company's reliance on cheap wood was clearly a major factor in its operation. The Saint-Stanislas and Saint-Prosper mountains were partially deforested in order to provide fuel for the operations.[15] Only once the company had closed did the government express interest in controlling access to the forest.[16]

The establishment of this large-scale enterprise contributed to a new attitude towards the landscape, one which favoured the economic value of trees and mineral resources and focused much more on their removal than their replacement with crops. External markets, more than local needs, determined land use. Nonetheless, logging did not preclude agricultural activity. The directors of the ironworks conceded small plots of land to forty-eight employees in 1809.[17] By encouraging what were probably small gardens, the owners wished that the workers would contribute to their own subsistence so as not to rely exclusively on wages from the company. Habitants were quick to sow crops on recently cleared land, even if the Batiscan Iron Works wanted to maintain such land as a road.[18] The directors of the company conceded property in the seigneury of Champlain with the understanding that the new owner would cut the trees on the lot and turn them into charcoal for heating the forge's furnace.[19]

Changes in imperial policy during and following the Napoleonic Wars seemed finally to offer a clear boost to merchants and seigneurs who wished to invest capital in the timber trade. Among other attributes, the timber resources in Sainte-Anne promised great profits to prospective buyers. Elizabeth Hale reported, with some exaggeration, that "no Timber has hitherto been cut down but for the purposes of fuel, & there is now such a demand for Timber for the Shipping (for exportation) that being so near the River we should make a good sum of that almost directly."[20] In fact, before the Hales took possession of the seigneury of Sainte-Anne, small entrepreneurs had already been active in the area cutting and selling timber.

In the state-owned seigneury of Batiscan, vigilance over the cutting of trees on unconceded land seems to have been particularly lax: after many such warnings over the years, the commissioners of the Jesuit estates again heard in 1824 that "Considerable Supplies of Billets of Pine and other kinds of Timber are furnished to the Merchants at Quebec from the Seigneury of Batiscan and Cape Magdalaine, which have been cut upon the Lands not Conceded." Once again, the official concluded, "Steps ought to be taken to prevent a deterioration of this Nature."[21] However, such small-scale operations could easily escape the unobservant eye of the seigneurial agent.

Thus for seigneurs, merchants, and some habitants by the early nineteenth century, the timber trade offered an alternative use of the landscape. The trees were seen as an economic end in themselves, at least by certain merchants and presumably by the habitants whom they paid to cut them. It might still be some years away, but forestry was the industry of the future in the Saint-Maurice area, particularly along the Rivière Batiscan.[22] This commercial perspective involved no particular plan to replace the felled forests with new land uses. Yet the timber industry did not conflict with agrarian purposes. This industry, given its seasonal patterns, allowed marginal farmers to combine wage labour with agriculture and thus permitted the expansion of the local economy beyond its subsistence level.

Even before the timber industry fully turned its sights on the area, deforestation had had ecological repercussions. By the early 1820s, habitants established as far up the Rivière Batiscan as Saint-Stanislas complained about the lack of trees on their concessions. Pierre Trepanier answered a query concerning the availability of timber for building and fuel on the "old Lands of the Seigniory of Batiscan" by declaring, "There are Lands on which there is no Timber for building, and but little for Fuel. I have been myself obliged to go three quarters of a League off for my Fire-wood."[23]

The removal of the forest cover and the introduction of extensive farming techniques both contributed to a reduction in the soil's capacity to hold water. Spring runoff became a larger problem as settlement proceeded up the Batiscan and Sainte-Anne rivers. In both seigneuries, churches built on the river banks had to be protected from the ravages of spring flooding. In 1822 church officials consented to change the building site for the church at Saint-Stanislas, "judging that the continued clearing of lands would only increase each year the level of the spring runoff in the river."[24] In this way, deforestation altered the landscape beyond its intent. Even before the important phase of forestry development that began in the 1820s, inspired by increased imperial demand, the local landscape was already experiencing the effects of this externally influenced perspective on the terrain.

THE BATISCAN IRON WORKS COMPANY, 1799–1813

The Batiscan Iron Works Company, one of the few relatively large-scale industrial enterprises in the colony, was established on the basis of the extensive timber and mineral resources of the backcountry of Batiscan seigneury.[25] The entrepreneurs and government officials Thomas Coffin and John Craigie located their company in Batiscan for a variety of reasons. The necessary resources (bog iron and timber for charcoal) and the area's accessibility to the St Lawrence provided the prerequisites. Given the structural changes in agriculture and the demographic pressures, it is likely that they could tap a local labour pool, but this was undoubtedly true of other parts of the colony too. The issue of land title in Batiscan seigneury was also important. The two men were able to lay claim to local resources during a particular historical moment: the transfer of proper land title from the Jesuits to the government.

Between 1799 and 1813 the ironworks employed a local workforce. It also brought in workers from afar and linked the region more closely to distant markets. The enterprise presaged the spatial economic orientation that the timber industry represented: founded on capital derived externally, it focused the activity of the local habitants on the hinterland of the seigneuries. In so doing, it turned their economic horizons geographically inward.

To evaluate the company's implications for the seigneury, I shall discuss the labour which the company employed, the markets for its products, and its demand for supplies. The Batiscan Iron Works Company represented the closest link that the economy of the local region had to colonial markets during the period under study.

Labour

Thomas Coffin, John Craigie, and Benjamin Joseph Frobisher, the directors of the ironworks,[26] relied heavily on skilled labour from outside the seigneury; the unskilled workers were recruited both locally and elsewhere in the St Lawrence valley. Like the Saint-Maurice ironworks, the Batiscan company called upon a specialized workforce. Many of the most highly skilled employees came from elsewhere in the colony or the United States. The directors of the company tried on a number of occasions to bring in foundry-men from Vermont, where a similar ironworks existed. They requested Joshua Bates, a forgeman from Vergennes who had already worked for the company in 1807, to return in 1808.[27] In the same year they invited Isaac Williams, who lived in Foucault seigneury (Caldwell's Manor), near the Vermont border, to join the workforce.[28] The moulders John, Thomas, and Robert Slicer, from a family of ironmasters at the Saint-Maurice forges, were in Batiscan as early as 1803.[29]

There was both a local and an external recruitment of colliers and lumbermen. It is possible that, as time passed, local employees substituted more and more for distant workers. Lord Selkirk, in his discussion of the different ironworks in North America, noted in 1804 that the Batiscan company employed Americans. "They contract with American workmen for Charcoal at 2½ or 3$ a load of 108 Bushels & they reckon this a more oeconomical plan than to employ different people to cut & to char."[30] There were still American colliers at Batiscan in 1808, but that same year the company hired a few former employees of the Saint-Maurice forges. The directors claimed to have taken on some twenty lumberjacks in February 1808. It was common practice to bring in lumbermen from other parishes. The company's merchant contacts sent some from Lotbinière and Sainte-Croix in 1808 and 1811, and in the latter year the directors tried to convince a merchant in Rivière-du-Loup (near Trois-Rivières) to send others.[31]

Apparently the habitants of the region did not fill the demand for labour. Nonetheless, a certain number of workers, in particular some of the less skilled, were recruited locally. Among them were quarrymen, carpenters, and porters. It is difficult to say much about their working conditions on the basis of the available documentation; such considerations were, after all, unlikely to find a place in the company's outbound correspondence. The forges undoubtedly employed men (and perhaps women too)[32] and provided them a seasonal income.

With no census during the period of the company's operation, it is difficult to know how many people were involved in the forges at any given moment. At the time that a fire destroyed the works in 1801, about sixty men were said to be living there.[33] A series of notarial documents from 1809 provides a list of forty-eight resident employees.[34]

The ironworks operated on a seasonal basis. The furnace was not lit before the end of spring runoff. In 1808, for example, the furnace was lit on 20 June and extinguished probably during the first week of December. In 1811 it was in operation from 21 June to 30 November. Thus it functioned only five months per year. But labour in the works did not completely conform to this seasonal pattern. When the furnace was shut down, workers cut wood and prepared coal. The directors naturally did not want to maintain the ironworkers at their expense on the site while the furnace was extinguished: they would have preferred them all, and especially the Americans, to return home. However, when the merchants who sold the forges' ironware were slow to send cash, the workers remained on the site at the company's expense.[35] Some workers established themselves permanently in Sainte-Geneviève. In addition to the directors' grants of small plots of land in the vicinity of the forges in 1809, Lanaudière, the seigneur of Sainte-Anne, had ceded larger pieces of land two years earlier.[36]

Although the managers of the works, Nicolas Bayard, Thomas Coffin, and Benjamin Joseph Frobisher, apparently functioned in both English and French, the small village at the works was not a direct reflection of its surrounding region. Some of the managers' decisions show how they differentiated themselves from the French-speaking population around them. Bayard brought in an English-speaking servant. Benjamin Joseph Frobisher ordered a copy of the *Encyclopaedia Britannica*.[37] The ornamentation of the company's stoves appealed to a sense of British imperial identity: busts of Admirals Nelson and Duncan appeared on them.[38]

Distribution of Products

The choice of these imperial symbols for the ironworks is not surprising; after all, the company owed its existence to the colonial government's benign neglect. The principal partners' enviable political connections were useful in their efforts to sell the products of the ironworks. Craigie was particularly well placed in this regard, since he served as deputy commissary general to the army, the official responsible for purchasing supplies for the single largest internal market in the colony. Between 1800 and 1806, when he came under criticism for the practice, he purchased at least £762 worth of products from his own company.[39] When Joseph Frobisher participated in the commission for the building of a prison in Montreal, his son wrote to him to bid on the contract for furnishing bars for the windows. The company did receive the contract, but nonetheless experienced difficulties in receiving payment.[40]

According to the company's letter book, the enterprise principally sold its products to small merchants. It established an extensive network of merchant-clients both in rural parishes and in the cities. From the Rivière Ouelle to Saint-Denis, William Henry (Sorel), Berthier, L'Assomption, La Prairie, Vaudreuil, Saint-Charles-sur-Richelieu, and Varennes, the products of the ironworks spread throughout the St Lawrence valley. The company even sold its goods in Upper Canada: one agent took wares to Queenston in order to find buyers during a period when the company was experiencing a particularly serious lack of cash.[41] The directors sought clients in York (Toronto), Upper Canada, when they tried to attract Quetton de Saint-George's business away from the Saint-Maurice ironworks[42] (they did not succeed in doing so). They also exported some products eastward to Nova Scotia.[43]

However, a large proportion of the output of the ironworks was sent to two or three merchants. Jacques Leblond in Quebec received about 27 per cent of the production of 1807 (according to the amounts of delivered products indicated in the surviving letters for that year). George Platt, a merchant in Montreal, received even more: 34 per cent of the total in 1808 (the year with the most complete data).

The agents sold on commission. The company sent castware (such as stoves, pots, and ploughshares) as well as pig iron to the merchants. The latter were to sell according to a fixed tariff, deducting 12.5 per cent for themselves from the sale price. In certain cases, the directors permitted a commission of 15 to 17.5 per cent to the smaller merchants, without informing their principal customers. For his part, Platt was allowed 2.5 per cent for storage and 5 per cent commission.

In order to facilitate payments, the directors added to his terms, "You will do your endeavours to sell for Cash and when you give credit, it must not extend beyond six months & at the expirations of that Term you must take every possible means to compel the Debtors to pay."[44] Pig iron was to be sold for cash, while castware were to be sold according to the merchant's terms. The company accepted delays in payment, but as the accounts lingered, the directors reminded their agents more and more insistently to send money. The calls for payments became particularly forceful in January and February, when the furnace was extinguished.

In fact, according to the letters, the lack of cash represented one of the major problems faced by the company. The enterprise had to accept rather often that the merchants would send them food or other products in exchange. It made similar offers to barter with various merchants.

The directors of the firm raised time and again the difficulties of collecting payments from their merchant-clients. This issue reveals perhaps a general problem of confidence among merchants at this time. In many cases a representative of the company had personally to visit the merchants; often the clerks did this work, but on occasion the directors did so as well. George Platt, their most important agent, caused them many difficulties. He was slow to send money, and he complained about the commission he was allowed. The company's relations with Jacques Leblond in Quebec deteriorated after the latter refused to honour a draft for fifteen pounds on the account of the now former manager of the company, Nicolas Bayard.[45] The enterprise conducted much less business with Leblond following this incident.

According to the letter book, financial difficulties were not the only ones that the company faced. Transportation also caused problems. As the ironworks was located at some distance from the St Lawrence, few boats could reach it and only at times of high water. The foundry not only produced heavy charges of wares but also consumed large amounts of products brought in from a distance. The boats generally loaded and unloaded at the church of Sainte-Geneviève or even at the merchant Marchildon's at the mouth of the Rivière Batiscan.

Not all boats wanted to stop at Batiscan. More interested in conducting trade between Montreal and Quebec, they did not find the cargoes profitable enough to stop at smaller centres. In fact, the firm had to purchase boats on its own account; in 1811 the directors planned to acquire "flat-boats."[46] But up to 1812 (the end date of the letters) the problem persisted. It is even possible that the introduction of steam-driven boats did not help the company. Monro and Bell of the Saint-Maurice forges complained in 1810 about the rise in transportation costs: "The advance for the last two Years upon all kinds of Labour, Freights &c has been so great, that we feel it in a very serious degree."[47]

Of course, the company in Batiscan was in competition with other enterprises. The letters provide only a few indications of the nature of the competition with Monro and Bell. The two firms produced the same products and sometimes hired the same workers. In 1808 three workmen from the Saint-Maurice ironworks offered themselves at Batiscan after they had had difficulties with Monro and Bell.[48] The same year Nicolas Bayard asked Ezekiel Hart to purchase a potash kettle from the other company; he wanted to use it as a model for production at Batiscan.[49]

Coffin and Craigie had forced up the rent of the state-owned Saint-Maurice forges in 1800, thus ensuring themselves a more competitive position. By 1806 they were no longer able to play the same role. Thomas Dunn, colonial administrator and an investor in the ironworks, later informed the British colonial secretary, "The Batiscan Company as I can assure your Lordship from dear bought knowledge were not in circumstances to enter into the Competition."[50] In 1808 Monro and Bell asked for a reduction in the rent paid to the Crown for the Saint-Maurice forges, complaining that there were too many ironworks in the colony, which had "occasioned a Glut of manufactured Articles in our limited Market; and this joined to our competition lessened the Value of these Articles. There had also been for several years previous to 1806, short crops by which the sales of Iron Ware were greatly diminished, which served to increase the accumulation of manufactured stock and lessen its Value still more, & with it, the Value of the Works."[51] In the following years it seems that the companies came to a better understanding. For example, in 1811 Bell told Coffin how much he was paying for wheat in the Richelieu valley.[52] In the same year Coffin established the tariff prices for Batiscan products on those of his firm's competitors.[53] Such examples of cooperation indicated that the Saint-Maurice forges had won the battle between the two companies.

Both companies also had to deal with competition from metropolitan – in particular, Scottish – firms. During the 1810s a large number of Scottish stoves were sent to the Lower Canadian market. However, even if the Scottish prices were lower "in consequence of the great Discount on Bills," the directors of the ironworks were confident of the quality of their products. Their stoves, they assured their clients, resisted fire better than did Scottish ones.[54] Whatever the quality of the Batiscan products, however, the company did not long survive the death of John Craigie in late 1813.

Supplies

Between 1798 and 1813 the firm offered a market for local agricultural production. It purchased the seigneurial shares of wheat from the banal gristmill.[55] When the mill at Sainte-Geneviève ceased functioning in 1806, the director of the company complained to the commissioners of the Jesuit estates. In the end, the firm contributed to the repairs itself, without asking for payment from the commissioners.[56]

Other suppliers in the immediate region profited from the situation by selling their surpluses to the company. Thomas Coffin explained to Xavier de Lanaudière his desire to purchase wheat from the latter's mill across the St Lawrence in Saint-Pierre: "We find that it is more advantageous to purchase wheat for our workers' consumption in the neighbouring parishes than to buy it from afar."[57] Xavier's brother, Charles-Louis, and a merchant from Gentilly sold flour, oats, and hay. From Portneuf the company received bran.

But a number of times the directors of the ironworks mentioned that there was not enough grain in the region. Therefore they had to purchase supplies from their merchant-clients. To an extent, the difficulties were caused by the lack of mills in the seigneury. Over time, the board of commissioners had let all the mills in Batiscan seigneury fall into disuse, to the point that the directors planned to construct one themselves. In fact, Coffin built a gristmill in the nearby (and also former Jesuit) seigneury of Cap-de-la-Madeleine.

But the company also called upon more distant supplies: wheat and oats from Rivière Ouelle; wheat, peas, and oats from Verchères; peas from Lachenaie; oats and peas from Saint-Denis; oats from La Prairie; hay from Rivière-du-Loup. In fact, at certain moments the company found itself requiring grain urgently.[58] For the years of the letter book, there was an increasing tendency to acquire provisions in the Montreal region and in the Richelieu valley. Pierre Guerout, a merchant at Saint-Denis, sent more than 2,300 *minots* of wheat in 1811.

In addition to Guerout, the company's main suppliers were George Platt from Montreal and Jacques Leblond from Quebec, their agents in the two cities. Coffin himself was in charge of finding beef and pork for the company in 1808, but after he began to spend more time at Batiscan, the two merchants took his place. Platt sent wheat and pork (fifteen barrels of pork a month in 1811), but also products for sale: shoes, tea, tobacco, soap, candles, and alcohol. According to the directors, the company intended to favour Canadian products: "this Comp[an]y appearing disposed to purchase in Canada rather than to import."[59] However, it also brought in imported products, particularly alcohol, from Quebec.

The ironworks operated a store for the workers, a way to link them more closely to the enterprise. But the directors did not want to allow the workers to rack up large debts. The manager Nicolas Bayard reprimanded his clerks in 1808, "I have constantly given orders not to make advances from the Store or warehouse either to the employees or the day-labourers beyond the value of their present work."[60] Still, local workers managed to become indebted to the company. In December 1811 it launched court actions in order to recover a number of small debts, challenging people who "have hitherto refused either to pay or do work for the amount of their respective Debts."[61] The ironworks, like rural merchants in general, increased local consumption of commercial products.

However, it is not clear that the company stimulated local agricultural production, despite the fact that the seasonal labour requirements did not always preclude work on the farm. In 1807 Sainte-Geneviève provided the lowest average wheat tithe per communicant of the four parishes in Batiscan and Sainte-Anne (table 3.8). The proportions were twice as high in Saint-François-Xavier and Saint-Stanislas parishes. As the firm's correspondence shows, many of the necessary foodstuffs were brought in from more prosperous regions in the colony.

Thus the impact of the Batiscan Iron Works on the region was somewhat ambiguous. It sold most of its products in distant markets. It provided employment for a number of local and outside workers. When it could not obtain its supplies locally, it purchased them elsewhere. Its "backward linkages," to use the staples thesis terminology, often led elsewhere. Nonetheless, some local workers were employed by the company, and some of the workers from outside settled at least temporarily in the parish. For the locals who worked for the firm, their economic horizons turned towards the hinterland of the seigneury. During the fifteen years of the company's operation, local habitants found an alternative to the declining opportunities in the fur trade; they were also able to supplement an agricultural economy in some difficulty. Not surprisingly, the short-term consequences of the closing of the ironworks were negative.

LOCAL ENTREPRENEURS

With the failure of the ironworks in 1813 and the general lack of attention shown by the commissioners for the Jesuit estates, economic activity in Batiscan seigneury relied more than before on individual initiatives. In 1817 Joseph Charrest and Antoine and Augustin Neaux signed an agreement to build a gristmill in Saint-Stanislas parish.[62]

The same year François Massicotte, a former employee of the iron-works, signed an agreement with Benjamin Joseph Frobisher to build a gristmill on the forge's property.[63] Sexton Campbell purchased a mill at the Rivière des Envies in 1822.[64] The commission was informed of these actions and at the time expressed its opposition to them.[65] By 1826 it had reasserted its seigneurial monopoly.[66] As the case of François Massicotte suggests, it is possible that the ironworks served as a training ground for entrepreneurs. In addition to his grist-mill, Massicotte proposed building a carding mill in 1828.[67]

Sainte-Anne provides even more evidence of economic activity than does Batiscan. The 1825 census schedules for the seigneury list a number of small enterprises. In addition to the gristmill, there were in operation a carding mill, a tannery, and a brewery. The six sawmills and two potash manufactures provide evidence of the nascent timber industry.[68] The labour force for these small companies was probably found among marginal farmers and their offspring.

During this period, local entrepreneurs, often merchants and inn-keepers, attempted to sell wood in colonial markets. For instance, in a March 1816 issue of the *Gazette de Québec*, Charles Gouin advertised for sale 4,000 planks, 200,000 cedar shingles, 400 cedar beams, and 100 cords of spruce wood. In the same issue Joseph Gouin tried to sell 25,000 feet of squared pine, 2,000 planks of red birch, and 6,000 white pine planks.[69] Louis Guillet, a local notary, advertised his sawmill in Saint-Stanislas parish for sale in November 1820, along with 600 spruce logs.[70] Joseph Pacaud of Batiscan gave notice of 500 cords of spruce wood early the following year.[71] Finally, in 1823 two sawmills, one in Sainte-Anne three leagues north of the village and the other on the Rivière des Chutes, came up for sale or lease. The purchaser or tenant had the possibility of acquiring the privilege of cutting wood in the area behind the mill of Sainte-Anne.[72]

These various advertisements suggest the relatively small scale of the industry at this time. The process by which timber came to form the basis of the local economy was barely underway by the 1820s. Nonetheless, this evidence illustrates the outcome of the processes of social differentiation: a few rich habitants, merchants, and innkeepers were reinvesting their capital locally and employing some of the less-prosperous members of the community. Some of the business activity reached a larger scale: in 1806 a consortium of French-Canadian entrepreneurs had come close to bidding for the lease of the Saint-Maurice forges. Among these men was Louis Gouin of Sainte-Anne, whom Thomas Dunn described as "a Country Sto[re]keeper supposed to have acquired a decent competency in his line."[73] But other investments were much more localized: most of the buildings in

Sainte-Anne village in 1830 were located on the properties of Charles and Antoine Gouin.[74] The prominence of the Gouin family, long linked to seigneurial and state privilege, demonstrates the possibilities inherent in petty accumulation in the countryside.

Despite the important activities of local entrepreneurs, this was not the principal path to economic development in this area. Like the Batiscan Iron Works before it, the timber industry was soon dominated by outside capital. The time when entrepreneurs from outside the area, such as William Price, would take control over the local timber industry lay just a short while in the future.[75]

THE IMPACT OF "DEVELOPMENT"

It is difficult to assess the impact of changing economic relations in the early nineteenth century in the two seigneuries. A few indirect methods can be presented: the rate of payment of seigneurial dues in Batiscan, the evolution of local prices, the extent of land division, and the marriage rate for men under twenty-five. Although the fur trade, local commerce, the Batiscan Iron Works, and the nascent timber trade may have provided some economic opportunities, by the 1820s the average habitant did not appear particularly prosperous.

One measure is provided by the seigneurial agent's account book for Batiscan for the years 1782 to 1822.[76] This *répertoire* was first used by the Jesuits' agent, F.-X. Larue, and was taken over by the commission's agent, Joseph Badeaux. The register is a confusing document. The personal knowledge of the agent was required to decipher it, as Badeaux noted when he transmitted it to the commission: "I believe that it would not be very useful for the operations which have begun [that is, drawing up a new plan of the seigneury], in that the plots are not organized sequentially or by concession line."[77] The register proceeds by individual lots, sometimes indicating when the land was transferred or subdivided, though the reliability of cross-referencing is uncertain. Each entry lists the years in which the *cens et rentes* were partially or fully paid; however, the final years are difficult to interpret because a lack of notations may indicate either nonpayment or transferral of title. As a result, the proportions obtained from the analysis of the register are the minima, especially for the last few years. Moreover, as payment was indicated for each lot of land and not for individual tenants, if certain habitants owning various lots tended to avoid payment, this fact would skew the results.

Figure 7.1 shows the percentage of lots on which seigneurial dues went fully or partially unpaid between 1782 and 1821. On average, about one-fifth (22.6 per cent) of the tenants did not pay their dues

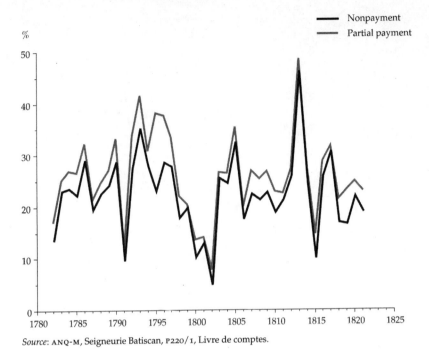

Source: ANQ-M, Seigneurie Batiscan, P220/1, Livre de comptes.

Figure 7.1   Percentage of lots for which seigneurial dues were not paid, Batiscan, 1782–1821

each year. Always more than half paid their dues, and in three years (1791, 1802, and 1815) 90 per cent or more did so. In eleven years, over 30 per cent of the tenants did not pay all or part of their dues (1786, 1790, 1792–97, 1805, 1813, and 1817). Although the commission's agent, Badeaux, was criticized for his laxness, he was apparently more successful than the Jesuits' representative.

The data from the seigneurial register indicate a few years of difficulty, but general consistency in ability or willingness to pay. Local price movements for wheat and lard (figure 7.2) provide elements of explanation. There is some correlation between the prices for lard and wheat and the proportion of unpaid dues. When prices reached high levels, the tenants were generally able to pay their dues the following year. However, specific local conditions also explain some of the fluctuations. In 1793 a grasshopper infestation undoubtedly caused many habitants to leave their dues unpaid.[78] The highest levels of nonpayment, reached in 1813, were probably connected to wartime conditions and the difficulties of the Batiscan Iron Works. In certain years, increased vigilance on the part of the agent was important. The years

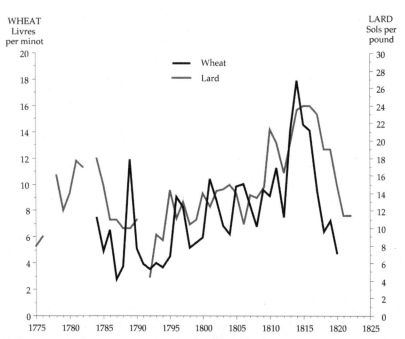

Source: Ouellet, Hamelin, and Chabot, "Les prix agricoles," tableau B.4, "Prix moyen du minot de blé" (Champlain, Cap-de-la-Madeleine, and Pointe-du-Lac); tableau B.7, "Prix moyen de la livre de lard" (Batiscan, Champlain, Cap-de-la-Madeleine, and Pointe-du-Lac).

Figure 7.2   Average prices for wheat and lard in the region, 1775–1822

of highest payment, 1800, 1802, and 1815 (after the government took over the seigneury), coincide with times when the agent paid more attention to collecting the dues.[79]

But the generally rising price levels between 1775 and 1822, combined with the shift in agriculture away from wheat, suggest the increasing impoverishment of certain families. The lists of habitants owing arrears provide evidence of this development. In 1801 the commission's agent compiled one such list for Batiscan.[80] This document shows the ways in which habitants fell behind in their payments. Of the 77 habitants listed, about half (46.8 per cent) owed arrears only for the past year. About one third (35.1 per cent) owed arrears for five years or more. Those habitants who owed capons as part of their dues tended to be more delinquent: 36 households owed at least one capon, and the average length of time for which they owed arrears was 5.6 years (the average time for the 42 households owing no capons was only 1.9 years).

There is other evidence to confirm the difficulty habitants had in paying capons. On a few occasions, poor individuals gave partridges instead of chickens to the agent.[81] Those habitants who did not pay their arrears were likely not refusing on a whim, but were unable to do so. Under agent Badeaux, the policy concerning capons apparently changed. He commented in 1803 that "the capons have been paid for in cash."[82] A second roll, drawn up in 1807, showed similar proportions of nonpayment.[83] Now 118 habitants were listed, 43 (36.4 per cent) owing arrears for the previous year. Forty (33.9 per cent) were five or more years behind in their payments (6 habitants had not paid in over ten years). The proportion of habitants who owed between one and five years of back dues had increased from the previous list.

In 1813 almost half the tenants did not pay their seigneurial dues for that year. When the Batiscan Iron Works closed for good in 1813, the local population found itself in temporary difficulty. Some workers would never receive their wages. John Craigie's post-mortem inventory recognized £919 in wages due to employees; it also mentioned some £1,205 owed by employees to the company.[84] The master founder John Slicer was still waiting for his £550 in 1828.[85] From the seigneur's point of view, the cumulative amount of arrears kept growing: in 1815 the agent noted that some £425 (10,197 *livres tournois*) and about thirty-eight *minots* of wheat were due in Batiscan.[86]

During the general crop shortages of 1816, the three parishes of Batiscan seigneury were among the hardest hit in the colony. The bishop evaluated the extent of hardship and found them to be "Parishes presently lacking all resources for their subsistence and without hope of acquiring the means for sowing in the spring."[87] It is possible, though difficult to prove definitively, that the weakness in local agriculture was due to the fact that the forges had offered a more attractive market for labour and that the habitants took time to reorient themselves towards agriculture.

In any case, the presence of the ironworks, and its control of large parts of the seigneury, had slowed down the colonization of new lands. The commission's agent reported in 1821 that "actual Settlements have not been made on this large portion of his Majesty[']s Seigneury."[88] Still, the government took more than ten years to acquire title to the lands that belonged to the Batiscan company.

The restrictions on new concessions were not limited to Batiscan. Habitants in both Batiscan and Sainte-Anne complained about not having access to land. As a result, land division became an issue. In 1804 Lord Selkirk had commented on the process: "I understand however from Lanaudière & others – that this division seldom takes place in fact except among very poor peasants – all that are in a thriving way, set out their children on new lots, as they come up, giving them some money to stock them."[89] Twenty years later the habitants from Sainte-Anne and Batiscan who appeared before a committee of the House of Assembly all grumbled about excessive land division. Louis Gendron complained of the high rents that the seigneurs of Sainte-Anne charged on new titles, and he suggested, "Were I to make any research I might find about forty Families who have partitioned their Lands, which occasions poverty and suffering."[90] Pierre Trepanier of Saint-Stanislas noted that the commission's policy of restricting land grants had had the same effect in Batiscan:

Q. Do the Lands begin to be Subdivided?
A. Yes, as they [young people] cannot obtain any Grant of lands they are obliged to come to an agreement with their Father, that is to say, to obtain a part of their Father's Land for Rent or otherwise.
Q. What is the effect of the Subdivision of these Lands?
A. Much misery is thereby occasioned, because double Expenses, twice the quantity of Buildings, Enclosures and Ditching are required. – The Parish is thereby impoverished.[91]

The habitants were anxious to avoid dividing their land, realizing that they would suffer by the negative economic consequences of the practice. However, if they chose to keep their land intact, they had to pay a price: their children would remain dependent on them longer and would have to delay their marriages, if indeed they were not forced in the meantime to work in the villages or in the towns as day labourers.

The 1825 census provides one final measure of the economic opportunities available in the seigneuries. It noted the number of men between eighteen and twenty-four years of age who were married (table 7.1). As marital rates tend to respond to economic conditions, the percentages reveal the availability of land or capital. The data indicate that the older parishes along the St Lawrence offered the least opportunity for young men. The newer parishes, which were still in the process of expansion (although the soil may have been poorer) and which presumably supplied lumberjacks for the timber trade, provided the same level of opportunity as the relatively wealthy agricultural parish of Saint-Denis. None of the parishes came close to the high rates of marriage for Sorel, where more part-time wage labour existed. In Batiscan and Sainte-Anne by the 1820s, for many young habitants, economic opportunities in their traditional agriculture appeared to be shrinking.

Table 7.1
Percentage of married men among those aged between eighteen and twenty-four,
Sainte-Anne and Batiscan parishes, 1825

	Married	Total	Percentage
Saint-Stanislas	6	30	20%
Sainte-Geneviève	19	92	21%
Saint-François-Xavier	5	43	12%
Sainte-Anne	14	139	10%
Sorel			40%
Saint-Denis			19%

Sources: Census of 1825. For Sorel and Saint-Denis, see Greer, *Peasant, Lord, and Merchant*, 192,
292n34. Greer explains the high rate of marriage in Sorel parish by the availability of part-time
wage labour.

CONCLUSION

Although the opening of the Batiscan Iron Works at the turn of the century may have promised economic opportunities for the local population, its closing exacerbated economic difficulties. The iron-works village near Sainte-Geneviève did not create an immediate, large-scale industrial focus for the area. With Craigie's death in 1813, the ironworks closed definitively, and government officials were careful to ensure that it could not open again. Land on one bank of the Rivière Batiscan was sold separately from the rest of the property, thus ensuring that future owners would not be able to rebuild a dam to power an ironworks.[92]

At the beginning of a long, colony-wide period of transition between an agricultural economy and an industrial one,[93] the people of the area would now experience economic development on a smaller scale. The future lay with increasingly capitalized forestry, mixed with subsistence agriculture. Still, in neighbouring Sainte-Anne seigneury another attempt at the imposition of British perspectives would be undertaken.

8 A Picturesque Landscape

A lake I found, whose smooth pellucid face
Expos'd to view each pebble at its base.
Devoid of eddy, down Stymphalia's grove
Stole the slow tide, and scarcely seemed to move.

Ovid, *Metamorphoses*, 199

While an industrial focus emerged and then disappeared from Batiscan seigneury, in Sainte-Anne seigneury another effort at establishing a new landscape was attempted. More than on economic interests, though these were certainly present as well, this perspective relied on aesthetic principles, developed through late-eighteenth-century art and estate design.

In 1819 John and Elizabeth Hale purchased the 130,000 acre seigneury of Sainte-Anne de la Pérade. The family's appropriation of the seigneury involved more than a simple monetary transaction. The Hales perceived an opportunity to fashion a new landscape in the St Lawrence valley. An examination of their actions reveals aspects of the English imperial project in the colony of Lower Canada. The Hale family imposed its own cultural understandings as it attempted to make a home for itself in this "new" land. Its members applied lessons of history, morality, and aesthetics in their quest for dominion.

This imposition of a "picturesque" sensibility did not involve, as it did elsewhere, the creation of a fanciful landscape out of "wilderness". Rather, it built on the decades of agrarian modification of the landscape undertaken by French-Canadian habitants.

A EUROPEAN LANDSCAPE

By the late eighteenth century it was possible to describe the landscape of Sainte-Anne and Batiscan according to European conventions. This result of generations of habitant farming and forest removal was of particular interest to elite British visitors to and residents of the colony. The habitants had cut trees around their buildings (often too many for English tastes) and had established extensive fields. Distancing indigenous wildlife and vegetation from their settlements, French farmers had filled the landscape with their buildings, fences, crops, and animals. Without fully resembling an English agrarian landscape, the habitants' farmland was nonetheless recognizable and often "picturesque."

The first recorded comparison of this area to European vistas occurred in 1776, when the German officer wrote from Batiscan about the nature of the landscape: "Whoever has seen the fences and enclosed fields on the marshlands of Bremen can clearly imagine it."[1] A decade later Robert Hunter Jr compared the region to England. Describing his 1785 trip, he made a telling comment on the area near Sainte-Anne: "Here and there you see some charming plantations, by the side of the river, which you might imagine to have been planned by a [Capability] Brown, but being natural exceed him as much as nature surpasses art ... This stage is quite romantic, and beautiful beyond description. What a show would such a noble river make running through England, with the noblemen's seats to adorn it instead of the habitants' huts."[2] Hunter's comparison implied that the landscapes of the area surpassed the designs of the leading English garden architect of the day. Canada, in particular this part, naturally offered more than invention could in England, but the landscape could be further improved by the imposition of an English social structure on it. A re-evaluation of the landscape along different European ideals from those of the early French explorers was under way.

Taking their perspectives from the royal road or from the St Lawrence, commentators increasingly focused on the humanmade aspects of the landscapes of Sainte-Anne and Batiscan. By the late eighteenth century, Sainte-Anne was increasingly seen as a "picturesque" spot. For British writer John Lambert, the picturesque qualities of the area had to be stressed, if only because "the inhabitants ... are no great admirers of the beauties of Nature." Lambert described the post road in Sainte-Anne, for example, as "wind[ing] along the summits of the lofty banks which overlook the river, or along the borders of delightful valleys."[3] Likewise, American traveller James Glennie considered Sainte-Anne "a very pleasantly situated village."[4] And from the other side of the St Lawrence, the entire region was a pleasing tableau for Elizabeth Simcoe: "The mouths of the rivers Batiscan and St Anne are seen on the opposite shore, with distant blue hills. This is the finest point on the river and a good military position."[5] For his part, Joseph Bouchette stressed the picturesque setting of the seigneurial manor house of Sainte-Anne: "The manor-house, agreeably situated near the point formed by the Ste. Anne and the St. Lawrence, is surrounded by excellent gardens and many fine groups of beautiful trees ... At the mouth of the Ste. Anne lie the isles, ... being well clothed with wood they afford several very pleasing prospects."[6]

However, when travellers and writers remembered Batiscan, the prospects of industrial activity dominated their attention. Apparently without having visited the site, Lord Selkirk, John Lambert, George Heriot, and Hugh Gray all mentioned the Batiscan Iron Works, usually commenting on the firm's tribulations.[7] Their descriptions indicate, when compared with the view of Sainte-Anne, a double vision of the colony. Either writers responded to the aesthetic qualities of the landscape, and thereby embraced their own cultural past, or they emphasized the economic activities that the colony offered. In either case, they made reference to human reshaping of the landscape.

THE HALE FAMILY

John Hale and his wife, Elizabeth Amherst Hale, were well placed to bring an English noble aesthetic to Lower Canada. Both the Hales and the Amhersts had built their careers in large part on the appropriation of Quebec. General James Wolfe had sent John Hale's father to take the news of the 1759 military victory to the king. John, the eldest child in his Yorkshire gentry family, came to North America in the 1790s as aide-de-camp to the Duke of Kent. Elizabeth's uncle, General Jeffrey Amherst, had been promised the Jesuits estates in recompense for his role in conquering New France. But he died before the transfer of titles took place, and the claims to the properties fell to his heir, Elizabeth's brother.

Elizabeth and John Hale, who maintained a lengthy correspondence with the second Lord Amherst, were quickly disillusioned by the political wranglings involved in the transfer of the estates. Declaiming the untrustworthiness of Governor Robert Shore Milnes and his "Yankee" attorney-general, Jonathan Sewell, they complained about the obstacles that Amherst faced. Finally, Amherst accepted an annuity from the king in exchange for his pretensions to the Jesuit estates. The Hales, in contrast, were more fortunate in receiving land grants: the Crown awarded them property in Upper Canada. Elizabeth Hale explained to her brother, with no irony whatsoever, "Surely if any one has right to lands in a Country it must be the Children of those who were at the Conquest of it."[8]

Despite their successes, the Hales felt trapped professionally in the colony. The lengthy Napoleonic Wars had produced too many candidates for the relatively few lucrative positions in the British civil service. The Hales filled letter after letter with pleas for patronage and speculations concerning various posts.[9] John did receive certain commissions and important employments in the colony as deputy paymaster general and inspector of public accounts.[10] In 1808 Governor James Craig appointed him to the Legislative Council, describing him as "a Gentleman of high character."[11] However, Hale's dreams of greater grandeur – for example, the governor generalship of New Brunswick or the lieutenant-governorship of Lower Canada – were not realized. Lord Amherst seems to have used his influence when he could, but he had little success in providing Hale with a much better position. Even the Duke of Kent admitted that his influence could do little for him: "I am not likely to participate in the loaves and fishes, but *that* no one will appreciate *more highly* than yourself; only for a moment I wish I possessed that influence with Government which I do not, to enable me to use it for your benefit."[12] The Hales' enviable connections did not always ensure them the sympathies of all the governors. In 1825 Lord Dalhousie recorded businessman Mathew Bell's description of Hale: "a clever man, called generally 'the old fox,' cunning, insincere & insatiably greedy of emolument in public office."[13]

The Hales' disillusionment with Canadian politics was partially compensated by their enthusiasm for the landscape. In one of her first letters, Elizabeth exclaimed to her brother, "This country is very beautiful," although she persisted in thinking that the family estate in Kent, tellingly named "Montreal," was "the prettiest spot I know."[14] The town of Quebec was particularly attractive from a picturesque point of view. Its topography provided a multitude of perspectives from which to admire the surrounding scenery.

Like many other well-educated women of her period, Elizabeth Hale was a trained artist.[15] Claiming no talent for portraits,[16] she preferred to sketch scenery, her aesthetic sense strongly influenced by the canon of the picturesque.[17] In 1802 she advised her brother on improvements to the landscape of the estate in Kent, specifically telling him to avoid geometric lines in favour of "natural" variation: "I used to think a Beech tree would have a very good effect where the single Poplar stood, opposite the Bow room window, & would not shut out any view. The line of hills in that part is rather too strait [sic] & wants something to cut it."[18] Elizabeth sent sketches of the new country back to her brother and her aunt, continuing the aesthetic exchange between the two landscapes. She collected botanical specimens for transplanting in the home country, and she and her husband requested seeds in order to grow an English garden in their backyard in

Quebec. With satisfaction, Elizabeth invited her brother to visit in 1799: "I wish you c[oul]d see our pretty house & garden, it is just like an English one."[19]

The Hales were particularly keen on country living. They rented country homes for Elizabeth and the children during the summer; John joined them in the evening after work or on weekends. Escaping the heat of the city and of colonial politics, they retreated into an idyllic, stable world with obedient servants. But at this time they did not trust the French-Canadian population (nor for that matter, the "Yankees"). They were fearful that the entire French-Canadian population would support a French invasion if one ever came to pass.[20] As war with the United States approached in 1812, Elizabeth Hale returned to England together with the children. During her time there she undoubtedly came into contact with the views of landscape designer Humphry Repton, one of the leading proponents of the picturesque approach. In 1812 Repton completed his commission to provide suggestions for the renewal of Montreal estate in Kent.[21]

On the Hale family's return to Lower Canada after the war, its members seemed more secure in their position in the colony. With the successes of the War of 1812, the generally strong showing of French-Canadian support, and the end of the Napoleonic threat, the British elite in Lower Canada felt reassured. The Hales now began to consider the possibility of establishing themselves in the colony. They were less concerned than previously about the possibility of Lower Canada falling back into the hands of the French: "Canada is now no longer likely to become again a French Province; and though it may in a few years be one of the United States of America, it is not probable that the same proscriptions would in that event attend the English settlers, as might have been apprehended from the French Government."[22] By 1818 the Hales had begun considering the purchase of a family estate in the New World. They continually stressed to their relatives in England that such an investment would not preclude their return to the home country, given the right circumstances.

As they looked for an estate, their interests coincided with the demographic and financial fortunes of the Lanaudière family. Only one of Charles-Louis de Lanaudière's children had survived into adulthood. Following Charles-Louis's death in 1811 and his widow's in 1817, Marie-Anne de Lanaudière, at forty-two years of age, found herself the sole heir to Sainte-Anne seigneury. After overseeing a number of concessions to habitants, she decided to dispose of the property. Elizabeth Hale reported that the seigneury "is sold in consequence of being now the property of a Lady not likely to marry & who cannot bear the trouble of looking after it."[23]

By the summer of 1819 the Hales had a "grand Speculation in view."[24] Various elements of the sale recommended themselves to them: the timber resources, the accessibility of the seigneury to Quebec, the promise of a return of 4½ to 5 per cent on their investment, and the escape from Quebec's summer heat. Impressed by the perceived beauty of the location and their belief in the effectiveness of agricultural "improvement,"[25] the Hales offered £12,000 for the seigneury. More than anything, the purchase represented the investment of their future in the colony, the acquisition of a property with possibilities for their many children.

However, not all members of the Lanaudière family were content to accept the sale of their ancestral seigneury (other seigneuries, such as Saint-Vallier and Lavaltrie, were now owned by various members of the family). Charles-Louis's half-siblings and their heirs plotted ways to employ the *retrait lignager*, by which they would repay the purchase price and thereby maintain their family rights to the land. According to Elizabeth Hale, "all these annoyances have arisen from two extravagant young Men who have spent all they had, & having nothing to lose, thought they might as well make the attempt to gain something."[26] She claimed that the family wanted to hold onto title to the seigneury, but was willing to leave the demesne to the Hales, "a most unjust, & unhandsome idea, & would never have enterd the head of an english Gentleman."[27] But other members of the Lanaudière family considered the financial risks involved in the case and decided to pursue it no further. As one of the sisters wrote to her sister-in-law, "Dear Agathe made us promise not to reclaim [*retraire*] Ste Anne, and to speak truthfully, the scarcity of money at this time and the court case would have ruined us. Therefore, it is more prudent that we remain quiet, because neither Madame Baby nor Agathe wish to reclaim the seigneury."[28]

From the Hales' point of view, it was the well-timed intervention of the vendor, Marie-Anne de Lanaudière, which was decisive: "The Lady of whom we purchased it, I imagine put a stop to the 'Retraite liniagere' [*sic*] by declaring, that should the family interfere, they would never see any part of the £12,000 she had received for it."[29] With the threat of losing the seigneury in the past, Elizabeth Hale concluded, "I do not wonder that a family should feel a little vexed at such a property going out of their hands, but they may thank themselves for that."[30] Her annoyance with the Lanaudières was coloured by a sense of superiority over a decadent French gentry. She claimed that the Lanaudières had not paid the appropriate attention to the agricultural potential of the land: "the late proprietors would never lay out 6 d. on it but were draining away the money as fast as they could."[31] Like other French Canadians, whose farming techniques also she criticized, the previous seigneurs were uninterested in agricultural improvement.

Once the purchase was finally concluded in 1820, the Hales were content. At least in part because Sainte-Anne happened to fill English aesthetic criteria, it had earlier attracted Elizabeth's eye. As she considered the prospect of purchasing the seigneury, she recalled, "I was there many years ago & admired the place, when there was no chance of its being sold."[32] Typical in many ways of the British gentry's attitude towards the moral qualities of rural living,[33] the Hales believed that investment in the countryside was the most legitimate use of their capital. They revelled in the prospect of owning so much more land than could ever have been possible in England. "Only consider," Elizabeth Hale exclaimed to her aunt, "what an immense tract of land [is] 60 square miles!"[34] For Elizabeth, their ownership of the land made all their endeavours worthwhile: "I was always partial to the Country & when the place is your own & all the alterations & improvements made for the benefit of your children, your interest in it is naturally increased & your attention almost engrossed by them."[35] The Hales were thrilled with the exotic seigneurial tributes they could exact: every twelfth fish, part of the maple syrup production, the right of passage over the Rivière Sainte-Anne, not to speak of the more lucrative yearly *cens et rentes*, the occasional *lods et ventes*, and the mill toll.[36] Timber sales also promised great profits, which John Hale was quick to exploit. In 1822–23 he contracted with local habitants for some 2,300 pine and spruce logs, to be cut in the unconceded parts of the seigneury.[37]

In addition to its economic benefits, the seigneury allowed the Hales to ignore current troubles. One of its appeals was the escape it represented from the tribulations of contemporary England, such as the Peterloo massacre of 1819. About a year after they purchased Sainte-Anne, Elizabeth Hale wrote to her brother, "here we enjoy peace & quiet at present & all the comforts of a Country life far from all political alarms."[38] Referring to the popular unrest related to Queen Carolina's trial for adultery, she commented that "some of them [the British ministers at Westminster] might envy us enjoying the quiet of the Country amongst well-disposed habitants."[39] Sainte-Anne offered a refuge from the vagaries of imperial and colonial politics.

But the seigneury did not only allow a retreat into a rural idyll. It also represented an investment of the family's future in the continent, an attempt to remain in step with a particular historical narrative, which Elizabeth Hale revealed in 1819: "for my own part I cannot but consider America as the rising Country & thus our Children or

GrandChildren will be very glad to have property here – in history we find that as one Country begins to decline another rises & generally to the Westward & I cannot but think that our children may see something of the kind during their lives."[40] With its promises of present peace and future prosperity, Sainte-Anne would become home to the Hales.

APPROPRIATION

Explorers, seigneurs, habitants, merchants, and industrialists all imposed new perspectives on the landscape of Batiscan and Sainte-Anne, perspectives that owed much to the economic uses to which they thought the land should be subjected. Yet behind their economic perceptions lay differing beliefs of what constituted an ideal landscape. The clearest example of an attempt to perceive and create such a landscape in this area was undertaken in the first few years of the Hale family's proprietorship of Sainte-Anne. It was one thing to purchase the land; it was another to take possession of it. For the Hales, the appropriation of their land proceeded along some lines typical of all seigneurs. Other elements of their approach were more specific to their class and cultural background.

In the process of negotiating the purchase, as a first act of possession, Elizabeth Hale compared the seigneury to a fashionable London suburb. "The village is remarkably pretty & the whole scenery reminds me very much of the Thames towards Putney," she claimed to her brother in England, "only that the St Anne's is a finer river & nothing like Mud."[41] So that they could enjoy fully the seigneury's many qualities, an inventory of present and absent elements had to be compiled. Establishing proprietorship over land implied taking stock of nature.[42] John Hale observed nature in a scientific spirit: he studied the sexual reproduction of crickets for a paper he later presented in Quebec.[43] Elizabeth Hale made the link between ownership and inventories of nature even more clearly in writing to her brother: "if we get the estate I have mentioned before to you, I shall make a point of endeavouring to collect seeds & roots."[44]

In the Hales' perception of landscape, and in that of the English gentry in general, trees conveyed the highest metaphorical value.[45] The forests in the deepest parts of the seigneury held the promise of economic benefits for the seigneur. Closer to the manor house, Elizabeth Hale deplored the lack of the proper trees. In the garden there were no fruit trees, not even a fine gooseberry bush.[46] To remedy this shortcoming, the Hales planted an orchard of plum and apple trees.[47] But they were not content to stop there. Oaks, because of their identification with British patriotism and by extension with the British gentry,[48] represented the most significant absence. "I am sorry to say," Elizabeth wrote, "there is not an Oak to be seen here or in the neighbourhood, but I intend trying some for the honor of my native country."[49] The Hales believed that the natural beauty of Sainte-Anne could be greatly improved by adding the proper English elements.

Thus garden plants were imported to improve the demesne. Elizabeth Hale's sister-in-law in England sent flower seeds, and son Jeffrey, on naval duty, promised to keep looking for exotic specimens.[50] In 1822 the Hales planted hedges, possibly to disguise the many fences, which were anathema to the proper noble landscape.[51] For Elizabeth Hale, the activities represented the improvement of the landscape: "I am very busy planting & neatifying which is (altho' not to be found in [Samuel] Johnson['s dictionary]), more descriptive of my occupations than beautifying would be."[52] Having moved into the manor house, the Hales expected to enhance the perspectives they could command, planning "at our leisure to build on higher ground."[53] Though they never replaced the manor house, their vista was appropriately noteworthy. An 1822 visitor recalled the setting: "a roomy, lightsome house, built mansion-like, one hundred yards from a trout-stream, the St. Anne de la Perade, on the upper edge of a large park-like meadow, which runs down to the St. Lawrence. From the house we saw the river, a woody islet or two, close in shore, and had between them a momentary glimpse of the passing steamers."[54] The Hales' desire to catalogue, reshape, and dominate the demesne reflected their hopes for the seigneury as a whole.

A second, rather typical, element of their appropriation was to commission maps of the property. This process was necessary in order to fix the exact boundaries of the seigneury, to locate *censitaires'* lands, and to permit future modifications in tenure. More than an objective representation of geography, maps also have political purposes.[55] Large-scale maps, such as seigneurial surveys, contain their ideological implications in their project: to justify and take stock of the hierarchical distribution of land. An 1825 map (map 4) presents a logic of appropriation. Except for the boundaries of the concessions, the rivers, and some indications of the density of buildings in the village, relatively few details appear on the map. In the northern part of the seigneury in particular, a great blank appears where the seigneurs could write their own history. In fact, the surveyor had begun to do so, providing the title in that space. John Hale's occupations coincide with and explicate his status as seigneur. The few details noted near the northwestern boundary promise future expansions: small rivers, lakes, pine forests, and prairies.

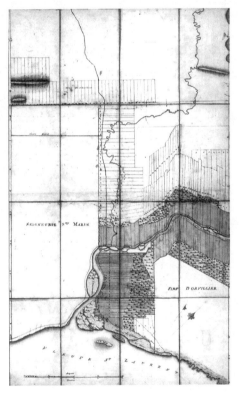

Map 4 An 1825 copy of the survey, begun in 1820, of Sainte-Anne de la Pérade
(NMC-8982)

The Hales were attentive to the surveyors' findings. Elizabeth Hale wrote of the results to her brother in 1820: "The Surveyors have been at work & about 5 Leagues from our house came to a beautiful little Lake covering about 6 acres of Land with large Trees & a very rapid river full of Trout – they found a very compleat [sic] Beaver dam which Mr Hale intends seeing but the road not being yet made I have no chance of getting there – He describes the Land as very rich & very fine Timber with-

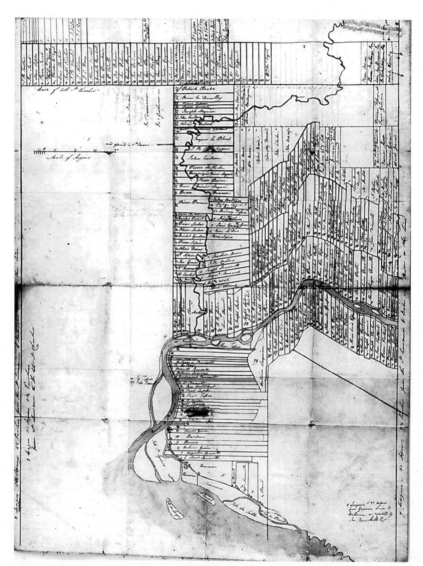

Map 5   A second map, from 1830, identifying by name each *censitaire*'s land
(NMC-15665)

out under wood."[56] A second survey, which dates from 1830 (map 5),
places the names of each plot-holder within the boundaries of his or her
land. The exception to the rule is telling: the Hales' land is referred to
only as the "Domaine." Although they occupied no other lots in Sainte-
Anne, the Hales' centrality is thus implicit in the construction of the
map at the same time as their name is omitted.

Figure 8.1   Elizabeth Hale's sketch of scenery near the manor house of Sainte-Anne
(NA/C-13077)

With surveyors trampling through the backcountry and family members busy making physical changes to the landscape, the Hales went about establishing proprietorship. Elizabeth Hale also expressed the family's appropriation of Sainte-Anne in her sketches. Only days after acquiring the seigneury, she sent her brother a drawing of a scene a short distance from the manor house: "the stream you see is a branch of the river St Anne's which falls into the St. Lawrence about a quarter of a Mile from the house & being wooded on each side is very pretty."[57] A watercolour painter of some talent, Elizabeth Hale sometimes demonstrated a more explicit political aim in her art. In 1824, anxious to establish closer relations with Governor Dalhousie, she sent him sketches of Quebec: "I request your Lordship's acceptance of the enclosed sketches, & trust they may serve to remind you of a place where the return of your Lordship & Lady Dalhousie will be most anxiously expected."[58]

Elizabeth Hale applied her talents to the scenery of Sainte-Anne, casting the landscape as a picturesque summertime idyll. A small sketchbook, dated between 1823 and her death in 1826,[59] illustrates the particular scenes she found worthy of depiction. In figure 8.1 she portrayed the stream that ran along the front of the manor house, using stock picturesque techniques to present a unified landscape. Framed by coulisses of trees, the picture is composed in three planes, the play of light attracting the eye towards the horizon. The dead tree in the foreground contributes pictoral unity as it echoes the direction of the stream. The canoe to the left humanizes the middle ground.

Figure 8.2   One of six views by Elizabeth Hale of the manor house of Sainte-Anne
(NA/C-13078)

Elizabeth Hale employed picturesque motifs in other sketches: ruins
of a windmill, blasted pines, and coulisses of trees.

In theory, she could have sketched many different landscapes in the
seigneury, showing habitant farms, bucolic labouring scenes, or wilderness views. In practice, she did not stray very far from the manor house,
and consciously or not, she chose to depict views in which the family's
proprietorship formed a symbolic presence. Of the twenty-four sketches
pertaining to Sainte-Anne seigneury, six portray different views of the
manor house. In figure 8.2, for instance, a dominating coulisse of trees
frames the manor house, which occupies the centre of the sketch.

As the first two sketches demonstrate, Elizabeth Hale usually chose
to illustrate perspectives visible from land belonging to her family.
Figures 8.3 and 8.4 were probably painted from islands in the Hales'
possession at the mouth of the Sainte-Anne. Figure 8.3 depicts the
ferry across the Sainte-Anne, a privilege worth £12 per year to the
seigneur, Elizabeth Hale had reported in a letter to her brother.[60]
Other sketches implicitly celebrated different seigneurial privileges:
the family's sawmill or the mere act of fishing on the Sainte-Anne.
The Hales' proprietorship is subtly present in all these drawings. In
this sense, Elizabeth Hale's art reflects the received views of the picturesque in their celebration of proprietorship.

As in her correspondence, trees occupied a prominent place in her
drawings. The predominance of deciduous trees in her views of an

Figure 8.3   Elizabeth Hale's depiction of the ferry across the Rivière Sainte-Anne
(NA/C-13092)

Figure 8.4   The only portrayal in Elizabeth Hale's sketchbook of the village of Sainte-
Anne (NA/C-13093)

area where pines were not uncommon illustrates her desire to portray
the landscape in English terms. Like other artists of the picturesque,
she did not attempt to provide a strict, empirical reproduction of the
landscape; rather, a natural-looking, but nonetheless ideal, landscape

was more important.[61] Aesthetic perspectives determined Elizabeth Hale's ability to see Putney along the Sainte-Anne as much the area's natural characteristics did.

Equally important for this analysis is what she chose not to depict. Without being unoccupied, her landscapes were certainly not over-populated with humans (or animals). There are very few humans in her sketches, especially French Canadians. Some people fish; others canoe and pole across the Rivière Sainte-Anne. But generally the local habitants do not form an important presence. Although the fences suggest agricultural activity, and fishing could be important in an economic sense, there is little acknowledgment of habitants' labour. No one actually works the land. Indeed, it is possible, given their clothing, that many of the figures represent members of the Hale family itself. Although fishing may have been work for the habitants, it was recreation for the Hales. Everything, or almost everything, was leisure in this ideal landscape.

Outnumbered by the sketches of the manor house is Elizabeth Hale's one drawing of the village of Sainte-Anne (figure 8.4). Like the peasants who had actually shaped the landscape, the village occupied a shadowy part of her picturesque world. In her letters to England, she seldom mentioned the village or the activities of habitants, except when it came to decrying their deficiencies (and expressing a desire to "improve" them). She pitied her daughter's isolation at Sainte-Anne: "we have not a single being above the capacity of a common farmer in the neighbourhood."[62] Rather than expressing interest in Canadian habitants, Elizabeth Hale saw the future promise of the seigneury as relying more on livestock and immigrant Yorkshire farmers.

Part of their belief that the demesne farm could be so quickly made profitable came from their sense that it had been so neglected by the Lanaudières: "We are very busy opening & deepening drains, which had not been touched for these 12 years certainly – & cleaning the land which had been suffered to get full of weeds, so that a very large field has been left without any produce this year."[63] With a picturesque perspective in mind, the Hales dreamed of the changes they could effect. Their appropriation of the environment focused on, but was not restricted to, the area around the manor house. They wanted to "improve" the land. For them, "improvement" implied the importation of English farmers, livestock, and techniques. For instance, the common had to be enclosed: "we might make great use of it if we had the right to enclose it when cleared, a great deal of Timber has already been cleared there but being in common it is no one's business to take care of it or improve it."[64] The belief that they were improving the seigneury justified the Hales' appropriation of it.

Of course, their superior attitude towards the previous seigneur was compounded by their class disdain for the habitants. The Hales complained that habitants did not know how to use manure, and they tried to show them how to run a farm. In an attempt to introduce English techniques, John Hale taught the French-Canadian farmers English agricultural methods. In this limited sense, the habitants were important to the Hales' world view, but only as pupils to be taught. Being seigneur of Sainte-Anne fulfilled John Hale's desire to see acknowledged his social prestige, a feeling undoubtedly enhanced by his many disappointed attempts to receive patronage.

But the Hales could not rely solely on their efforts to impose new agricultural techniques on the Canadian peasants. Forming a population of some 2,178 in 1822, local habitants complained of land shortages. The Hales maintained the high rents of the previous seigneurs and posited that the future growth of the seigneury depended upon the immigration of Yorkshire farmers. John Hale sent an advertisement to the *Farmers' Journal* in Yorkshire, requesting twenty or thirty families to settle in his seigneury.[65] He particularly tried to attract the Chandler family.[66] Ultimately, the Hales wanted to create a rival for the village of Sainte-Anne. They projected the clearing of a second demesne six or eight miles back of the St Lawrence in order to establish another village: "we might perhaps be able to make a Protestant village of it from the many settlers who come here & then have a Protestant Church."[67] For the Hales, then, this was the promise of Sainte-Anne. They could reshape the landscape, physical and human, and create a "new" England in the St Lawrence valley.

Ultimately, the development of the seigneury would coincide with that of their family. As their family grew and prospered, so would Sainte-Anne. "I sometimes amuse myself," Elizabeth Hale confided to her brother in 1823, "with looking forward to the improvements [son] Edward will make some years hence when he returns from India – we have not yet received much from it, but it goes on well & we still hope will be advantageous to the young ones."[68] A permanent desire for improvement should, she thought, transform the local landscape.

RESULTS

The Hales' picturesque landscape never fully took root in Sainte-Anne, however. Of the seventy-two concessions that John Hale granted between 1821 and 1831, only four went to people with English names.[69] There would be no Protestant village in the seigneury of Sainte-Anne. The manuscript census for 1825 lists few Protestants and no Chandler family.[70] Elizabeth Hale died of cancer in 1826. The following year John Hale, who relished his position as seigneur, successfully applied to the governor to have the northern part of Sainte-Anne (the blank area on the 1825 map) transmuted to free and common socage.[71] By 1833 the Anglican minister at Trois-Rivières was warning that the few Protestants in the area "are much in danger of being seduced from the Protestant faith or of having their children brought up in the Romish Communion."[72] The Hales' dreams had not come to fruition.

As long as John Hale lived, there seemed to be no question of selling the seigneury.[73] Although his son George planned at various points to move into the manor house, no Hales appear in the government censuses of the area after 1831. Within a year of John's death, son Edward began speaking of placing the property on the market. By the 1830s the habitants had greatly reduced their wheat crops, which in turn limited the seigneurial mill toll. John's brother Edward commented in 1840, "I really dont know how those manage who depend of their seign[euria]l property for a livelyhood [sic]."[74] A calculation of seigneurial profits between 1841 and 1844 showed an average net total of about £286 per year, for a return of 2.4 per cent on the initial investment.[75] In the latter year uncle Edward Hale disparaged the materialistic turn of seigneurs at the same time as he agreed that Sainte-Anne should be placed on the market: "the taste for this kind of property is I fear on the decline ie. all look to the £.S.D. return without (as formerly) attaching the least value to the imaginary dignity of Seignior, but something must be done, this property cannot be sold as the U[pper] C[anada] Land in lots."[76] But the Hales were not able to find a buyer.

Despite their willingness to sell Sainte-Anne, the Hale children had nonetheless imbibed many of the cultural proclivities of their parents: they botanized and sketched and fanned out across the British empire. Son Edward built a new estate near Sherbrooke, and in 1846 he commissioned artist Cornelius Krieghoff to commit it (and the ancestral manor houses at Sainte-Anne and in England) to canvas.[77] Edward Hale's name for his estate reflected in many ways his mother's expectations of hers: he called it "Sleepy Hollow."

CONCLUSION

On a small scale, the Hales attempted to apply in the St Lawrence valley the lessons of English imperialism that were reshaping the world in the early nineteenth century. This project was not merely political or economic; it also involved an aesthetic appropriation. Elizabeth Hale's sensibilities and work were of particular significance in the attempted appropriation of Sainte-Anne seigneury. Bounded by her picturesque sense, she could not see Sainte-Anne – or by extension, North America – as a fundamentally different world.

The Hales' attitude towards their property ultimately bore a close resemblance to other European imperialist projects of the period.[78] Celebrating the social and economic satisfactions of their proprietorship, the Hales viewed the land in a way that left little place for its local inhabitants. They ignored the specificity of the new context in order to recreate their homeland.

To assume that the Hales' project was impossible would be to read history backwards. They could not know in the early 1820s that their visions would not be realized, just as the earliest seigneurs also could not have known. More important is the fact that they posited alternative visions of the landscape of this region. Their inspirations usually had an economic foundation: perspectives of the land were influenced greatly by how one thought one could profit most from it.

Thus the Europeans' earliest glimpses hinted of agrarian futures. As these predictions were fulfilled, seigneurs and peasants argued over the nature of land distribution and of control over resources. As external markets for wood expanded, seigneurs, merchants, industrialists, and some habitants focused on the commercial opportunities of woodland. The anglicized Charles-Louis de Lanaudière recognized early on that the land conferred on him prestige and potential profit; the Hales saw an opportunity to create an English landscape in North America.

With the Hales most clearly, but with the other individuals as well, the appropriation of landscape in Batiscan and Sainte-Anne involved not merely economically but also culturally defined motives. Altering the landscape involved creating boundaries of "civilization." The Hales' desire to create a "new" England, and their distancing of the local population, was not so fundamentally different from the French creation of New France. The shape that the area would assume had almost as much to do with the European newcomers' background as it did with the actual resources of the region. Nonetheless, creating a home in the New World was not a linear process which inexorably led to a picturesque village on the banks of the Sainte-Anne or to an ironworks on an island in the Batiscan. It was a history of changing cultural perspectives and contested visions, in which the agricultural economy, the peasants' demography, and the developing sense of a French-Canadian community had the most durable consequences.

Conclusion: Three Journeys

His native shore,
With dying glance, he strives to see once more,
But strives in vain.

Ovid, *Metamorphoses*, 430

In the 1780s the Huron chief Isawanhonhi (Nicolas Vincent) hunted along the Rivière Batiscan, travelling all the way from its source to its mouth.[1] From seemingly endless boreal forests filled with blackflies and wild game during the summer season, he would have finally approached large-scale human activity as he arrived at the clearings and the small chapel at Saint-Stanislas. The village of Sainte-Geneviève downstream provided stronger indications of agrarian developments, as did the settled banks at the mouth of the river.

In the 1820s Lieutenant Ingall of the 15th Regiment undertook a journey in the opposite direction. The purpose of his trip was different: to ascertain the agricultural potential of the lands beyond the old seigneurial grants. His conclusions were optimistic: "A great proportion of good land has been discovered to exist in the valleys of the Batiscan and St. Anne extending as far as the river Jacques Cartier, capable of supporting a large population."[2] Like those of the early French explorers, his account emphasizes the trees, and indeed, he would have witnessed much evidence of forestry activity. The slopes of the Saint-Stanislas and Saint-Prosper mountains, partially denuded for the purposes of the Batiscan Iron Works, would have begun regenerating their forest cover. He would have travelled past the increasingly decrepit chapel at Saint-Stanislas and later the ruins of the ironworks themselves, the furnaces cold and the tools rusting. By the time he passed, small groups of lumber workers had begun felling the trees in the depths of the seigneuries. There was little reason for Ingall to comment on the cohesive French-Canadian communities closer to the St Lawrence. Their crowded nature was, indeed, one of the reasons for his visit.

In mid-century the American author Henry David Thoreau passed by Batiscan and Sainte-Anne on his way to Quebec. For him, the St Lawrence valley "appeared as old as Normandy itself, and realized much that I had heard of Europe and the Middle Ages. Even the names of humble Canadian villages affected me as if they had been those of the renowned cities of antiquity." Thoreau exaggerated the backwardness of the colony, but he did acknowledge the transformation of the St Lawrence valley landscape that some two centuries of European settlement had effected. In Quebec, he noted, "I thought it would be a good place to read Froissart's chronicles. It was such a reminiscence of the Middle Ages as Scott's novels."[3]

But the St Lawrence valley was not an "ancient" landscape. Its differences from the states of New England may have misled Thoreau, but its villages and cities were as young as the ones he had left behind. It was just beginning to discover its own past. At the same time as Thoreau visited, an increasingly strong consciousness of French-Canadian history and traditions was developing. François-Xavier Garneau had committed its history to the bookshelves, and painter Joseph Légaré had celebrated its mythic origins. Nationalist politicians such as Jean-Baptiste-Éric Dorion were attempting to garner support by appealing to a long history of survival in the face of the British threat.[4]

The mid-century mobilization in defence of French-Canadian culture and history had its roots in the recent past. From the 1820s, local elites throughout the colony had roused opposition to British policies. In Batiscan and Sainte-Anne, as in hundreds of other localities throughout the colony, the leading laymen signed a petition in 1821 to protest the proposed union of Lower Canada with Upper Canada.[5] They wanted to maintain its distinctiveness, its French language, its Catholic religion and its civil code. These small groups of men were increasingly successful at harnessing the political fervour of their fellows. Communities throughout the colony were witnessing the development of nationalism on the local level.

Grown out of the local soil of Batiscan and Sainte-Anne, as elsewhere, such sentiments represented the work of some seven generations of settlers. Never entirely cut off from waves of immigration and economic fluctuations, the local society had become increasingly more centred by the turn of the nineteenth century. At the same time, it could not absorb all of its natural increase in population. Still, the inhabitants of the two seigneuries remained dedicated primarily to agrarian pursuits.

The locality had seen more than just demographic growth, it had also witnessed the attempt and failure to develop two new landscapes in the area. The Batiscan Iron Works, whose origin owed so much to conditions external to the locality, did not succeed in creating an industrial focus for the area. Waged labour did not disappear with – and indeed, was not invented by – this industrial endeavour. Rather, for many years it supplemented the agrarian pursuits of the vast majority of the population.

In the neighbouring seigneury of Sainte-Anne, the attempt to create a picturesque English landscape also failed, though again for some reasons external to the locality. The death of Elizabeth Hale in 1826 and the lack of interest on the part of English farmers in the land meant that the seigneury remained essentially a bulwark of French-Canadian sentiment. In the distant future, the nationalist premier of Quebec, Honoré Mercier, leader of the Parti National in the 1880s, would purchase the manor house at Sainte-Anne for his periodic escapes from the politics of the Quebec legislature.[6]

In the historiography of early French Canada, the questions of colony-wide nationalistic sentiment and agrarian economic potential are closely intertwined. One historiographical trend has focused on the development of capitalistic relations in the countryside. This debate emphasizes the ability of "feudal" property relations to permit profit-oriented managerial strategies. In Batiscan and Sainte-Anne the seigneurs were not as important figures as they appear to have been elsewhere. Although their vigilance increased during the period of relative prosperity in the 1720s and 1730s, in the aftermath of the British conquest both areas experienced a decline in seigneurial influence, though for markedly different reasons.

More in keeping with what had happened in other areas of the St Lawrence valley, an important process of differentiation had occurred. Lower down the social scale, a significant divergence in wealth levels developed in these two seigneuries. Already during the French regime but more noticeable by the late eighteenth century, a process of economic differentiation had produced an identifiable local elite. In Sainte-Anne and Batiscan this elite succeeded in fostering a more effective sense of community than had been the case under the French regime.

A second debate examines whether French-Canadian nationalism, as it developed in the early nineteenth century, was born of poverty and desperation or was rather the result of commercial success and the full integration of the colony into the burgeoning North Atlantic economy. These two positions are not irreconcilable if one acknowledges the degree of economic differentiation that had occurred at a local level. While some families benefited from the economic opportunities, others were constrained by the same forces.

Moreover, the local economic elite assumed a vital function in providing the bases for increased political activity in the area. It is possible to see the birth of nationalism along the banks of the Sainte-Anne and Batiscan rivers in the early nineteenth century, but these areas also witnessed the variations in nationalism that were occurring. Liberal nationalist leaders the Dorion brothers were born in Sainte-Anne, as was their next-door neighbour Louis-François Laflèche, later bishop of Trois-Rivières, one of the leaders of ultramontane nationalism of the late nineteenth century. It was not obvious by the 1820s which of the types of nationalisms would prevail. Nationalism was not, and never has been, a single-minded force, although at particular times one thrust may indeed hold sway. Two of the dominant strains of nineteenth-century French-Canadian nationalism found their expression through the words and lives of sons of Sainte-Anne de la Pérade.

This study has also emphasized the imperial context of local social relations. Just as the French seigneurs and settlers displaced the aboriginal inhabitants of the region, so did British entrepreneurs and seigneurs believe that they could rewrite the historical destiny of the area. But unlike the achievements of the French seigneurs and settlers, the British activities were to prove illusory.

The irony of settlement in the so-called New World countries was the facility with which newcomers could envisage utterly transformed landscapes and utopian futures. This is a theme which runs through Canadian history and literature, beginning with the idealism of the Catholic visionaries who established Ville-Marie in 1649. Batiscan and Sainte-Anne de la Pérade experienced a series of utopian dreams, but only the habitants' ideal landscape emerged.

In the 1820s little sense of the future of the colony was certain. The only fair prediction was that this territory would not become a homeland for British workers or farmers; it would remain the cultural and economic centre for French-Canadian agrarian society. And if necessary, it would be worth defending.

Yet at the time of the Rebellions of 1837–38, unrest did not beset this area. No battles were fought; no individuals joined the fight against British rule. Instead, in mid-winter 1838 the habitants of Batiscan humbly petitioned the commissioner of Jesuit estates to construct a mill for grinding oats.[7] But the cultural bases for nationalist sentiment were here as elsewhere in the colony, and locals had shared the nationalist fervor of the 1830s. Jean-Baptiste-Éric Dorion remembered having learned his first political words (*Patriotes* and *bureaucrates*) at rallies in his hometown.[8]

Studies of the growth of nationalism place rightful emphasis on the role of colonial elites in creating a sense of "imagined community."[9] The importance of a broadly based elite is ineluctable, but as this study suggests, the development of a cohesive community allows that spirit to pervade right down to the local level. In this sense, there is an organic nature to nationalism as well, expressed in an increasingly coherent community sentiment, in addition to its "invented" character.

This was a metamorphosis in the identity and community of the French-Canadian people. In the mid-seventeenth century, French settlers had barely touched the two seigneuries. Some 150 years later a clearly focused French-Canadian community existed. The sense of nationhood would galvanize the French-speaking population of the St Lawrence throughout the nineteenth and twentieth centuries, and the people of Batiscan and Sainte-Anne also undertook that journey.

Abbreviations
Used in the Sources

AAQ Archives de l'Archevêché du Québec
ANQ-M Archives nationales du Québec à Montréal
ANQ-Q Archives nationales du Québec à Québec
ANQ-TR Archives nationales du Québec à Trois-Rivières
ASQ Archives du Séminaire de Québec
ASTR Archives du Séminaire de Trois-Rivières
BJ Terres et forêts, Biens des Jésuites (ANQ-Q)
BRH *Bulletin des recherches historiques*
CFB Registre de lettres de la Compagnie des Forges de Batiscan (Parcs Canada)
CHR *Canadian Historical Review*
CPJN Collection des pièces judiciaires et notariales (ANQ-Q)
DCB *Dictionary of Canadian Biography*
Duclos Greffe Nicolas Duclos (ANQ-M)
FS Fonds Seigneuries (ANQ-Q)
NA National Archives of Canada
NA-Baby Baby Collection (NA)
NA-Hale Hale Family Collection (NA)
NMC National Map collection (NA)
PDCJ Pièces détachées des cours de justice de la Nouvelle-France (ANQ-M)
RAPQ *Rapport de l'archiviste de la province de Québec*
RHAF *Revue d'histoire de l'Amérique française*
TL Tarieu de Lanaudière (ANQ-Q)
UM-Baby Baby Collection (Université de Montréal)
UT-Hale Hale Family Collection (Thomas Fisher Rare Book Library, University of Toronto)

Notes

PREFACE

1 NA, Neilson Collection, MG 24, B 1, vol. 186, 2849, Account owed by B.J. Frobisher to John Neilson.
2 Vance, "Ovid and the Nineteenth Century," 21; Pearcy, *The Mediated Muse*.
3 Barkan, *The Gods Made Flesh*, 19.
4 Fernand Ouellet, "Frobisher, Benjamin Joseph," DCB, 6: 267–8.
5 It is impossible to know which edition of Ovid's *Metamorphoses* Frobisher received. For the epigrams at the beginning of each chapter, an 1811 edition of a translation by Thomas Orger was used.

INTRODUCTION

1 Hunter, *Hunter's Panoramic Guide*, 52.
2 Among others, Dechêne, *Habitants and Merchants*; Greer, *Peasant, Lord, and Merchant*; Lavallée, *La Prairie*; and Noël, *The Christie Seigneuries*.
3 Sabean, *Power in the Blood*; Sabean, *Property, Production, and Family in Neckarhausen*; Isaac, *The Transformation of Virginia*.
4 Anderson, *Imagined Communities*.

CHAPTER ONE

1 Thwaites, *Jesuit Relations*, 48: 215–17.
2 For example, Sansom, *Sketches of Lower Canada*, 159–60.

3 Cronon, *Changes in the Land*; White, *Land Use, Environment, and Social Change*, 22.
4 Lévesque, Fitz Osborne, and Wright, *Le gisement de Batiscan*.
5 Biggar, *Works of Samuel de Champlain*, 1: 132; 2: 67–8.
6 Douville, *Les premiers seigneurs et colons*, 18–26.
7 Day and Trigger, "Algonquin," 794–5.
8 Carter, *The Road to Botany Bay*, 336.
9 Thwaites, *Jesuit Relations*, 35: 253.
10 Ibid., 31: 209.
11 Biggar, *Works of Samuel de Champlain*, 2: 67.
12 Douville, *Les premiers seigneurs et colons*, 19.
13 Testimony of Nicolas Vincent (Isawanhonhi), a Huron (Wendat) chief, before the House of Assembly: "At the age of Fifteen, I hunted along the Branches of the River Batiscan, which I have descended as far as the River St. Lawrence" (*Journals of the House of Assembly of Lower Canada*, 1823–24, app. R, "Seventh Report from the Special Committee … [on] the Settlement of the Crown Lands"; app. A (testimony), 9 December 1823).
14 For example, Laurent Aubry reported to the bishop that some native families wanted him to minister to them: "Quelques familles Sauvages qui sortent des terres de temps en temps par la Rivière des Envies, me Regardent comme leur père." ASTR, Fonds Paroisses, DR-285, no. 120, Saint-Stanislas, Aubry à l'Evêque, 1 mars 1789).
15 Todorov, *The Conquest of America*, 9–10; Carter, *The Road to Botany Bay*, 56.
16 Cartier, *The Voyages of Jacques Cartier*, 57.
17 Ibid., 58.
18 Biggar, *Works of Samuel de Champlain*, 1: 133.
19 Ibid., 135.
20 Ibid., 2: 67.
21 Morissonneau, *Le langage géographique de Cartier et de Champlain*, 220. See also Lemire, "Champlain: Entre l'objectivité et la subjectivité," 44–5.
22 Boucher, *Histoire véritable et naturelle … de la Nouvelle-France*, 33.
23 Bertrand, "Pour une histoire écologique de la France rurale," 86; Dommergues, "La forêt en Nouvelle-France au dix-septième siècle."
24 "ainsi qu'un Vrai possesseur a accoutumé faire" (ANQ-Q, Terres et forêts, E21, BJ, vol. 70, Title Deeds, 80–1, Prise de possession du fief Batiscan par les Jésuites de la Nouvelle France, 10 octobre 1662).
25 ANQ-M, Seigneurie Batiscan, P220/1, Aveu et dénombrement, 29 décembre 1677.
26 *Le Journal des Jésuites* (1657); quoted in Douville, "Les lents débuts," 252.
27 Douville, "Les lents débuts," 255.
28 Thwaites, *Jesuit Relations*, 48: 217.
29 Douville, *Les premiers seigneurs et colons*, 18–36.

30 "ce qui le plus souvant les réduisoit dans une si grande nudité qu'yls se trouvaient hors d'estat de pouvoir aller à la chasse" (ANQ-M, Conseil supérieur, Insinuations, M9 (mf. 1208), f. 52v, 16 février 1674).

31 Jaenen, *The Role of the Church in New France*, 80–1.

32 P.-G. Roy cites ten *congés* from 1682 involving men from the two seigneuries, in *Ordonnances, commissions*, 2: 301–7.

33 Dechêne, *Habitants and Merchants*, 119.

34 Ibid., 120, 370n136. Lavallée finds similar patterns among *engagés* from La Prairie (*La Prairie*, 217–30).

35 ANQ-Q, Cour des plaidoyers communs, T50–301, District de Québec, 37, no. 3129, 1786.

36 Ouellet, "Dualité économique et changement technologique," 269.

37 "Capitaine Lanouette … n'a pas plus de vingt deux Miliciens, dont La majeure partie Sont Voyageurs" (UM-Baby, mf. 2584, Requête du capitaine Belletête, 12 mars 1783). It is not clear whether the total number of militiamen equalled twenty-two, or whether that was the number absent. In 1794 there were fifty-three militiamen in the parish (ibid., mf. 3468, Tableau général du nombre d'hommes mariés et garçons présens portant les armes, Infirmes etc … Québec, 31 octobre 1794).

38 Cf. Greer, *Peasant, Lord, and Merchant*, 187–8.

CHAPTER TWO

1 For the importance of naming and drawing boundaries in the appropriation of land, see Carter, *The Road to Botany Bay*.

2 Biggar, *Works of Samuel de Champlain*, 1: 132.

3 Carter, *The Road to Botany Bay*, 47–54.

4 Thwaites, *Jesuit Relations*, 48: 215.

5 UM-Baby, mf. 2584, Requête des habitants de Baptiste Camp à François Baby, 15 février 1783. John Knox recorded the name as "Batiste camp" (Doughty, *An Historical Journal*, 2: 478).

6 Douville, *Les premiers seigneurs et colons*, 9–10.

7 Trudel, *Les débuts du régime seigneurial au Canada*, 20–1; Harris, *Seigneurial System*, 23–5.

8 FS, vol. 3, Batiscan, Acte de Concession de Messire Jacques de La Ferté aux Pères Jésuites, 3 mars 1639.

9 NA, France, Archives des colonies, Des limites et des postes, Transcriptions, MG 1 série C 11 E (mf. F-409), 14, Estat des Terres que les Reverends Peres Jesuistes Possedent en Canada suivant leurs declarations du 26e novembre 1667.

10 ANQ-M, Seigneurie Batiscan, P220/1, Aveu et dénombrement, 29 décembre 1677.

11 Jarnoux, "La colonisation de la seigneurie de Batiscan," 169.

12 "ayant pas meme sur les Lieux aucune Justice formée ni assurée" (BJ, vol. 70, Title Deeds, Jesuits Estates, 82–4, Acte de Monsieur de Bouteroue Intendant pour suppleer au defaut d'insinuation des Donnations des fiefs Batiscan & Champlain, 27 nov. 1668).

13 Douville, *Les premiers seigneurs et colons*, 13–36.

14 C.-M. Boissonault, "Gamelain de La Fontaine, Michel," DCB, 1: 320–1.

15 Harris, *Seigneurial System*, 26–31.

16 "en Considera[ti]on des bons utils et louables services quil[s] ont rendus a sa ma[jes]te en differents endroicts tant en lancienne France que dans la nouvelle depuis quils y sont passez par ordre de sa ma[jes]te et en veue de ceux quils temoignent encore vouloir rendre cy apres" (FS, vol. 52, Sainte-Anne de la Pérade [Ouest], Acte de concession par Jean Talon, 29 octobre 1672).

17 Ibid., Sainte-Anne de la Pérade (est), Extrait d'un Contrat de vente par Moses Hart à Pierre Charay [*sic*] et uxor, 26 février 1816.

18 NAC-Hale, vol. 2, Acte de foi et hommage, 23 décembre 1819.

19 ANQ-M, Seigneurie Batiscan, P220/1, Aveu et dénombrement, 1.

20 UM-Baby, mf. 2104–5, Contrat de concession d'une place au village de Batiscan, 13 septembre 1674.

21 Douville, *Les premiers seigneurs et colons*.

22 Carte de Catalogne, 1709, in Trudel, *Atlas de la Nouvelle-France*, 169. This map does not, in fact, indicate the presence of a common in Sainte-Anne, though one was established.

23 Hamelin, "Le rang d'arrière-fleuve en Nouvelle-France," 113–14, notes that the St Lawrence formed the principal axis for concessions in the majority of cases. Still, according to Catalogne's map of 1709, other seigneurs also assured themselves of the most prominent geographic positions.

24 Douville, *Les premiers seigneurs et colons*, 122–8.

25 NA, Sainte-Anne de la Pérade, Transcriptions, MG 8, F 83, 10–13, Copie du contrat de donation faite par feu messire de Suève, 8 aoust 1691.

26 NMC-10842, Murray Map (1760), section FI.

27 For the male Lanaudières' military activity, see Roy, *La famille Tarieu de Lanaudière*. As for the women, besides Madeleine de Verchères, Philippe Aubert de Gaspé discussed his aunt, Agathe de Lanaudière, in his *Mémoires*, 402–4.

28 Raymond Douville, "Lanouguère, Thomas de," DCB, 1: 417–18.

29 Douville, *Les premiers seigneurs et colons*, 56, 62.

30 FS, vol. 52, Sainte-Anne de la Pérade (Est) [*sic*], Acte d'abandon et cession de la seigneurie de Sainte-Anne par Marguerite-Renée Denys à Pierre-Thomas Tarieu de la Pérade (Greffe Genaple), 4 novembre 1704.

31 "Ordonnance qui déclare bonne et valable la saisie …," in *Pièces et documents relatifs à la tenure seigneuriale*, 120–4.

32 ANQ-M, Conseil supérieur, Registres, M9, (mf. 1197), vol. 28, folio 39r–v, Esmond et Jean Tessier et al. versus Thomas Tarrieu de la Pérade, 18 août 1721; vol. 32, folio 51v–52v, François Chorel Dorvilliers vs Thomas Tarrieu de la Pérade, 12 mars 1725.

33 NA, Nouvelle-France, Correspondance officielle, 3ᵉ série, MG 8, A 1, vol. 12, 2657–8, Lettre de Beauharnois et Hocquart au ministre, 15 octobre 1731.

34 Ibid., vol. 11, 2427–8, Lettre de Beauharnois et Hocquart au ministre, 25 octobre 1729; NA, France, Archives des colonies, Lettres envoyées, MG 1, série B, vol. 54, folio 423 1/2, Lettre du ministre à Beauharnois, 4 avril 1730.

35 Bégon, *Lettres au cher fils*, 53.

36 Ibid., 72; Franquet, *Voyages et mémoires sur le Canada*, 129, 141.

37 NA-Baby, vol. 1, 511a, Beauharnois à Lanaudière, 22 juillet 1744; vol. 3, 1722–3, Marquis de Vaudreuil à Mr de Lanaudière, 23 juillet 1759.

38 Ibid., vol. 30, 18725–61, Inventaire des biens de la communauté entre De La Perrade [Lanaudière] et feue Geneviève de Boishébert, sa première épouse, 5 juillet 1762 (according to this document, Lanaudière held some 63,000 livres in France in the hands of various merchants); TL, vol. 1, Accord entre M. de Lanaudière et M. Varin, 16 octobre 1753, and Cession de Gaultier, 4 avril 1754.

39 NA-Baby, vol. 30, 18759, Inventaire des biens de la communauté entre De La Perrade [Lanaudière] et feue Geneviève de Boishébert, sa première épouse, 5 juillet 1762.

40 Ibid., vol. 4, 2139–40, Thouron & Frères à Lanaudière, 22 avril 1764.

41 Ibid., 1886–8, M. Duparquet, lieut. colonel, commend[an]t du 2ᵉ bataillon de la Sarre à M. de Lanaudiere, 1ᵉʳ juillet 1762.

42 "Mon oncle de Lanaudière … ne faisait jamais allusion à sa carrière militaire; je savais qu'il avait fait la guerre sur le continent où il avait été blessé de nouveau assez grièvement … 'J'ai fait, dit-il, en riant, des exploits bien glorieux en France contre messieurs les contrebandiers!' " (Aubert de Gaspé, *Mémoires*, 83).

43 NA-Baby, vol. 5, 2652–8, Thouron & frères à Lanaudière, 10 mars 1768.

44 "on ne peux pas être plû heureux que je le sui avec Mr Le generalle" (ibid., 2968, Lanaudiere à son père, 14 septembre 1770).

45 "joui des plaisirs de la vie et de la bonne compagnie, dont il est tres naturel qu'un jeune homme profite" (ibid., vol. 42, 27489–90, District de Québec, Cour des plaidoyers communs, Charles Tarieu de la Perade … contre Dame Catherine Lemoine de Longueil veuve DeLanaudière, 20 décembre 1777).

46 Thompson, *Whigs and Hunters*.

47 NA-Baby, vol. 30, 19052, Inventaire et procès-verbal de vente des biens de la succession de Lanaudière, avril 1788.

48 Letters in NA-Baby between 1774 and 1783 were written in March, July, September, October, and December.

49 "Vertrauliche Briefe aus Kanada," 304–5. A French translation of this passage is in Wilhelmy, *Les mercenaires allemands au Québec*, 119.

50 UT-Hale, E.F. Hale to Lord Amherst, 17 September [1819].

51 NA-Baby, vol. 6, 3570–1, Lanaudière fils à Vercher, 24 juillet 1773.

52 Porter, *English Society in the Eighteenth Century*, 73–8.

53 "comme nesséscairement il fautdra que le gouvernement fasse, Dotorité faire, faire le bois, – je propose sesi, si lon veux me donner les paroisses – Déchambaut, grondine, *St anne* & tous batiscand – qui ne fournisse jamais Du bois, avec pouvoir de commender Les hommes Dont jorei besoin pour bucher" (NA-Baby, vol. 8, 4398–9, Lanaudière à M. François Baby, 17 septembre 1778; emphasis in original).

54 "en fesant l'affaire Du gouvernement il faut que je fasse les miéne" (ibid., vol. 8, 4406, Lanaudière à François Baby, 30 septembre 1778). Evidence that the enterprise was undertaken is shown by a further letter in the same collection (4736–7, Lanaudière à F. Baby, 6 mars 1781).

55 See the criticism of Charles de Lanaudière in the handbill *Commentaire sur le discours de l'honorable Chas. Delanaudiere (qui a paru hier)*, reprinted in Hare, *Aux origines du parlementarisme québécois*, 177–9.

56 "cest le devoir de toutes hommes quis est atachés a son rois de faire c'est [cet] effort" (TL, vol. 2, Agathe de Lanaudière à Gaspard Lanaudière, 2 avril 1810).

57 Legault, "Les aléas d'une carrière militaire," 113–15.

58 *Gazette de Québec*, 15 mai 1783.

59 ASTR, DR-285, no. 120, Saint-Stanislas, L. Aubry à l'Evêque, 27 septembre 1788.

60 "pourrons nous … croire que ces mêmes Personnes qui auront quittés leur patrie pour prendre des Terres dans cette Province, voudront donner la preférence, à nos Seigneuries pour s'y Etablir, Etant régies par un Systeme de Loi qu'ils ont en Horreur, & qu'ils ne pourroient Entendre" (NA, Lower Canada Land Papers, RG 1, L 3 L, vol. 118 [mf. C-2538], 57737–8, Petition de Charles-François de Lanaudière à Lord Dorchester, 26 janvier 1788).

61 "Answers submitted by Charles de Lanaudière to various Questions relating to the Seigniorial System, October 11, 1790," in Munro, *Documents Relating to the Seigniorial Tenure in Canada*, 273.

62 *Gazette de Québec*, 24 mars 1791; supplément, 28 avril 1791.

63 ANQ-TR, Cour de banc du roi (dossiers), T25, Terme de septembre 1808, no. 1, Pierre Bureau vs Jos. Riv[ar]d Lanouette et L'Honorable De Lanaudière.

64 "ayant toujours ardemment désiré de tenir ses Terres en franc et commun Soccage en préférence de Féodalité" (NA, Lower Canada Land Papers,

RG 1 L 3 L, vol. 188 [mf. C-2538], 57763–4, Petition de Charles de Lanaudière à Sir James Craig, 21 décembre 1810).

65 Lambert, *Travels through Canada*, 461. Lord Selkirk was similarly impressed with Lanaudière: "a very gentlemanly old Canadian Officer, & a man of reflexion" (NA, Selkirk Papers, MG 19, E 1, Lord Selkirk's Diary, 19749).

66 *Gazette de Québec*, 22 juillet 1802.

67 Jarnoux, "La colonisation," 173–5, quotation from 173. See also Douville, "Les lents débuts."

68 BJ, vol. 97, St-Agnian vs. Antoine Trottier, 29 avril 1745. See also CPJN, Mesager vs. François Massicot, 6 avril 1748. Lavallée notes that the Jesuit seigneurs of La Prairie became more vigilant in the 1730s, launching a number of court cases for nonpayment of dues in the following decade (*La Prairie*, 100).

69 The following section dealing with the disposition of the Jesuit estates is summarized from Dalton, *The Jesuits' Estates Question*, chaps. 1–6.

70 NA, Executive Council and Land Committee, RG 1, L 7, Jesuit Estates, vol. 38, 11, Extrait de l'aveu & dénombrement des Fiefs & Seigneuries des Jésuites, 12 décembre 1781.

71 BJ, vol. 96, Rapport de l'Etat actuel des Moulins situés en les Seigneuries qui appartenoient ci devant au Jesuites, dans le District des Trois-Rivières … (no date; probably July 1800).

72 "marchoient encore et étoient en assez bon ordre Lors de lextinction des Jesuites" (ibid., vol. 103, Moulin de la Seigneurie, 1824–28, L. Guillet à John Stewart, 2 juin 1826).

73 Ibid., vol. 99, Liste des Concéssions qui ont été faites dans les Seigneuries qui appartenoient ci devant à l'ordre des Jésuites dans le District des Trois Rivieres, en la Province du Bas Canada, depuis la conquête de ce pays, fait par l'agent des ditte Seigneuries dans le dit District en conséquence des ordres des Commissaires pour l'adminstration des dits Biens, Suivant une Lettre du secretaire en date du 18 janvier 1802.

74 NA, Earl Amherst Papers, MG 12, WO 34, packet 47 [mf. C-1215], Compte que rendent les Jesuites du Canada à Mr Guy Carleton, le 7 avril 1768; Executive Council and Land Committee, RG 1, L 7, Jesuit Estates, vol. 35, General Recapitulation …; ibid., vol. 38, Extrait de l'aveu & dénombrement des Fiefs & Seigneuries des Jésuites, 12 décembre 1781; Haldimand Papers, MG 21 [mf. A-779].

75 UT-Hale, John Hale to Lord Amherst, 6 May 1802.

76 "étant des restant entre des terres concédées, qu'il est obligé de faire mesurer, à payer un sol par arpent en Superficie" (BJ, vol. 99, Liste des concessions … 18 janvier 1802). The government finally was able to ascertain the extent of the three "grands compeaux" in 1828: 169 arpents behind the falls, 480 arpents behind the ironworks, and 420 arpents near the Rivière à Veillet (ibid., L. Guillet à J. Stewart, 24 septembre 1828).

77 Ibid., vol. 75, Lettres, 1787–1800, Jonathan Sewell to H. Ryland, 27 February 1800.
78 Ibid., vol. 99, Trépagny à Larue, 22 décembre 1799; vol. 257, Larue, 18 juin 1800.
79 UT-Hale, John Hale to Lord Amherst, 5 December 1800.
80 Ibid., John Hale to Lord Amherst, 20 October 1801.
81 Milobar, "The Origins of British-Quebec Merchant Ideology," 370.
82 Noël, *The Christie Seigneuries*, 136.

CHAPTER THREE

1 For lay seigneuries, see Douville, *Les premiers seigneurs et colons*; Greer, *Peasant, Lord, and Merchant*, 89–112; Wien, "Peasant Accumulation in a Context of Colonization," chapter 4; Noël, *The Christie Seigneuries*. For seigneuries owned by religious orders, see Dechêne, *Habitants and Merchants*, 205–7; Dépatie et al., *Contributions à l'étude du régime seigneurial canadien*, 229–30.
2 Lacroix, "Les origines de La Prairie, 170–1; Jarnoux, "La colonisation," 173–5; La Fleur, "Seventeenth Century New England and New France, 113–14; Lavallée, *La Prairie*.
3 Jarnoux, "La colonisation," 173.
4 Trudel, *Atlas de la Nouvelle-France*, 169; NMC-1725, Plan cadastral de Batiscan (ca. 1726).
5 Douville, *Les premiers seigneurs et colons*, 55–6.
6 BJ, vol. 100, Papiers terriers, 1669–1821, Avertissment aux habbitans de Batiscan, 3 Février 1669.
7 "o qu'il est fâcheux d'avoir affaire a des ingrats et des esprits mal faicts" (ibid., Responce a l'escrit du sr. Nicholas Rivard, vers 1700 [sic]). Ibid., vol. 99, Correspondance, Seigneurie, 1846–94, Response aux plaintes de quelques habitants de Batiskan (no date).
8 "rebelle et refrectairre aux ordre du roy" (ibid., vol. 97, Trois-Rivières – 1657–1745, Sentance au R Reverand Perre jesuitte contre antoinne trotie ce 19 avril 1745).
9 "quil on du teraint plus quil leur faut" (Duclos, [mf. 1456], Sentence entre le Révérend Père Mésager et Joseph Juinot Latulippe et Jean et Jacques Massicot, 4 janvier 1746).
10 CPJN, no. 2009–54, Sentance entre Jésuites et François Massicot, par St Sire, 6 avril 1748.
11 BJ, vol. 99, Liste des Concéssions qui ont été faites dans les Seigneuries qui appartenoient ci devant à l'ordre des Jésuites …, 18 janvier 1802.
12 Testimony, 6 December 1823, in *Journal of the House of Assembly of Lower Canada*, 1823–24, app. R, app. A.

13 NA, Nouvelle-France, Ordonnances des intendants, Transcriptions, MG 8, A 6, vol. 9A, 87–96, Ordonnance entre le sieur de la Pérade et le sieur Voyer, 22 février 1727.

14 CPJN, no. 2009–19, Procédure entre le Sr De La Pérade et ses habitants, 3 septembre 1735.

15 "pour rémedier aux abus qui se commettent que trop souvent" (*Journal of the House of Assembly of Lower Canada*, 1812, 112–17).

16 Wien, " 'Les travaux pressants' "; Saint-Pierre,"L'aménagement de l'espace rural en Nouvelle-France."

17 Cook, "Cabbages not Kings."

18 Gédéon de Catalogne, "Report on the Seigniories and Settlements," in Munro, *Documents Relating to the Seigniorial Tenure in Canada*, 123.

19 The land was cleared in greater proportion on the east half of the seigneury, and in fact, the western section – the area around the church, constituting the Jesuits' village – had a much smaller ratio of cleared land (comparison of the Batiscan map of ca. 1726 and the document drawn in preparation of the *aveu et dénombrement*, BJ, vol. 100, Papiers terriers).

20 "leurs intentions étant seulement d'en déteriorer les bois" (NA-Baby, 31557–61, Ordonnance de Dupuy, 4 avril 1727).

21 "attendu que les bois sont tres rares aud. Batiscan." Gouin himself took wood from his brother's property (CPJN, no. 2009–38, Nomination d'arbitres en question entre Gouin et Lahaye, par St Sire, 26 avril 1740).

22 Ibid., no. 2009–53, Sentence entre Morainville et Labissonniere, par St Sire, 15 mars 1746.

23 Ibid., no. 1751–5, Sentence entre Joseph Pezar et Louis Marchand, 28 novembre 1752.

24 "Der neue Habitant zündet alsdenn so viel Bäume an, als des zu machenden Ackerlands wegen ausgerodet werden sollen … Alle habitationen haben schon so viele Waldungen zu Acker gemacht, dass sie ganz vortrefliche Fluren von Feldern haben, und die Holzung schon ¼ Leuke von ihren Häusern entfernt ist … Die Waldung siehet daher scandaleux aus; und man glaubt oft nicht anders, als es müßte Feuer vom Himmel in den Wald gefallen seyn, wenn man halb verbrannte, halb dürre, und ganz dürre Bäume darin erblicht." ("Von Kanada, aus Briefen eines deutschen StabsOfficiers," 331–2).

25 Sansom, *Sketches of Lower Canada*, 52. Sansom exaggerates here the lack of fences. Other travellers who mentioned the sparseness of the trees include Stansbury, *A Pedestrian Tour*, 159, and Lambert, *Travels through Canada*, 462.

26 Testimony of Joseph Trepanier, in *Journal of the House of Assembly of Lower Canada*, 1823–24, app. R, app. A.

27 For instance, the case between Voyer and La Pérade (NA, Nouvelle-France, Ordonnances des intendants, MG 8, A 6, vol. 9A, 87–96, 22 février

1727); also BJ, vol. 80, Minutes of the Commissioners, 28 August 1810.

28 If we take the inventory prepared by Michel Sarrasin and Sébastien Vaillant as an example, the native plants used by habitants were those most easily comparable to European ones. For example, the *Dens Canis flore luteo*, which "approche pour le goût de celle de l'ail," or the *Crypototaenia canadensis*, which Sarrasin indicated, "On l'appelle *Cerfeuil sauvage*." The *Pedicularia canadensis* "[se] mange dans la soupe. Sa fleur et son fruit ressemblent à ceux de la pédiculaire." See Boivin, "La flore du Canada en 1708."

29 The statistics for Sainte-Anne are for the French regime censuses (NA, Censuses of New France, 1685–1739, série G1) and the militia captain's census of 1783 (UM-Baby, mf-1519, 3140–1). For Batiscan, only the French regime censuses list the amount of maize.

30 Crosby, *Ecological Imperialism*, 300.

31 ANQ-M, Greffe Jacques de La Touche, CN401–28 (mf. 1456), Sentence, 15 novembre 1668.

32 CPJN, no. 395, Cause entre Pierre Retou et le sr. Labissionnière, 1707.

33 "In der Nähe der Pariossen schießt man nichts von Erheblichseit. Die habitans haben in der Nähe der habitationen alle wilde Tiere ausgerottet" ("Vertrauliche Briefe aus Kanada," 298).

34 "Den ganzen Sommer lebt der Canadier von Brod, welches aber so weis wie Schnee ist, von Milch, Zugemüse, und Mehl: sein Vieh, Hüner etc. spart er auf den lieben langen Winter, und alsdenn sollen sie sehr gut leben" ("Von Kanada, aus Briefen eines deutschen StabsOfficiers," 335).

35 However, these data must be used with some caution. Critiques of the French regime censuses may be found in Wien, "Peasant Accumulation," 66–7; Lalou and Boleda, "Une source en friche"; and Saint-Pierre, "L'aménagement de l'espace rural," 180–3. In fact, there are a few years for which there is no information for Sainte-Anne.

36 Dechêne provides a detailed analysis of the internal colonial trade in agricultural goods in *Le partage des subsistances*.

37 "On y auroit encore l'avantage de trouver sur le lieu, les bleds, pois, lards et autres denrées nécessaires pour la subsistance de tous les ouvriers qui seront employez aux forges" (NA, Archives des colonies, Correspondance générale, Canada, Transcriptions, MG 1, série C 11 A, vol. 63, 117–18, Mémoire Instructif des observations à faire par le Sr Olivier, 1er septembre 1735).

38 The proximity of the three local rivers, the Batiscan, the Sainte-Anne, and the Champlain, may have been a contributing factor in that hemp required waterways for retting. Dechêne criticizes the emphasis that historians accord to the state's role in determining economic growth (*Le partage des subsistances*, 123). In this case, the importance of government subsidies seems ineluctable.

39 Lunn, *Développement économique*, 46–8.

40 "Les habitans de Champlain et Batiscant se sont vanter d'en apporter 150 milliers l'annéz prochaine." (NA, France, Archives des colonies, MG 1, série C 11 A, vol. 49-2, 310, Dupuy au ministre, 20 octobre 1727). It is not clear whether the figure refers to the value or the volume of the hemp; in either case, it implies a large amount.

41 "La Parroisse de Baptiscant ne porte quasi plus que du chanvre" (ibid., 313).

42 "Il y a même des paroisses qui autrefois n'avaient pas de supplément, et qui en ont grand besoin aujourd'hui, comme Lachine, Batiscan, Champlain, etc., et cela, ou parce que les terres ne valent rien et sont usées, ou parce qu'au lieu de blé on y fait venir le chanvre et le tabac" (Dosquet to the minister, 11 September 1731; quoted in Gosselin, *L'église du Canada*, 2: 151–2).

43 Lunn, *Développement économique*, 47.

44 Innis, *Select Documents in Canadian Economic History*, 371–2.

45 NA, France, Archives des colonies, MG 1, série C 11 A, vol. 60, 25, Hocquart au ministre, 2 octobre 1733.

46 "La culture du chanvre se soutient a l'ordinaire" (ibid., vol. 71, 218–19, Hocquart au ministre, 14 octobre 1739; vol. 73, 57–8, Hocquart au ministre, 29 septembre 1740 [quotation from the same sentence in these two letters]; vol. 75, 369–70, Hocquart au ministre, 3 octobre 1741).

47 Ibid., vol. 85, 68, Hocquart au ministre, 9–10 octobre 1746.

48 "cette culture n'exige pas autant de soins" (ibid., vol. 93, 250, Bigot au ministre, 25 septembre 1749).

49 "cette culture ne pourra s'établir en Canada assés considérablement pour en envoyer en france que lors qu'il y aura des Nègres" (ibid., vol. 34, 390, Bégon au ministre, 12 novembre 1714; vol. 43, 21–2, Lettre du conseil, 1er juin 1720 [quotation]).

50 "Les habitans le pouvant faire en toute sorte de terres indifférentes et y occuper leurs femmes et leurs enfants" (ibid., vol. 49-2, 316, Dupuy au ministre, 20 octobre 1727).

51 Murray quoted in Fowke, *Canadian Agricultural Policy*, 68.

52 "Was der Canadier an seinem Leibe trägt, macht er fast alles selbst" ("Von Kanada, aus Briefen eines deutschen StabsOfficiers," 337).

53 On these attempts, see Macdonald, "Hemp and Imperial Defense."

54 "au plus haut prix qui vous en sera offert … sachant que nombre de vous ne peuvent sortir pour porter dans les villes cet article de commerce"; "continuez à cultiver un article si essentiellement nécessaire à la vie de l'homme" (*Gazette de Québec*, 22 juillet 1802).

55 BJ, vol. 101, Administration, 1802–64, Account of Lewis Foy's expenses, 13 July 1821.

56 However, the entrepreneur François-Étienne Cugnet attempted to export

tobacco to France. In 1736 he sent samples collected in various parts of the colony, including "les Cantons des 3 Rivieres" (NA, France, Archives des colonies, MG 1, série B, vol. 64–3, 528–30, Ministre aux MM Beauharnois et Hocquart, 17 avril 1736).

57 NA, Haldimand Papers, MG 21, King's Manuscript 205, Return of the Lands granted by the Seigneurs ..., J. Bruyère, Secretary, 5 April 1762.

58 Lambert, *Travels through Canada*, 131–3.

59 This view runs contrary to Marjorie Cohen's contention that, in pre-industrial Canada, women did not participate in market-oriented economies (*Women's Work, Markets, and Economic Development*, 24).

60 The 1765 census, on which this material is based, was taken during a time of agricultural hardship (Ouellet, *Histoire économique et sociale*, 82).

61 This theme of differentiation within the colonial peasantry has been of particular interest to historians. As they demonstrate, already in the French regime, differing levels of economic ease were experienced. In focusing on this development for the British regime, I do not deny that similar disparities existed earlier. Rather, I attempt to link the growth of political importance of this local group to its economic importance in a way that was less evident under French rule. On the theme of differentiation, see Wien, "Peasant Accumulation"; Dessureault, "L'égalitarisme paysan"; Lavallée, *La Prairie*, 249–55; and Desbarats, "Agriculture within the Seigneurial Regime."

62 "Die Braatfelder geben die schönste Weide für das Vieh ab, und diese wechselsweise geben zu ihrer Zeit die besten Kornfelder ab ... Das Feld, welches das andre Jar besäet werden soll, wird in späten Herbste gepflügt, und bleibt so den Winter liegen: im Frühjar wird das Korn hineingesäet, und der Acker alsdenn mit drei guten Eggen geegget.

   "Man baut in Kanada sehr guten Weizen, und ziemliche Gerste und Haber. Roggen, ingleichen Sommer- und WinterSaat, wird gar nicht gebaut. Erbsen, wicken, Feldbohnen, baut man ebenfalls; und in den Gärten findet man weissen Kohl, Steckrüben, Kartoffeln, gelbe Rüben, Kürbisse, Gurken, Lauch, Zwiebeln, Petersilje, auch nicht sehr selten Sparges und Melonen" ("Von Kanada, aus Briefen eines deutschen StabsOfficiers," 321).

63 Dechêne argues that British immigrants living in urban areas represented a good market for potatoes, but I found no evidence to suggest that potatoes from this area reached urban markets (see "Observations sur l'agriculture du Bas-Canada au début du XIXᵉ siècle," in Goy and Wallot, *Évolution et éclatement du monde rural*, 198). Fyson points out that potatoes formed a small part of the diet of Montreal workers in the 1820s ("Du pain au madère," 75–7).

64 NA, Haldimand Papers, MG 21, B 171, Henry Rousseau (no date).

65 The schedules are in UM-Baby, mf. 1519, 3140–1. The schedules for the Batis-

can parishes are dated 15 February 1783. The Sainte-Anne listing is undated.

66 Ouellet, *Histoire économique et sociale*, 111, 132.

67 These men were or had been militia captains or lieutenants.

68 It appears that only the nominal schedules for Jesuit seigneuries survive (BJ, vol. 97, Population etc etc, Jesuits Estates, District of Three Rivers & of Montreal … a true Extract from the original recensement of the Province taken in the Year 1784 by Order of His Excellency General Haldimand then Governor of this Province, [signed] Geo. Pownall Sec[reta]ry, [no date]). The schedule indicates only total grain and therefore presumably includes both wheat and oats.

69 For instance, I make the rather large assumption for the purposes of this analysis that levels of nonpayment of tithes remain more or less the same from year to year. Excepting the few letters I discuss below, the bishops' correspondence with the local priests provides little evidence contradicting this assumption.

70 "les Patates dont on luy demande les dixmes, n'ont point eté plantés dans son Jardin potager mais dans un Champ ou il avoit coutume de Semer depuis plus de cinq ans du bled, avoine et autres grains" (UM-Baby, H1/ 93 [mf. 1926], Jugement contre Benony Marchand, 6 décembre 1798).

71 In 1818 the report of the pastoral visit for Saint-Stanislas included the following annotation concerning potatoes: "à voir par quelle autorité cette derniere dixme se perçoit" (AAQ, Cahiers des visites pastorales, 69CD, cahier 7, 165–70).

72 "Vous savez très bien que la dixme de patates n'est point dûe. La maigreur extrême de votre revenu, vous fait dériver ce supplément, et je consens que vous le demandiez, non comme dû en loi et en conscience, mais comme une aumône que de bons paroissiens ne sauroient refuser à leur pasteur. Quant à la quantité, ne la déterminer pas: recevez avec contentement et reconnaissance ce que chacun vous apportera, sans compter ni mesurer et sans faire de reproches à ceux qui n'apporteront rien" (ibid., Registres des lettres, 210A, vol. 9, ff. 263–4, lettre à Mr Hot, 14 novembre 1817).

73 However, the years for which potato tithes are noted do not always coincide with decreases in the average production of wheat, oats, or peas. It is possible that different fields were brought under cultivation for potatoes. The sparseness of the records makes firm conclusions difficult on this subject.

74 Christian Dessureault notes that, on poor soils, rye and buckwheat were grown instead of wheat ("Les fondements de la hiérarchie sociale," 261).

75 "Die Viehzucht ist in Canada sehr gut. Jeder Habitant hat seine Pferde, Ochsen, Kühe, Schweine, und Schafe; auch hin und wieder, jedoch selten, Ziegen. Die Ochsen sind von 3 bis 600 Pfund schwer, und sehr feist, und haben ein ungemein wolschmeckendes Fleisch … Milch und Butter kan

man sich nicht besser wünschen: Käse aber macht man wenig. Hühner, Puter, Gänse &c. hat jeder Habitant in Menge" ("Von Kanada, aus briefen eines deutschen StabsOfficiers," 322).

76 UM-Baby, mf. 1519, Paroisse de sainte anne – louis gouin capitaine – etat des grains et bestiaux (1783).
77 Lambert, *Travels through Canada*, 133.
78 Weld, *Travels through … Upper and Lower Canada*, 249.
79 UT-Hale, E.F. Hale to Lady Amherst, 17 July 1819.
80 NA-Hale, (mf. A-1085), J. Hale to Lord Amherst, 20 July 1820.
81 *Journal of the House of Assembly of Lower Canada*, 1823–24, app. F, no. 1, Report of the Agricultural Society of the District of Three-Rivers, L. Gugy, 29 November 1823.
82 NA, Civil and Provincial Secretary, Lower Canada, "S" series, RG 4, A 1, 175, J. Stewart to A.W. Cochran, 22 September 1828.
83 Ouellet shows that the Trois-Rivières district had grown proportionately more oats than the other two districts since the French regime ("Ruralization, Regional Development, and Industrial Growth," in *Economy, Class & Nation in Quebec*, 132, Table 7).

CHAPTER FOUR

1 "le pays Etant Lors troublé par les Courses continuelles et Massacres que les Iroquois faisoient des habitans" (BJ, vol. 70, Title Deeds, Jesuits Estates, 82–4, Acte de Monsieur de Bouteroue Intendant pour suppleer au defaut d'insinuation des Donnations des fiefs Batiscan & Champlain, 27 novembre 1668).
2 Jarnoux, "La colonisation," 183; Douville, *Les premiers seigneurs et colons*, 129–63.
3 Ouellet, "Ruralization, Regional Development, and Industrial Growth," in *Economy, Class & Nation in Quebec*, 125–6.
4 Jarnoux, "La colonisation," 186–8. Lavallée notes that some settlers in La Prairie seigneury had arrived from Batiscan as early as the 1670s (*La Prairie*, 34–5).
5 Fournier, *Les Européens au Canada*, 130. So also were Joseph Greenhill, Jean Willet, and Jean-Baptiste Jacob, *dit* Langlais; see 152, 165, and 260–1.
6 Anglican Church of Canada, Quebec Diocesan Archives (Lennoxville), Three Rivers, B24, Parish Report, 24 July 1816.
7 Trudel, *Dictionnaire des esclaves*, 7, 189–92, and 199.
8 Trudel, *L'esclavage au Canada français*, 179.
9 Ibid., 189.
10 Trudel, *Dictionnaire des esclaves*, 207.
11 NA, Nouvelle-France, Ordonnances des intendants, MG 8, A 6, vol. 9, 49–50, Ordonnance qui enjoint au capitaine de la coste …, 17 juillet 1726.

12 The data for the first three decades of British rule show less out-migration, though at least part of this is explained by the gaps in the parish registers for a few of the years (1766–1768 in Batiscan and 1766–73 in Sainte-Anne).

13 *Journal of the House of Assembly of Lower Canada*, 1823–24, app. R, app. A, Testimony, 6 December 1823.

14 Of course, the church played a fundamental role in socialization. Also, children from the area were sent to outside schools. The list of girls attending the Ursulines' school at Trois-Rivières between 1809 and 1825 shows the importance of schooling for the reproduction of the local elite. The daughters of local elite families dominate the list. See *Les Ursulines des Trois-Rivières*, 2: 517ff.

15 This case is discussed at length in chapter 5.

16 Cliche, *Les pratiques de dévotion en Nouvelle-France*, 70.

17 "yl a mal parlé de leur famille." "pour gens de probité et d'honneur" (ANQ-M, Conseil supérieur, Registres, M9, vol. 28, 13 janvier 1721 au 26 avril 1723: f. 15v, 31 mars 1721).

18 "deffence à toutes personnes de quelque condition et qualité qu'elles soient de composer, debiter ou chanter chansons diffamatoires" (NA, Nouvelle-France, Ordonnances des intendants, MG 8, A 6, vol. 7, 404–5, Ordonnance au sujet des chansons calomnieuses ..., 4 juin 1723).

19 Duclos, Sentence entre Lefebvre et Trépanier, 30 avril 1742.

20 ANQ-Q, Magdeleine Lonval, P-1000–1314, Certificat de Dizy, 11 avril 1730.

21 NA, Nouvelle-France, Archives judiciaires, Transcriptions, MG 8, B 4, vol. 1, 375–7.

22 Haskell, "Capitalism and the Origins of the Humanitarian Sensibility, Part II."

23 ANQ-Q, Cours des plaidoyers communs, District de Québec, T50–301, vol. 37, no. 3129, Défenses de Joseph Gouin et al., 19 avril 1786.

24 NA-Baby, 2885–6, Lanaudière fils à cousin Vercheres, 1770; 3570–1, Lanaudière fils à Vercheres, 24 juillet 1773.

25 ANQ-TR, Forges de Batiscan (copies), DR-8, Greffe Planté, no. 4680, Dépôt de documents, vente par Craigie à Joseph Frobisher, 30 janvier 1804.

26 NA, British Military and Naval Records, RG 8, series C, vol. III, 88–90, Craigie to Colonel I. Brock, 23 March 1807.

27 UT-Hale, E.F. Hale to Lady Amherst, 17 July 1819.

28 Greer, *Peasant, Lord, and Merchant*, 76–80.

29 Barthe, *Analyse des actes de François Trottain*, Révocation d'une obligation, 8 mai 1689, 19–20.

30 "auberger le dit Pierre Retor chez lui et comme eux, le regardant comme un de leurs enfans propres" (ibid., Donation, 1690, 26–7).

31 "par une donnation en forme quil m'a tousjours promise, sans effectuër cette promesse" (CPJN, no. 395c, 1707).

32 Duclos, Sentence, 8 août 1747.

33 PDCJ, Sentence entre Baril et Massicot, 25 juin 1743.
34 "se serva[i]t même de violence à leur égard" (ANQ-Q, Cours des plaidoyers communs, T50–301, vol. 3, no. 841, Supplication de Lefebvre et Morant contre leur fils, vers 22 janvier 1770).
35 Sabean makes a similar argument concerning family relations in *Property, Production and Family*, 298.
36 "suivant la Loy on ne doit rien prendre a autruit sans sa permission Ce qui est Contraire a tous coutumes d'agir et prendre sans permission" (CPJN, no. 2009–38, Nomination d'arbitres en question entre Gouin et Lahaye, 26 avril 1740).
37 "sa ditte mere ne luy a jamais rien donné" (Duclos, Ordonnance, 9 juin 1731).
38 Ibid., Sentence, 14 juillet 1742.
39 Ibid., Sentence, 4 avril 1742.
40 CPJN, no. 2009–17, Sentence entre Lafond et la veuve Ignace Baril, 19 juillet 1735.
41 "demande toute et prend toutes les qualitéz" (ibid., no. 1212–11, Entre Marguerite Jarret de Verchères et Joseph Levreau de Langy).
42 "contre l'Esprit et la Véritable intention des Lois de cette province … qui défendent et prohibent Très expressement de Traiter de la succession d'un homme vivant" (ANQ-Q, Cours des plaidoyers communs, T50–301, vol. 11, Requête de Charles Tarieu de Lanaudière contre Dame veuve de Lanaudière, signé Cugnet, 14 novembre 1777).
43 "Il n'est point étonnant qu'une dame n'ait point fait réflections sur le véritable sens de l'acte de Québec; Les Dames n'étant point éduquées pour être jurisconsultes" (NA-Baby, vol. 42, 27499, District de Québec Cour des Plaidoyers Communs, Charles Tarieu de la Perade ecuier Sr de Lanaudière … demandeur contre Dame Catherine Lemoine de Longueil veuve de Lanaudière defenderesse, 20 décembre 1777).
44 "d'allieur M[a]d[a]me je ne veux pas perdre mon droit *dénesse* [d'aînesse] étant le seul autorisé" (ibid., vol. 7, 4291, Lanaudière fils à Madame veuve Lanaudière, 5 novembre 1777).
45 "Les croix naissent sous les pas des veuves" (ibid., 3798, Longueüil veuve Lanaudière à Messieurs, 4 novembre 1774).
46 Gadoury, *La noblesse de Nouvelle-France*.
47 "le dit Claude Devaux est venu garçon (libre de mariage) en France en Canada, étant employé comme garçon sur la liste des faux-sauniers et contrebandiers" (ANQ-M, Registres d'état civil, Église Sainte-Anne de la Pérade, ZQ2-8, 1 février 1742).
48 Trudel, *Le régime militaire*, 51–2. The marriages do not appear in the parish records.
49 ANQ-M, Registres d'état civil, Église protestante St-James, Trois-Rivières, CE401–50.

50 "son nom annonce un étranger" (AAQ, Registres des lettres, 210A, vol. 10, f. 275, à Côté, Sainte-Geneviève, 9 octobre 1821).

51 Serge Gagnon provides a detailed discussion of the church's role in ensuring that prospective marriage partners were not indeed previously married (*Mariage et famille*, 110–18).

52 Trudel, *Initiation à la Nouvelle-France*, 273–4.

53 AAQ, Registres des lettres, 210A, vol. 10, ff. 82–3, à Xavier Coté, Saint-Stanislas, 12 mai 1820.

54 Greer notes the same phenomenon in the lower Richelieu area by the early nineteenth century (*Peasant, Lord, and Merchant*, 49–50). For a broader discussion of the phenomenon, see Gagnon, *Mariage et famille*, chaps 1–2.

55 AAQ, Registres des lettres, 210A, vol. 3, ff. 151–2, à Gallet, Batiscan, 6 juin 1801.

56 "Enfin je n'ai pu résister aux instances et aux larmes du jeune homme ni à sa piété envers des parens infirmes et des frères et so[e]urs en bas âge" (ibid., vol. 5, ff. 231–3, à Alexis Dorval, Sainte-Geneviève, 19 décembre 1806).

57 "Louis Normandin et Madeleine Normandin sa cousine que vous voyez en pénitence au milieu de cette église depuis trois dimanches, demandent pardon à Dieu et à la paroisse, du grand scandale qu'ils ont donné par leur commerce criminel" (ibid., vol. 7, f. 262, à Dorval, Sainte-Geneviève, 11 février 1811).

58 Ibid., vol. 8, f. 320, à Hot, Sainte-Geneviève, 30 mars 1815.

59 "Il est inutile de m'adresser votre Aug. Frigon. Ni ses instances, ni sa folie ne sauroit me donner un pouvoir que je n'ai point. Ce n'est pas pour gratifier une famille particulière que l'Eglise dispense dans le degré dont il s'agit" (ibid., ff. 458–9, à Hot, Sainte-Geneviève, 17 février 1816).

60 Gagnon, *Mariage et famille*, 23.

61 This is true especially for rural areas up to the early eighteenth century: see Paquette and Bates, "Les naissances illégitimes," 242; and Bates, "Les conceptions prénuptiales," 258.

62 ANQ-M, Registres d'état civil, Église Saint-François-Xavier de Batiscan, ZQ1-14, 20 avril 1728.

63 Even if they did not identify the father in church, women were supposed to make a *déclaration de grossesse* before the courts. However, as Cliche shows, relatively small numbers of women in New France took advantage of the legal rules in their favour to extract payment from the father ("Filles-mères, familles et société sous le Régime français").

64 Duclos, Rapport sur enfant trouvé, 2 septembre 1747.

65 "je suppose que tu na pas perdû La coutume ordinaire que quand on na pas sa fem[m]e on en trouvent" (NA-Baby, 3570–1, Lanaudière fils à Vercher, 24 juillet 1773).

66 AAQ, Registres des lettres, 210A, vol. 10, f. 117, à Morin, Sainte-Anne, 27 octobre 1820.

67 "Il avoit feint d'abandonner son concubinage tout en y perséverant" (ibid., ff. 350–1, à Gauvreau, Sainte-Anne, 2 février 1822).

68 Ibid., vol. 9, ff. 246–7, à Morin, Sainte-Anne, 23 octobre 1817.

69 "il doit la renvoyer dès que le public s'en offense" (ibid., vol. 7, ff. 386–7, à Viau, Sainte-Geneviève, 21 mars 1812).

70 Ibid., vol. 2, ff. 197–8, à Morin, Sainte-Anne, 1 mai 1795.

71 "qui a commis secretement plusieurs fornications"; "pourvû qu'elle soit tout à fait hors de l'habitude et de l'occasion prochaine" (ibid., vol. 7, ff. 386–7, à Viau, Sainte-Geneviève, 21 mars 1812).

72 "il fera en sorte d'en tirer lui-même adroitement un nouveau consentement, sans lui faire soupçonner son péché" (ibid., vol. 10, f. 90, à Xavier Coté, Sainte-Geneviève, 26 juillet 1820).

73 ANQ-TR, Cour du banc du roi (plumitif), T25, Terme de mars 1808, Angélique Deveau vs François Nobert.

74 ANQ-TR, Cour du banc du roi (dossiers), T25, Terme de janvier 1823, no. 59, A. Toubin dit Boisvert vs P. St Arnault.

75 Mintz and Wolf, "An Analysis of Ritual Co-Parentage (Compadrazgo)."

76 Sabean, *Power in the Blood*, 12; Sabean, *Property, Production, and Family*.

77 Tebbenhof, "Tacit Rules and Hidden Family Structures," 575.

78 Saint-Vallier, *Rituel du diocèse de Québec*, 24.

79 Lange, *La nouvelle pratique civile*, 278, 367.

80 Bates, "Stock, caractéristiques et mode de transmission des prénoms," 170.

81 ANQ-M, Registres d'état civil, Église Sainte-Anne de la Pérade, ZQ2-8, 7 janvier 1733.

82 ANQ-M, Registres d'état civil, Église Saint-François-Xavier de Batiscan, ZQ1-14, 4 janvier 1702.

83 ANQ-M, Registres d'état civil, Église Sainte-Anne de la Pérade, ZQ2-8, 4 septembre 1707.

84 Ibid., 19 novembre 1717.

85 ANQ-M, Registres d'état civil, Église Saint-François-Xavier de Batiscan, ZQ1-14, 1er janvier 1733.

86 The functions of the seigneurial court are analyzed in chapter 6.

87 The nature of the local elite is discussed at greater length in chapter 5.

88 The methodology of these calculations must be explained, as certain assumptions are involved. For this analysis, the family names of the godparents were compared to those of the parents. If one of the godparents' surnames matched one of the parents' surnames, it was counted. The principle behind this decision was that it represented a relatively quick way of determining the proportion of close family members who were chosen as godparents. In order to maintain the integrity of the selection

process, even when the priest noted the relationship between godparent and child, when the family names did not match, the case was excluded. This analysis unfortunately excludes grandmothers, maternal cousins, and in-laws. But it does capture the parents' siblings, the grandfathers, the infants' siblings, and the paternal cousins of both the parents and the infants. In the absence of a reason for believing that the excluded kin members were more likely to serve as godparents, this calculation provides a relatively accurate picture of the importance of choosing family members as spiritual kin.

89 All the baptisms in the parishes of Batiscan and Sainte-Anne were included in this analysis of the periods 1700–03 and 1750–51. For the third period, a random selection of eight baptisms in each of the three parishes in 1800, 1802, and 1804 was performed.

CHAPTER FIVE

1 NA, Nouvelle-France, Archives judiciaires, Transcriptions, MG 8, B 4, vol. 2, 1032, Acte d'assemblée des seigneur, curé et habitants de Sainte-Anne du 22 mars 1737.

2 We have two complementary, though somewhat different, records of the trials. A photocopy of many of the documents is available at the ANQ-Q, Verchères/Naudière – Procès avec le curé de Batiscan, ZQ27. At the NA is a transcription. The quotation is from NA, Nouvelle-France, Archives judiciaires, MG 8, B 4, vol. 1, 218. Each collection contains material lacking in the other, though both include most of the documents.

3 NA, Nouvelle-France, Archives judiciaires, MG 8, B 4, vol. 1, 214.

4 Lachance, *Crimes et criminels en Nouvelle France*, 25–6.

5 Moogk, "'Thieving Buggers' and 'Stupid Sluts,'" 546–7.

6 Burke, *The Historical Anthropology of Early Modern Italy*, 101; David Garrioch, "Verbal Insults in Eighteenth Century Paris," in Burke and Porter, *The Social History of Language*, 115.

7 Dareau, *Traité des injures*, 116–20.

8 This was the widow La Bissionnière's claim, discussed in chapter 4, that M. and Mme Langis had beaten her in 1720.

9 NA, Nouvelle-France, Archives judiciaires, MG 8, B 4, vol. 1, 242–8.

10 Ibid., 248–51.

11 Ibid., 251–3.

12 "Je me f.[ous] de cela, J'ay toujours eu 25 minots de bled" (ibid., 276).

13 Ibid., 336.

14 "Si tu ne soutiens pas le certificat que J'ay donné, Je passerai pour un Jean Foutre" (ibid., 518).

15 Ibid., 630.

16 Ibid., 634.

17 Ibid., 612–13.

18 "jusqu'aux genoux chair nue" (ibid., 613–15).

19 "semblable à cette femme laquelle tenant en sa main le manteau de l'innocent Joseph, demandait justice du crime qu'il n'avait pas fait" (ibid.,
396–7).

20 Sabean, *Power in the Blood*, 137–8.

21 "Le mari ... a-t-il lieu de suspecter la vertu de sa compagne, les noirs sou-
cis l'obsèdent, tout l'inquiète, tout lui déplaît. Il ne se sent plus ces tendres
mouvemens qu'inspire une paternité certaine. Ses enfans, auparavant si
chers, n'ont plus les mêmes charmes à ses yeux" (Dareau, *Traité des injures*, 295–6).

22 See Darnton, "Workers Revolt: The Great Cat Massacre of the Rue Saint-
Sévérin," in his *The Great Cat Massacre*, 98–9; and Dorinda Outram, "*Le
langage mâle de la vertu*: Women and the discourse of the French Revolution," in Burke and Porter, *Social History of Language*, 125.

23 NA, Nouvelle-France, Archives judiciaires, MG 8, B 4, 490.

24 Ibid., 665–6.

25 "elle ne s'amusoit pas à une canaille comme luy" (ibid., 664).

26 "par consequent à leur solde" (ibid., 366).

27 NA, Nouvelle-France, Ordonnances des intendants, MG 8, A 6, vol. 10,
345–6, Commission de notaire royal ..., 12 septembre 1730.

28 NA, Nouvelle-France, Archives judiciaires, MG 8, B 4, vol. 1, ibid., 692.

29 Ibid., 367, 709.

30 Ibid., 271; ANQ-M, Registre d'état civil, Église Sainte-Anne de la Pérade,
ZQ2-8, 5 June 1730.

31 ANQ-M, Registres d'état civil, Église Saint-François-Xavier de Batiscan,
ZQ1-14, and Église Sainte-Anne de la Pérade, ZQ2-8, passim.

32 NMC-1725, Plan cadastral de Batiscan (ca. 1726).

33 "Il n'y a pas de semaine depuis l'ynstance qu'on ne les ayt vue les uns
chez les autres pour combiner la perte du s. Lefebvre" (ANQ-Q,
Verchères/Naudière, ZQ 27, 199).

34 "La Cour est trop penetrante pour ne pas sapercevoir de la caballe
concertée entre parents; alliés; et amis pour perdre le sieur Lefebvre"
(ibid., 13).

35 "sa passion l'a emporté audessus de la raison" (NA, Nouvelle-France,
Archives judiciaires, MG 8, B 4, vol. 1, 294).

36 "La Religion auroit deu leur imposer silence mais la fureur la passion les
ont emporté et aveuglé" (ANQ-Q, Verchères/Naudière, ZQ 27, 181).

37 "[ils] se disent noble comme le Roy" (ibid., 189).

38 "se croyent au dessus de tout le monde et agissent en souverains"
(ibid., 14).

39 "Lefebvre reconnoit pour Superieur dans ce pays que Mr le Marquis de
Beauharnois qui luy represente la personne de notre Ynvinsible

Monarque, yl a pour Superieur Monseigneur de Samos coadjouteur de quebec qui luy represente la personne sacrée de son Evecque Mgr du Mornay eveque de Quebec, Yl a pour Superieur Mr Hocquart Yntendant de toute la Nouvelle France a la Teste de Tout le Conseil Sup[érieu]r de Quebec; Yl a pour Superieur Mr La Tour grand vicaire de ce Diocese, Yl a pour Superieur Mr de Lotbiniere archidiacre dans ses visites, yl a pour Superieur Mr le Gouverneur des Trois rivieres dans le Gouvernement Duquel sa paroisse est scituée" (ibid., 183–4).

40 "une personne aussi honorable que l'est le premier du pays, tel qu'est Monsieur le marquis de Beauharnois" (NA, Nouvelle-France, Archives judiciaires, MG 8, B 4, vol. 1, 385).

41 Ibid., 476.

42 "Lefebvre attaque s'il le juge à propos mon dit seigneur le gouverneur-général" (ibid., 671).

43 "alors public dans toute la ville" (ANQ-Q, Verchères/Naudière, ZQ 27, 131).

44 "le sr Portail et la dame la Pérade prononcent tant dinormités aux cotes et à la ville" (ibid., 31).

45 "Un pasteur ou curé, dont la vie doit être le model[e] de son peuple, et dont les mauvais exemples causent un scandal universel dans toute l'Eglise" (NA, Nouvelle-France, Archives judiciaires, MG 8, B 4, vol. 1, 309).

46 ANQ-Q, Verchères/Naudière, ZQ 27, 2.

47 NA, Nouvelle-France, Archives judiciaires, MG 8, B 4, vol. 1, 368.

48 NA, France, Archives de colonies, MG 1, série B, vol. 59–1, folio 458 ½, Ministre à MM. de Beauharnois et Hocquart, 12 mai 1733.

49 "qu'il ne soit plus parlé ny question des différents" (quoted in Roy, "Madeleine de Verchères, plaideuse," 69).

50 ANQ-Q, Verchères/Naudière, ZQ27, 200. This would appear to be Marguerite Dizy.

51 Ibid., 100.

52 "lui dit les connoissances qu'il avoit de ses crimes d'Impureté, d'Yvrognerie et d'impiété … afin que les peuples ne soupçonnassent rien … il n'a pû garder le secret" (NA, France, Archives des colonies, MG 1, série C 11 A, vol. 106, 235–6, M. le Coadjuteur, 29 septembre 1731); ANQ-M, Registres d'état civil, Église Saint-François-Xavier de Batiscan, ZQ1-14, 1731, passim.

53 NA, Nouvelle-France, Ordonnances des intendants, MG 8, A 6, vol. 9, 37–45, Ordonnance qui enjoint aux habitants … de payer les dixmes au Sieur Joriant curé, 6 juillet 1726; NA, Nouvelle-France, Correspondance officielle, MG 8, A 1, vol. 11, 2071–3, Maurepas à Beauharnois et Dupuy, 11 mai 1728. This incident is dealt with in more detail in chapter 6.

54 ANQ-Q, Verchères/Naudière, ZQ 27, 1.

55 NA, Nouvelle-France, Ordonnances des intendants, MG 8, A 6, vol. 10, 102–4, Accord entre les R. P. Jésuites et le sieur Lefebvre, 21–2 mars 1730.

56 Ibid., vol. 9A, 87–96, Ordonnance entre le Sieur de La Pérade et le Sieur Voyer, 22 février 1727.

57 "d'un esprit de mutinerie et de desobéïssance" ("Ordonnance qui déclare bonne et valable la saisie …," in *Pièces et documents*, 120–4).

58 "Ordonnance … qui condamne le Sr Dorvilliers …," in ibid., 117–20.

59 NA, France, Archives des colonies, MG 1, série C 11 A, vol. 107, 198, Beauharnois et Hocquart au ministre, 2 octobre 1731.

60 "Un titre ne sert souvent qu'à rendre le pasteur indépendant et plus indocile, et à faire murmurer les paroissiens, quand la nécessité oblige d'agir contre un curé" (quoted in Gosselin, *L'église du Canada*, 2: 189). See also Provost, "Le régime des cures au Canada français."

61 Gosselin, *L'église du Canada*, 2: 76n.

62 UM-Baby, H1/26, (mf. 1888), Protestation du curé Voyer, 22 mars 1730.

63 I deal with the links between these local issues and the cathedral chapter's actions following the death of Bishop Saint-Vallier in "Authority and Illegitimacy in New France."

64 "attaque les RR PP et les taxe de Chicane luy qui ne debvroit avoir que des respects pour Eux il scait les obliga[ti]ons qu'il leur a" (BJ, vol. 100, Papiers terriers, 1669–1821, Responce a l'escrit du sr. Nicolas Rivard, vers 1700 [*sic*]).

65 "ces Signeur pour qui il doit avoire tout respec et honneur" (ibid., vol. 97, Trois-Rivières – 1657–1745, Sentance au R Reverand Perre jesuitte contre antoinne trotie ce 29 avril 1745).

66 "voila un enfent qui est bien malin" (CPJN, no. 550 ½, Entre Jean Ricard et Pierre Thomas de la Perrade, 1715).

67 "le d. curé reconnait mon d. sr de la Pérade comme le premier des fidels de la d. paroisse, et, comme tel, le respecte; non seulement l'aîme tendrement comme sa brebie la plus chere en vôtre Seigneur" (NA, Sainte-Anne de la Pérade, MG 8, F 83, Copie fidelle des actes publics que se sont fait signifier … Mr de la Pérade … et J. Voyer, prêtre, 24–30 décembre 1737, 3); "il n'a point été surpris du Baiser de Juda[s] que lui a fait le d. sr Curé" (ibid., 5).

68 "n['] a travaillie quand [qu'en] bonne enseigne" (BJ, vol. 100, Papier terriers, 1669–1821, Alexis Raux dit Morinville vs Joseph Trottier dit Labissonniere, 16 février 1746).

69 CPJN, no. 1240 (1740).

70 Lettre de M. de Lamothe Cadillac, 29 septembre 1694, *RAPQ*, 1923–24, 80–3; George F.G. Stanley, "Desjordy Moreau de Cabanac, François," *DCB*, 2: 186–7; André Vachon, "Dizy, Marguerite," *DCB*, 2: 189–90.

71 Gosselin, *L'église du Canada*, 1: 123.

72 Ibid., 430.

73 ANQ-M, Registres d'état civil, Église Saint-François-Xavier de Batiscan, ZQ1-14, 8 septembre 1728.

74 "ne m'allegant autre chose sinon quen consequence du procés que je venois davoir avec les Sr et dame la perade je ne ferois aucuns biens dans ma parroisse" (UM-Baby, H1/25 (mf. 1888), Protestation de Gervais Lefebvre, 5 mars 1731).

75 "C'est un sujet peu sensé, peu appliqué à instruire, contre qui il y eu plusieurs plaintes par cidevant" (quoted in Gosselin, *L'église du Canada*, 3: 74–5).

76 CPJN, no. 2009–21, 21 octobre 1735.

77 Dumas to Governor Vaudreuil, 18 April 1760, in *Report concerning Canadian Archives for the year 1905*, 1, part 4: 27–8.

78 Except for the period of the American invasion, the principal instance of direct disobedience of superiors in the region occurred in 1764, when the habitants of Batiscan and Sainte-Geneviève refused to volunteer to fight in Pontiac's war (Trudel, *Le régime militaire*, 184–5).

79 "la plus grande partie de cette paroisse vous est entièrement opposée" (AAQ, Registres des lettres, 210A, vol. 1, f. 55, à Mr Aubry, 7 septembre 1789).

80 "il avait trop de rancune contre moi pour en agir de la sorte … il n'a d'autre vocation que celle de courir du matin au soir et du soir au matin, de maison en maison, pour lire un papier à l'un et en écrire un à l'autre, pour conseiller celui-ci et souffler celui-là, le tout ne tendant qu'à la procédure, ce qui est son unique gagne-pain … Comme il est fin et rusé et que les habitants sont simples et grossiers, il les mène et conduit comme il veut." "ce lieu de désordres et d'affliction" (ASTR, Fonds Paroisses, DR-285, no. 120, Saint-Stanislas, 7, Aubry à l'Evêque, 14 septembre 1789).

81 Ibid., 10–2, Aubry à l'Evêque, 21 janvier 1790.

82 Ibid., 14, Aubry à l'Evêque, 16 mars 1790.

83 "Vous vous êtes fort mal à propos servi du nom de l'Evêque pour engager lesdits habitants à bâtir leur presbytère lorsque je vous ai demontré l'inutilité de cette bâtisse vous m'avez dit que vous y étiez poussé par les habitants. Aujourd'hui il paroît que vous avez été le seul moteur et entrepreneur de toute cette affaire. Tout cela, si vous n'y prenez garde, finira mal pour vous" (AAQ, Registres des lettres, 210A, vol. 1, ff. 127–8, à Aubry, 30 mars 1790).

84 ASTR, Fonds Paroisses, DR-285, no. 120, 15–7, Aubry à l'Evêque, 12 avril 1790.

85 ASTR, Fonds fabrique de la paroisse Sainte-Geneviève de Batiscan, FN-287, Protêt de Laurent Aubry, 25 juillet 1790.

86 Ibid., Accord entre la fabrique de Ste Genevieuve Rivière de Batiscan et Michel Veillet, 4 juillet 1790.

87 AAQ, Registres des lettres, 210A, vol. 1, ff. 191–2, à Mr Aubry, 10 janvier 1791.

88 Ibid., vol. 1, f. 238, à Mr Aubry, 11 août 1791.

89 ASTR, Fonds Paroisses, DR-285, no. 120, 18–9, Différend à l'occasion d'une terre de Saint Stanislas appartenant au curé de Sainte-Geneviève de Batiscan, 18 octobre 1791. Among Aubry's two supporters was the militia captain Pierre Trépagnier.

90 AAQ, Registres des lettres, 210A, vol. 1, ff. 312–3, à Mr Aubry, 15 mars 1792.

91 "Quel est l'homme public qui persiste être à l'abri de la critique?" (ASTR, Fonds Paroisses, DR-285, no. 120, 23, Aubry à l'Evêque, 24 mars 1792).

92 AAQ, Registres des lettres, 210A, vol. 1, f. 325, à Mr Jean, 3 juin 1792; ff. 344–5, à Mr Jean, 24 septembre 1792; f. 342, à Mr Aubri [sic], 24 octobre 1792.

93 "je concois que L'intérest n'est-pas ce qui le guide" (AAQ, Notre-Dame-de-Québec, C1 CD, 1–50, De Lanaudière à Monseigneur, 19 juillet 1792).

94 AAQ, Registres des lettres, 210A, vol. 1, ff. 344–5, à Mr Jean prêtre à Contrecour, 24 septembre 1792; vol. 5, f. 28, à Mr Alexis Dorval ptre curé à Saint-Nicolas, 29 octobre 1804.

95 ASTR, Fonds Paroisses, DR-285, no. 120, 26–7, Hot à l'Evêque, 24 mars 1817.

96 AAQ, Registres des lettres, 210A, vol. 8, ff. 458–9, à Mr Hot, Sainte-Geneviève, 17 février 1816; vol. 9, f. 422, à Mr Hot, 19 septembre 1818.

97 Trudel, Le régime militaire, 51.

98 On the institution, see Ouellet, "Officiers de milice," 49–52.

99 The lists of names of bailiffs were printed in the Gazette de Québec.

100 "vous lui ferez rendre les mêmes honneurs que l'on rendait ci-devant aux capitaines de milice" (Têtu and Gagnon, Mandements, lettres pastorales et circulaires, 2: 213–14).

101 "Vor den Häusern der Cap, und Lieut. de milice sind hohe abgeschelte Tannenbäume aufgerichtet, an deren Spitze eine kleine Jane wehet: auf diese Art kan man gar leicht den Vorgesetzten der Paroisse finden" ("Von Kanada, aus Briefen eines deutschen StabsOfficiers," 329).

102 "Mais avons-nous eu beaucoup de divertissements cet hiver? Je réponds: tout à fait! Vous voyez, il y a bon nombre de 'seigneurs' et de 'curés' dans notre voisinage … Grâce à cet homme, nous avons eu droit à plusieurs petites 'fêtes' données à son château. Les 'curés' eux non plus, ne sont pas à dédaigner. Ils sont de bons royalistes et, ayant la possibilité d'être de bons vivants, ils sont capables de fournir à dîner à vingt personnes et de les approvisionner avec du bon vin" (French translation in Wilhelmy, Les mercenaires allemands, 118–19). The words in single quotation marks were in French in the original. The German original for château is hiesigen Rittersitze, or indigenous knight's seat.

103 "Rien, Monsieur, rien n'etoit capable de m'empêcher d'accélerer les opérations désirées, si le délais des sus-dits seigneurs n'y eu mit un obstacle jusqu'à ce jour" (NA, Lower Canada Land Papers, RG 1, L 3 L, Jesu-

its Estates, vol. 18, Laurent Aubry, ptre, à Mr Hugue Finlay, 15 avril
1790).

104 "Je ne leur en ai rien dit. J'ai même affecté de les regarder comme des
Criailleries d'habitants" (AAQ, Registres des lettres, 210A, vol. 1, ff.
191–2, à Mr Aubry Ptre, Curé à Sainte-Geneviève, 10 janvier 1791; also
vol. 1, ff. 312–13, 15 mars 1792).

105 Ibid., ff. 243–4, à Mr Morin, ptre Curé à Sainte-Anne, 14 septembre 1791.

106 "je n'aime pas à donner le tort aux curés devant des habitants, quand
bien même ces premiers seroient en faute" (ibid., vol. 12, f. 412, à Xavier
Coté, Sainte-Geneviève, 22 décembre 1825).

107 "Journal par Messrs Fran[çoi]s Baby, Gab[riel] Taschereau et Jenkin Williams … [1776]," RAPQ, 1927–28, 454–7.

108 NA, Adjutant General, Lower Canada, Correspondence, RG 9, 1 A 1,
vol. 5, 1065–8, Nord des Trois-Rivières, 1812, T. Coffin à Lt Colonel
Vassal, 31 mai 1812.

109 ANQ-Q, Ministère de l'agriculture, E9, vol. 1, Seigneurie Batiscan, 1824,
A.G. Douglas to George Railand [sic], 11 January 1824.

110 "il s'est attiré l'indignation du plus grans nombre de sa paroisse"; "il a
été pillé, désarmé & insulté en plusieurs occasions"; "laquelle assemblée
les a tous continué chacun dans leur charge respective"; "Il parait que
Pierre Frigon n'a été cassé cet hivert par la paroisse que par ce qu'il avait
fait executer les ordres du Roy avec trop de fermeté" ("Journal par
Messrs Fran[çoi]s Baby," RAPQ, 1927–28, 452–7).

111 Quoted in Tousignant, "Problématique pour une nouvelle approche de
la Constitution de 1791," 186.

112 Hare, *Aux origines*, 15–46.

113 "Il m'a été rapporté qu'il courroit un bruit parmi mes compatriotes que
Monsieur de Lanaudiere et moi avons eu un différent occasionné par la
prochaine election. Je déclare sur mon honneur que personne ne peut me
ravir, et encore bien moins les méchans, que je ne diffère en rien sur ce
point avec lui ainsi que bien d'autres notables du comté; et qu'il y a plus
de cent trente ans, que mes ancêtres ont été continuellement au service
de sa famille, et qu'il y a pres de cinquante ans que je les régie moi
même" (*Gazette de Québec*, 31 mai 1792).

114 Benjamin Joseph Frobisher served as a member of the House of Assembly from 1808 to 1810 for the county of Montreal.

115 *Gazette de Québec*, 5 décembre 1822.

116 Ouellet points out the general decline of French nobles' influence by the
early nineteenth century ("Le régime seigneurial dans le Québec (1760–
1854)," in his *Élements d'histoire sociale*, 96–101). However, as the case of
Gabriel Christie demonstrates, bourgeois seigneurs remained influential
(Noël, "La gestion des seigneuries de Gabriel Christie").

117 NA, Selkirk Papers, MG 19, E 1, Lord Selkirk's Diary, 19750.

118 Ibid., 19754.

119 BJ, vol. 93, Recette de 1793, 23 novembre 1793; vol. 100, Recettes de 1794–98.

120 "des personnes protegées l'ont devancées dans cette démarche" (ibid., vol. 1875, Requêtes, 1800–10, Larue au Lieutenant-governeur Milnes, 17 juin 1800; Larue aux Commissaires, 17 juin 1800). Joseph Badeaux and Ezekiel Hart had already made applications.

121 "une personne me fis dire que je n'etois autorisé qu'à recevoir, mais non a demander" (ibid., vol. 97, District des Trois-Rivières, Correspondance par Badeaux, 1800–23, Badeaux à Pyke, 23 octobre 1807).

122 Ibid., vol. 101, Administration, 1855–60, Abstract of the Moneys received and spent by the Agent in the Seigniory of Batiscan from the 1 November 1823 to the 1 April 1824.

123 "Ce nouveau plan qui est Désiré par les habitants depuis Longtems, est un agent résident dans chaque Seigneurie, Sous la Surveillance du Procurateur de la commission, qui Seroit chargé de visiter les Seigneuries de tems a autres, Ecouter les reclamations des habitants" (ANQ-Q, Ministère de l'agriculture, E9, vol. 54, Agence de la Seigneurie Batiscan, 1825–96, L. Guillet à L'honorable Mathieu Bell, 24 novembre 1824).

124 BJ, vol. 99, Correspondance – Seigneurie – 1822–24, Lewis Foy to the Commissioners, 21 August 1824; Lewis Foy to the Commissioners, 20 September 1824; vol. 103, Moulin de la Seigneurie, 1800–23, Petition de François LeSieur etc., 12 juillet 1823, in letter from Mr Sec[retar]y Cochran, 24 July 1824.

125 Ibid., vol. 97, District of Trois-Rivières, Correspondance générale, 1767–1839, John Hale to John Stewart, 8 March 1827.

126 Bigsby, *The Shoe and Canoe*, 1: 49.

127 NA, Adjutant general, Lower Canada, RG 9, 1 A 1, vol. 25, 3rd Battalion de Trois-Rivières (Nord) – 1821 – Sainte-Anne, J. Hale to Lt Col. Vassal de Monveil, 17 February 1821.

128 NA, Quebec, Lower Canada, and Upper Canada, Petitions and Addresses, RG 1, E 16, vol. 2, part 1, petition of 3 February 1830. This issue is discussed in greater detail in chapter 6. A few similar petitions from Batiscan seigneury in 1831 included the local priest, who was usually one of the first to sign (NA, Grand Voyer, RG 1, E 17, vol. 5, Requête à Aylmer des habitants de Saint-Stanislas, 15 janvier 1831; Requête à Aylmer des habitants de Sainte-Geneviève et Saint-Stanislas, 25 janvier 1831; Requête à Aylmer des habitants de Champlain et Batiscan, 20 janvier 1831).

CHAPTER SIX

1 "Yls ont continué ce desordre Jusqua la fin comme sy fut eté Un pillage" (CPJN, no. 1240). On lotteries in the French regime, see Massicotte, "Des loteries à Montréal en 1701."

2 However, the following works make contributions to the question of community in the colony: Greer, "L'habitant, la paroisse rurale et la politique locale"; and Dickinson, "Réflexions sur la police en Nouvelle-France," 520. See also Dickinson, "La conception populaire de la tenure en Normandie et en Nouvelle-France," in Goy and Wallot, *Évolution et éclatement*, 169–70. Dechêne refers to "l'absence d'institution communautaire" in *Le partage des subsistences*, 174. In his study of La Prairie seigneury, Lavallée asserts, without proving, "la belle unité habituellement maintenue au sein de la communauté" (*La Prairie*, 168).

3 Nelson, *Dispute and Conflict Resolution in Plymouth County*, 152.

4 Mann, *Neighbors and Strangers*; Lockridge, *A New England Town*.

5 Rutman, "Assessing the Little Communities."

6 Cohen, *The Symbolic Construction of Community*.

7 This view is similar to the "dramaturgical" approach of Isaac in *The Transformation of Virginia, 1740–1790*.

8 Sabean, *Power in the Blood*, 29.

9 Jones, *Politics and Rural Society*, 5.

10 ANQ-M, Conseil supérieur, Registres, M9 (mf. 1197), vol. 32, folio 51v–52v, François Chorel Dorvilliers vs Thomas Tarrieu de la Pérade, 12 mars 1725.

11 NA, Nouvelle-France, Ordonnances des intendants, MG 8, A 6, vol. 8, 193–4, Ordonnance entre le Sr Loranger et Jean Bary du Chesny, 21 juillet 1724.

12 CPJN, no. 2099–11, Décision du juge prévôt Duclos, 10 avril 1733.

13 "un coup de poing de sur la Teste, et ensuitte un Coup de Canne sur la Teste" (ibid., no. 3882, Requête d'Etienne Prade au Lieutenant Général Civil et Criminel au siége de la Prévoste Royale de Québec, 29 août 1744).

14 AAQ, Registre des lettres, 210A, vol. 2, f. 162, à Mr Jean, Sainte-Geneviève, 23 octobre 1794.

15 "les femmes s'y introduisent et … il s'y commet de petites indécences" (ibid., vol. 9, ff. 263–4, à Mr Hot, Sainte-Geneviève, 14 novembre 1817).

16 CPJN, no. 2009–54, 6 avril 1748.

17 Ibid., no. 1378, Procès entre St-Agnian et Trottier dit Bellecour, 9 avril 1744.

18 "senveloper dant une fourbe chicannerie qui ne setant que pour embroüillier lesprit ynnocent dudit deffendeur …" (Duclos, Sentence entre la veuve dame de St Onge et François Baril maistre farinier, 1 mars 1746). It is likely that St-Onge was in fact acting on behalf of her son-in-law, who conducted a similar case against the miller at Rivière des Envies in 1749.

19 "il netes [n'était] pas entre libre de delibere d'un bien qui ne luy apartient pas [a]partenant a sa belle mere" (ibid., Sentence entre la veuve St-Onge et Charles Poquelot prestre, 15 mars 1748).

20 FS, vol. 3, Batiscan, Acte de concession de Messire Jacques de la Ferté aux Pères Jésuites, 3 mars 1639.

21 Guillaume De La Rue (Larue) is identified as "juge prévost de Batiscan" in notarial records between 1687 and 1699 (Barthe, *Analyse des actes de*

François Trottain, 2, 109, 167). A 1705 edict of Intendant Raudot refers to the judges of Champlain and Batiscan ("Réglement qui détermine que les juges seigneuriaux," in *Complément des ordonnances*, 118). However, in 1708 the intendant assigned the judge at Champlain to hear witnesses, "naiant point de Juge a Batiscan" (CPJN, no. 395d, Ordonnance de M. Raudot, 6 janvier 1708).

22 Raymond Douville, "Dizy, *dit* Montplaisir, Michel-Ignace," DCB, 2: 190.

23 Maurice Fleurent, "Dizy (Disy) de Montplaisir, Pierre," DCB, 3: 187.

24 CPJN, Information de vie et moeurs du Sieur Duclos du 14 juin 1725, no. 2053 ½.

25 Ibid., no. 2089 ½, Information de vie et moeurs sur Jacques Rouillard St Cir, juge à Batiscan, 24 mars 1738.

26 Fleurent, "Dizy," DCB, 3: 187.

27 The records of the court have been scattered over the years into a number of different archival collections. Each case was written on separate sheets of paper, and it is likely that some have been lost. I have compiled eighty-nine cases, which date from 1726 to 1758. For six years there are no records at all. This is not necessarily a representative sample of all the cases that came before the judges at Batiscan; we have left only what the hazards of record keeping and archivists' interests provide. Many of the cases are to be found in CPJN, no. 2009 (1–54). A few others are in the same collection, nos. 1212, 1240, 1378, 1751, and 2975. The clerk's records provide another thirty-nine cases: ANQ-M, Greffe Nicolas Duclos, CN401-30. The remaining cases were located in the following places: PDCJ; BJ, vol. 97, Trois-Rivières, 1657–1745; vol. 100, Papiers terriers, 1669–1821; ASQ, Polygraphie 18, no. 79; Polygraphie 37, no. 18F.

28 Unlike the seigneurial court at Notre-Dame-des-Anges near Quebec, this court did not hear criminal cases (Audet, *Les officiers de justice*, 16n60; Dickinson, "La justice seigneuriale").

29 As Dickinson suggests in "Réflexions sur la police," 513–20.

30 Dickinson, "La justice seigneuriale," 335.

31 Lachance, *La justice criminelle*, and Dickinson, *Justice et justiciables*, 170–5, reach the same conclusion for the other courts of New France.

32 Comaroff and Roberts, *Rules and Processes*, 29. Other anthropologists deal with the negotiation of "reality" through official courts; see, for example, Rosen, "Islamic 'Case Law' and the Logic of Consequence."

33 As Comaroff and Roberts point out in *Rules and Processes*, 130.

34 CPJN, no. 2009–39, 26 avril 1740.

35 Ibid., no. 2009–31, 23 mars 1738.

36 Duclos, Accord entre Antoine Trottier et Blondeaux, 9 août 1752.

37 CPJN, no. 2009–4, 4 août 1732.

38 Ibid., no. 2009–26 (no date, ca. 1728).

39 David Garrioch notes this phenomenon in eighteenth-century Paris; see *Neighbourhood and community in Paris, 1740–1790*, 51–4.

40 CPJN, nos. 2009–41, 42, 43, 17 mai, 5 juillet 1740.

41 Ibid., no. 2009–30, 20 septembre 1738.

42 Ibid., nos. 2009–18, 19, 3 septembre 1735.

43 Duclos, Sentence entre Richard et Lafont, 2 septembre 1748.

44 CPJN, no. 2009–27, 2 avril 1737.

45 Duclos, Sentence, 25 juin 1748.

46 PDCJ, Sentence entre Jacques Lezée et Joseph Levraus de Langis, 30 octobre 1742.

47 CPJN, no. 2009–34, 28 juillet 1739.

48 Ibid., no. 2009–33, 6 janvier 1739.

49 Hoffer, "Honor and the Roots of American Litigiousness," 306.

50 There is no record of a woman having sworn an oath before the judge. However, the notation that Elizabeth Blanchez, widow Juinot, *dit* Latulippe, "a Refusé a faire serment sur le susds. mémoire" suggests that it was possible for women to do so (CPJN, no. 2009–37, 21 mars 1740).

51 Ibid., no. 2009–32, 29 avril 1738.

52 BJ, vol. 100, Alexis Raux dit Morinville versus Joseph Trottier dit Labissonnière, 16 February 1746.

53 CPJN, no. 2009–33, 6 janvier 1739.

54 Duclos, Sentence, 1 mars 1746.

55 PDCJ, Sentence entre Jacques Lezée et Joseph Levraus de Langis, 30 octobre 1742.

56 Rosen, *Bargaining for Reality*, 123.

57 ASQ, Polygraphie 37, no. 18f, Sentance au profit de Thomas contre antoinne trottier, 28 avril 1744.

58 Dickinson, *Justice et justiciables*, 138.

59 Bruce H. Mann makes a similar claim in *Neighbors and Strangers*, 23.

60 Dickinson, "La conception populaire de la tenure," in Goy and Wallot, *Évolution et éclatement*, 169–70.

61 CPJN, no. 2009–54, 6 avril 1748.

62 BJ, vol. 97, Trois-Rivières – 1657–1745, Sentance au R. Reverand Perre jesuitte contre antoinne trotie, 29 avril 1745.

63 Duclos, Sentence, 9 janvier 1748.

64 "Sil navet [n'avaient] point ette borné quil nore [n'auraient] point paye de rante" (ibid., Sentence, 4 janvier 1746).

65 CPJN, no. 2009–2, 20 juillet 1728.

66 NA, Nouvelle-France, Ordonnances des intendants, MG 8, A 6, vol. 10, 213–4, Ordonnance rendue aux Trois-Rivières qui confirme celle de M. Raudot du 4 novembre 1707 au sujet d'un fossé …, 14 juin 1730.

67 CPJN, no. 2690, 21 septembre 1744.

68 Ibid., no. 2689, 22 septembre 1744.

69 "Journal par Messrs Fran[çoi]s Baby," *RAPQ*, 1927–28, 455–7.

70 ANQ-M, Procès-verbaux des grands-voyers, E2 (mf. 1243), 1er cahier, f. 53, 23 et 26 juin 1724.

71 CPJN, no. 2625, 21 mai 1732.

72 Sanfaçon, "La construction du premier chemin Québec-Montréal," 20–2; ANQ-M, Procès-verbaux des grands-voyers, E2 (mf. 1243), cahier 5, ff. 25–7, 29 mai 1732.

73 NA, Ordonnances des intendants, MG 8, A 6, vol. 10, 196–8, Ordonnance qui enjoint aux habitants de Batiscan de s'assembler pour faire un pont, 4 juin 1730.

74 CPJN, no. 2652, 26 avril 1737.

75 "tous les Ponts sont si mauvais et si Estroits que les Chevaux et meme Les Gens de Pieds ne Peuvent passer dessus sans Courir Risques de se Casser les jambes" (ANQ-M, Procès-verbaux des grands-voyers, E2 (mf. 1244), cahier 5, f. 25, 28 mai 1732).

76 "voyant Le Manquement des habitans et respects quil[s] doivent aux ordonnances" (CPJN, no. 2675, 26 juillet 1742).

77 Greer, "L'habitant, la paroisse rurale."

78 AAQ, Registre des insinuations ecclésiastiques, 12A, vol. A, ff. 500–1, Lettre aux habitans de Sainte-Anne et des Grondines.

79 Ibid., vol. C, f. 123 vo, Mandement pour achever l'eglise et le cimetiere de Sainte-Anne pres batiscan (no date).

80 Ordonnance au sujet de la Bâtisse d'une Eglise en la Paroisse Sainte-Anne, 25 janvier 1716, in *Arrêts et Réglements du Conseil Supérieur*, 447.

81 Ordonnance qui condamne les habitants de Sainte-Anne, près Batiscan, à fournir ce qui sera nécessaire pour la bâtisse d'un Presbytère, 22 août 1731, in ibid., 346–7.

82 NA, France, Archives des colonies, MG 1, série C 11 E, vol. 12, 171–6, 10 février 1721.

83 NA, Nouvelle-France, Ordonnances des intendants, MG 8, A 6, vol. 9, 37–45, Ordonnance qui enjoint aux habitants establis dans les proffondeurs de la Rivière de Batiscan de payer les dixmes au Sr Joriant curé de Champlain, 6 juillet 1726. The fact that Lefebvre was one of the few titular priests in the colony may have encouraged church and state authorities, desirous of reducing priests' independence, to take away this large proportion of his tithe revenues.

84 Ibid., 43–5, Ordonnance qui ordonne que le Sr Jorian curé de Champlain desservira par voye de mission la chapelle Sainte-Geneviève ..., 13 décembre 1726.

85 Ibid., 119–21, Ordonnance concernant la batise du Presbytere de la Nouvelle Paroisse de Sainte-Genevieve près Batiscan ..., 20 mars 1727.

86 ASQ, Polygraphie 18, no. 79, Assignation donnée à Chatoneauf, 22 avril 1727; CPJN, no. 2009–1, Sentence entre André Jorian et Jean Baptiste Adam, 17 juin 1727.

87 NA, Nouvelle-France, Correspondance officielle, MG 8, A 1, vol. 11, 2071–3, Maurepas à Beauharnois et Dupuy, 11 mai 1728.

88 NA, Nouvelle-France, Ordonnances des intendants, MG 8, A 6, vol. 10, 102–4, Accord entre les R. P. Jesuites et le Sr Lefebvre au sujet des paroisses de Batiscan et de Sainte-Genevieve, 21–2 mars 1730.

89 Sanfaçon, "La construction du premier chemin Québec-Montréal," 23.

90 Lavallée cites similar instances for La Prairie seigneury (*La Prairie*, 123–8).

91 AAQ, Registres des requêtes, 220A, vol. a, f. 9 vo – 10 ro, Requête des habitants de Saint-Stanislas, 1 février 1813.

92 ASTR, Fonds Paroisses, DR-285, no. 120, Commissaires civils, 1, Pétition du 12 juin 1814.

93 Ibid., 3, Humble Requête à Messieurs les Commissaires, 28 juillet 1817.

94 "les habitants n'ayant pu commencer à bâtir par leurs mauvaises recoltes et la rareté de l'argent" (AAQ, Registres des requêtes, 220A, vol. b, f. 74 ro – 75 vo, Procès-verbal de Mr Noizeux pour bâtir une Eglise etc à Saint-Stanislas, 10 septembre 1822).

95 "J'avais aussi moi-même abandonné ainsi que les Syndics, car après toutes les fatigues et les peines prises depuis environ deux mois, voir des ouvriers travailler pour la répartition, prendre les informations nécessaires pour le prix des différents ouvrages etc et voir si peu de bonne volonté, cela m'avait découragé" (ASTR, Fonds Paroisses, DR-285, no. 120, F.-X. Côté à l'Évêque, 7 avril 1825).

96 AAQ, Registres des requêtes, 220A, vol. b, f. 15vo, Requête des habitants du haut de la Rivière des Envies (Seigneurie de Sainte-Anne) pour contribuer à la batisse de l'église, Presbytère, de Saint-Stanislas, 16 avril 1820.

97 ASTR, Fonds Paroisses, DR-285, no. 120, 37, Pétition du 17 août 1825.

98 Ibid., 38, Pétition du 17 août 1825.

99 BJ, vol. 99, Correspondance – Seigneuries – 1822–24, Lewis Foy to the Hon[oura]ble the Commissioners, 20 September 1824.

100 AAQ, Registres des lettres, 210A, vol. 12, f. 412, à Xavier Coté, Sainte-Geneviève, 22 décembre 1825.

101 "vous n'avez pu vous accorder, les uns etant d'avis de construire en bois, les autres en Pierres, et … le projet est resté là, partie par le peu d'harmonie qui règne entre vous, partie par le peu de zèle que l'on a communément pour les travaux publics" (AAQ, Registres des insinuations ecclésiastiques, 12A, vol. G, f. 181 ro–vo, Lettre pastorale aux habitants de Sainte-Anne, 10 décembre 1809).

102 Ibid., vol. F, f. 214 VO, Procédures pour la construction d'un presbytère en pierres dans la paroisse de Sainte-Anne de la Pérade, 15 juin 1810. The parishioners signed a notarial document indicating their opinion on the matter: only three signatures opposed the construction of a new stone presbytery, and these individuals were not members of the local elite (ANQ-M, Greffe Augustin Trudel, CN401–91, Dépôt d'un Ecrit sous seing privé portant opinions sur la batisse d'un Presbitere, 6 juin 1810, no. 3504).

103 AAQ, Registres des lettres, 210A, vol. 8, f. 166, à Mr Morin, Sainte-Anne, 1 mars 1814.

104 "par la mauvaise volonté de ceux qui par pauvreté ou autrement n'ont pas fourni leur quot[e] part" (AAQ, Vicaires généraux, 1CB, IX – 132, Mr Noizeux à Mgr Plessis, 9 janvier 1816).

105 "vous savez combien cette paroisse a de peine à s'entendre pour les contributions publiques. Une partie des habitants apporteront de la terre: les autres n'en apporteront pas; une partie du cimetière sera comblée: l'autre sera négligée & les eaux y croupiront" (AAQ, Registres des lettres, 210A, vol. 12, f. 145–6, à Mr Moll, Sainte-Anne, 25 novembre 1824).

106 Moll's attitude was also tied up with his financial obligations to the previous priest, Coté (ibid., vol. 12, f. 192, à Mr Moll, Sainte-Anne, 19 février 1825).

107 NA, Grand voyer, RG 1, E 17, vol. 4, Proposal from Commissioners François Boucher, S. Grant and Etienne Mayrand, 6 December 1818.

108 BJ, vol. 99, Correspondance – Seigneuries – 1822–24, Lewis Foy to the Hon[oura]ble the Commissioners, 21 August 1824.

109 *Journal of the House of Assembly of Lower Canada*, 1812, 112–17, 170–1. The petition was apparently unsuccessful, though the reasons for the failure are not known.

110 BJ, vol. 97, District des Trois-Rivières, Correspondance par Badeaux, 1800–23, Badeaux à George Pyke, 16 septembre 1800.

111 Ouellet, "L'enseignement primaire: responsabilité des Églises ou de l'État (1801–1836)," in his *Élements d'histoire sociale*, 265–8.

112 "l'opposition que nous avons eu tant de la part du curé du Lieu que de quelque un de ses partisant qui son contre ces Ecole" (NA, School Records, RG 4, B 30, vol. 39, Tableau de l'école de Sainte-Anne de Lapérade … pour l'année 1829, Zéphirin Pepin, Maitre).

113 Ibid., Marguerite Le Maistre, Maitresse; J.O.L. Préquet, Maitre.

114 Ibid., vol. 52 (Saint-François-Xavier and Sainte-Geneviève, 1830) and vol. 72 (Saint-Stanislas, 1831).

115 NA, Quebec, Lower Canada, and Upper Canada, Petitions, RG 1, E 16, vol. 2, part 1, Petition de 1830. A similar request had been made during the French regime. In 1745 a number of habitants from Sainte-Anne and Grondines had asked the roads officer to approve the construction of a bridge over the rapids of the Rivière Portneuf. However, the habitants of

Grondines were careful to share the costs, "demandant a Estre aidés par leur voisins ..." (CPJN, no. 2696, 23 octobre 1745).

116 ANQ-Q, Poll Books, M46.1, Hampshire, 1826, vol. 1. Volume 2 of this poll book is missing from the archives. On Dorion, see Louis-Philippe Audet, "Dorion, Pierre-Antoine," DCB, 7: 254.

117 ANQ-Q, Poll Books, M46.1, Hampshire, 1827, 1 cahier. In both 1826 and 1827, Dorion was not elected, as other parts of the constituency supported the other candidates, F.-X. Larue and J. Cannon.

118 According to Ouellet, these localized voting patterns were common in rural areas (*Le Bas-Canada, 1791–1840*, 366ff).

CHAPTER SEVEN   ·

1 The fullest treatment of the history of this enterprise to date is in Hardy, *La sidérurgie dans le monde rural*, 51–5.

2 "il est impossible d'y rien faire ni d'en rien tirer" (ANQ-Q, Archevêché de Québec, P332, vol. 2, Copies de lettres, 2–3, Réponses et éclaircissements sur quelques propositions faites à M. de Pontchartrain contre les pères Jésuites, 1706).

3 Colonial censuses; Lunn, *Développement économique de la Nouvelle France*, 145–60.

4 Fauteux, *Essai sur l'industrie au Canada*, 70–2.

5 "il est des endroits ou l'on pouroit plus aisément placer des fourneaux, tant pour la commodité des bois, la proximité de la mine, que la plus grande quantité d'eau, la seigneurie de Mr de Tonnancour, la Rivière de Batiscan et terre bonne m'ont parus plus favorables que St-Maurice" (NA, France, Archives des colonies, MG 1, C 11 A, vol. 91, 228–32, M. de Beauharnois au ministre, 1 octobre 1748).

6 Hardy and Séguin, *Forêt et société en Mauricie*, 17.

7 "Alle Seigneurs haben noch Waldung genug, welche sie verkaufen können" ("Von Kanada, aus Briefen eines deutschen StabsOfficiers," 331).

8 On the importance of colonial policy to the timber trade, see Ouellet, *Histoire économique et sociale*, 188–90.

9 Lettre de Morin, ptre, Ste. Anne de la Pérade, in *First Report of the Committee of the House of Assembly*, 112–13.

10 Testimony of Louis Gendron, 11 December 1823, in *Journal of the House of Assembly of Lower Canada*, 1823–24, app. R, app. A.

11 Testimony of M. James McDouall, in *First Report of the Committee of the House of Assembly*, 47.

12 As Jeanne Dufour points out in the case of French enterprise ("Les forges et la forêt dans la Sarthe," 222).

13 BJ, vol. 1875, Correspondance des agents avec Pyke, 1810–12, Badeaux à Pyke, 28 juin 1811.

14 Ibid., vol. 99, Correspondance, Seigneurie, 1799–1821, Jean Trépagny à François X. Larue, 22 décembre 1799.

15 Hardy and Séguin, *Forêt et société en Mauricie*, 25.

16 ANQ-Q, Ministère de l'agriculture, E9, vol. 1, Seigneurie Batiscan, 1816, J. Badeaux à Lewis Foy, 1 janvier 1816.

17 Fortin and Gautier, "Aperçu de l'histoire des forges Saint-Tite et Batiscan," 13.

18 CFB, 105, Nicolas Bayard to John Antrobus, 8 June 1808.

19 See, for instance, ANQ-M, Greffe Doucet, CN601–134, Concession à John Marble, 24 mai 1809, no. 2117; Concession à Jonathan Huntingdon, 24 mai 1809, no. 2118; Concession à Ebenezar Miller, 24 mai 1809, no. 2118 (*sic*).

20 UT-Hale, E.F. Hale to Lord Amherst, 24 June 1819.

21 BJ, vol. 99, Correspondance – Seigneurie – 1822–24, Lewis Foy to the Hon[oura]ble The Commissioners for the Estates of the late Jesuits in Canada, 21 August 1824.

22 Hardy, Roy, and Séguin, "Une recherche en cours," 147–51.

23 *Journal of the House of Assembly of Lower Canada*, 1823–24, app. R., app. A.

24 "jugeant que le défrichement progressif des terres ne feroit qu'augmenter tous les ans, la crue des eaux de la Rivière le printemps" (AAQ, Registres des requêtes, 220A, vol. b, f. 74ro–75ro, Procès-verbal de Mr Noiseux pour bâtir une Eglise etc à Saint-Stanislas, 10 septembre 1822).

25 Of course, the ironworks at Saint-Maurice were even more considerable (Sansom, "Une industrie avant l'industrialisation").

26 Joseph Frobisher and Thomas Dunn played minor roles in the management of the enterprise. Between 1806 and 1810 Frobisher spent only seven days at the ironworks (McGill University, McLennan Library, Rare Book Department, Joseph Frobisher, Diary, 1806–10, Ms 433/2). Nicolas Bayard acted as manager up to 1808, leaving the company at the same time that Dunn withdrew his participation.

27 CFB, 69, Nicolas Bayard to Thomas Coffin, 7 December 1807; 93, Bayard to Joshua Bates, 4 April 1808.

28 Ibid., 116, Coffin to Isaac Williams, 21 July 1808; 131, Coffin to Isaac Williams, 15 August 1808.

29 ANQ-M, Registres d'état civil, Église protestante St-James, Trois-Rivières, CE401–50 (mf. 742).

30 NA, Selkirk Papers, MG 19, E 1, Lord Selkirk's Diary, 19770.

31 CFB, 88, Bayard à Jean-Baptiste LeMay, 12 mars 1808; 374, Coffin à Louis Legendre, 1 octobre 1811; 386, Coffin to Sueton Grant, 4 November 1811.

32 Bayard brought in a servant from Quebec, Elizabeth Mayer (CFB, 67, Bayard à Jac. LeBlond, 1 décembre 1807). Margaret Michlang, who bore the illegitimate daughter of Thomas Slicer, was described as being "late of Batiscand" in the baptismal record (ANQ-M, Registres d'état civil, Église

protestante St-James, Trois-Rivières, 2 February 1804). It is possible that women worked as cooks.

33 ANQ-TR, Forges de Batiscan, DR-8, Greffe J. B. Badeaux, 2 janvier 1801.
34 Fortin and Gautier, "Aperçu de l'histoire des forges Saint-Tite et Batiscan," 13.
35 CFB, 70, Bayard aux Messieurs Malhiot, décembre 1807.
36 ANQ-M, Greffe Louis Guillet père, CN401–46, 28 octobre 1809, nos 67–103; ANQ-M, Greffe Augustin Trudel, CN401-91, 24 août 1807, nos 2752–4, 27 août 1807, nos 2761–71.
37 CFB, 267, B.J. Frobisher to George Platt, 6 November 1809.
38 Ibid., 65–6, Bayard to George Alsopp, 24 November 1807.
39 NA, British Military and Naval Records, RG 8, series C, vol. 3 (mf. C-2678), 92, John Craigie, Statement of Stoves and Iron Pots purchased of the Batiscan Iron Works Company, 23 March 1807.
40 CFB, 119, B.J. Frobisher to Joseph Frobisher, 26 July 1808; 278, Coffin to W. Ermatinger, 4 December 1809.
41 Ibid., 128, B.J. Frobisher to J. Craigie, 12 August 1808.
42 Archives of Ontario, William Warren Baldwin and Robert Baldwin Papers, MS 88, Benjamin Joseph Frobisher to Quetton St. George, 18 March 1808.
43 CFB, 156, B.J. Frobisher to Benj. Tremain, 4 October 1808.
44 Ibid., 133–4, Coffin to Platt, 11 August 1808.
45 Ibid., 149, Benjamin Joseph Frobisher to Jacques Leblond, 23 septembre 1808.
46 Ibid., 345, Coffin à Pierre Guéroux, 18 juillet 1811.
47 Toronto Reference Library, Laurent Quetton de St-George Papers, S129, section II, Monro & Bell to Q. St. George, 29 December 1810.
48 CFB, 93, Bayard to Joshua Bates, 4 April 1808.
49 Ibid., 113, Bayard to Ez. Hart, 7 July 1808.
50 NA, Thomas Dunn Letterbook (copy), MG 24, B 10, 311, Dunn to Lord Castlereagh, 3 October 1807.
51 NA, Colonial Office Papers, Q series, MG 11, CO 42/109, 32–44, D. Monro and Mw. Bell to H.W. Ryland, 31 December 1808.
52 CFB, 317, Coffin à Jean Bte Raymond, 9 avril 1811; 323, Coffin à Etienne Duchesnois, 19 août 1811.
53 Ibid., 345, Coffin à Pierre Guérout, 18 juillet 1811.
54 Ibid., 379, B.J. Frobisher to George Platt, 7 October 1811.
55 BJ, vol. 100, État des cens, 1 septembre 1801; recette de 1801, 1 mars 1802; recette de 1803, 1 avril 1804; vol. 101, recette de 1806, 1 avril 1807.
56 Ibid., vol. 77, Minutes of commission, 14 March 1806, 14 March 1806; vol. 97, District des Trois-Rivières, Correspondance par Badeaux, Badeaux à Pyke, 25 novembre 1806.

57 "Nous trouvons qu'il est plus avantageux d'acheter le Bled pour la Consommation de nos ouvriers dans les Paroisses Circonvoisines de celle-cy que d'aller l'acheter au loin" (UM-Baby, mf. 4494, Coffin à X. de Lanaudière, 1 décembre 1804).

58 CFB, 112, Bayard to B.J. Frobisher, 1 July 1808 (concerning oats); 296, B.J. Frobisher to G. Platt, 28 July 1810 (wheat); 323, Coffin à Etienne Duchesnois, 19 août 1811 (wheat).

59 Ibid., 47, Bayard to George Platt, 14 September 1807.

60 "Les ordres que J'ay Constamment donnés ont été de Ne Point faires des avances du Magazin ou hengards Ni aux ouvriers Ni aux Journaliers au dela de leurs ouvrages Courant" (ibid., 81–2, Bayard aux Messirs Ch. Gouin, Thos. B. Ackers, Chs Taché ju., Robt Snatt, 12 février 1808).

61 Ibid., 392, B.J. Frobisher to Vezine (Trois-Rivières), 1 December 1811.

62 BJ, vol. 103, Moulin de la seigneurie, Société et convention entre Charrest, Neaux et Neaux, 25 janvier 1817. A few months later, Charrest left the agreement, but he kept the right to build his own gristmill on the same property (ibid., Cession d'une part de société par Joseph Charrest à Antoine Neaux, 2 avril 1817).

63 BJ, vol. 257, Notes de Foy, Marchés et convention entre Frobisher et Massicotte, 11 octobre 1817.

64 Ibid., 239–40, vol. 80, Minutes of commission, 26 July 1822.

65 Ibid., 6–7, vol. 80, Minutes of commission, 9 July 1817; vol. 99, Correspondance, Seigneurie, Lewis Foy to Joseph Badeaux, 17 August 1822.

66 Ibid., vol. 103, Moulin de la Seigneurie, L. Guillet à John Stewart, 2 juin 1826.

67 Ibid., vol. 99, Correspondance – Seigneurie, L. Guillet à John Stewart, 7 novembre 1828.

68 NA, 1825 Census (mf. C-718), 1676, Hampshire county.

69 Gazette de Québec, 14 mars 1816.

70 Ibid., 13 novembre 1820.

71 Ibid., 25 janvier 1821.

72 Ibid., 15 janvier 1824.

73 NA, Thomas Dunn Letterbook, MG 24, B 10, 309, Dunn to Lord Castlereagh, 3 October 1807.

74 Fourteen of the twenty-four buildings clustered on lots six to eleven were on their two properties (NMC-15665, Sainte-Anne de la Pérade [1830], H2/325).

75 Hardy and Séguin, Forêt et société en Mauricie, 23, 28.

76 ANQ-M, Seigneurie Batiscan, P220/1, Livre de comptes.

77 "je crois qu'il ne pourra être de beaucoup de secours en raison des opérations qui sont commencées, en ce que les terres n'y sont ni de Suite ni par rangé de concession" (ANQ-Q, Ministère de l'agriculture, E9, vol. 1, Seigneurie Batiscan, J. Badeaux à H.W. Ryland, 27 juillet 1821).

78 AAQ, Registres des lettres, 210A, vol. 2, f. 55, à Huot prêtre curé à Champlain, 12 juin 1793; ff. 60–1, à Jean, Sainte-Geneviève, 1 juillet 1793.

79 On 17 August 1815 a notice appeared in the *Gazette de Québec* exhorting the habitants on Jesuit seigneuries to pay their dues.

80 BJ, vol. 96, Administration par Badeaux, District des Trois-Rivières, État des Revenus provenants des Biens qui appartenoient ci-devant à L'Ordre des Jésuites, dans le District des Trois Rivières ..., 15 janvier 1801.

81 ANQ-M, Seigneurie Batiscan, P220/1, Livre de comptes, 62 (1790), 89 (1787); BJ, vol. 100, Recette de 1797, 24 novembre 1797.

82 BJ, vol. 100, Recette de 1802, 1 mars 1803.

83 Ibid., vol. 96, Administration générale des Biens des Jésuites, District des Trois-Rivières, Tableau des arrérages de cens et rentes & Lots & Ventes dus dans la Seigneurie de Batiscand, Jusqu'au onze Novembre 1806, 11 novembre 1807.

84 ANQ-TR, Forges de Batiscan, DR-8, Greffe Planté, Inventaire de feu John Craigie, février 1814.

85 ANQ-Q, Cour supérieure de Québec, T11–1, vol. 459, Cour du banc du roi, Rex vs John Craigie, 1829.

86 BJ, vol. 78, Minutes of commission, 434–5, 23 December 1815. Of course, the Batiscan Iron Works owed a large proportion of this total.

87 "Paroisses dès maintenant dénuées de toute ressource pour leur subsistance et sans espoir de se procurer les moyens de semer au printemps" ("Mémoire touchant l'état de la récolte dans les paroisses, en l'année 1816," 15 février 1816, in Têtu and Gagnon, *Mandements* 3: 127–32). Dechêne provides a cartographic representation of the impact of the crisis ("Observations sur l'agriculture," in Goy and Wallot, *Évolution et éclatement*, 193).

88 BJ, vol. 80, Minutes of commission, 190–3, 29 October 1821, Report by L. Foy, 17 October 1821.

89 NA, Selkirk Papers, MG 19, E 1, Selkirk's Diary, 19754–5.

90 *Journal of the House of Assembly of Lower Canada*, 1824, app. R., app. A, Testimony of Gendron, 11 December 1823.

91 Ibid., Testimony of Trepanier, 6 December 1823.

92 NA, British Military and Naval Records, RG 8, series C, vol. 134 (mf. C-2686), 54–6, John Hale to Colonel Darling, 31 August 1824.

93 Courville, Robert, and Séguin, *Atlas historique du Québec*, 126–7.

CHAPTER EIGHT

1 "Wer die Verschläge und die umschlossenen Cämpe in den Marschländern im Bremischen gesehen hat, kan sich davon eine deutliche Vorstellung machen" ("Von Kanada, aus Briefen deutschen StabsOfficiers," 321).

2 Wright and Tinling, *Quebec to Carolina in 1785–1786*, 25.

3 Lambert, *Travels through Canada*, 425, 460.

4 McGill University, McLennan Library, Rare Books Department, James L. Glennie, "Diary of a Journey commencing 18th June [1800]," 76–7.

5 Robertson, *The Diary of Mrs John Graves Simcoe*, 348.

6 Bouchette, *A Topographical Dictionary*, "Ste. Anne, seigniory" (no pagination). This is the English translation of a passage from Bouchette's 1815 book, *Description topographique*, 326–7.

7 NA, Selkirk Papers, MG 19, E 1, Lord Selkirk's Diary, 19769–70; Lambert, *Travels through Canada*, 461–2; Heriot, *Travels through the Canadas*, 231; Gray, *Letters from Canada*, 221. Bouchette probably also visited the site; see *Description topographique*, 322.

8 UT-Hale, E.F. Hale to Lord Amherst, 14 November 1811.

9 NA-Hale (mf. A-1085), E.F. Hale to Lord Amherst, 11 January 1820.

10 Christine Veilleux, "Hale, John," DCB, 7: 372–3.

11 NA, Colonial Office papers, MG 11, CO 42/136, Craig to Lord Castlereagh, 15 August 1808, ff 229–32.

12 NA-Hale, vol. 4, Edward, Duke of Kent, to John Hale, 14 December 1819, f 234 (emphasis in original).

13 Whitelaw, *The Dalhousie Journals*, 3: 31, entry for 9 October 1825.

14 UT-Hale, E.F. Hale to Lord Amherst, 22 July 1799; E.F. Hale to Lord Amherst, 1 October 1800.

15 On amateur noblewomen artists during this period, see Greer, *The Obstacle Race*, chapter 14, and Tippett, *By a Lady*, 5–9.

16 UT-Hale, E.F. Hale to Lord Amherst, 4 August 1804.

17 On the implications of the application of the picturesque approach to the Canadian landscape, see my "Like 'The Thames towards Putney'" and the references therein.

18 UT-Hale, E.F. Hale to Lord Amherst, 12 August 1802.

19 Ibid., E.F. Hale to Lord Amherst, 22 July 1799.

20 Ibid., John Hale to Lord Amherst, 2 February 1803.

21 NA, Documentary Art Division, "Report concerning Montreal in Kent a Seat of the Right Honorable Lord Amherst etc etc etc by H. Repton," 1812.

22 NA-Hale (mf. A-1085), John Hale to Lord Amherst, 16 May 1817.

23 UT-Hale, E.F. Hale to Lord Amherst, 24 June 1819.

24 Ibid., E.F. Hale to Amherst, 3 June 1819.

25 Ibid., E.F. Hale to Lord Amherst, 17 Sept. 1819.

26 NA-Hale (mf. A-1085), E. Hale to Lord Amherst, 25 November 1819.

27 UT-Hale, E.F. Hale to Lord Amherst, 11 December 1819.

28 "la chere agathe nous as fait promettre de ne pas retraire Ste anne, et à vous dire le vrais l'argent rare a trouvé comme il l'est dans ce temps ici et un procet à soutenir nous aurois ruiner, ainsi il est plus prudent que nous nous te-

nions tranquile, car Mad[a]me Baby, ni Agathe ne vouloient pas retraire" (TL, vol. 2, Marguerite Lanaudière à Mme G. de Lanaudière, 16 décembre 1819).

29 NA-Hale, (mf. A-1085), E.F. Hale to Lord Amherst, 25 November 1819.
30 UT-Hale, E.F. Hale to Lord Amherst, 15 December 1819.
31 Ibid., E.F. Hale to Lord Amherst, 17 September 1819.
32 Ibid., E.F. Hale to Lady Amherst, 25 June 1819.
33 Thomas, *Man and the Natural World*, 13.
34 UT-Hale, E.F. Hale to Lady Amherst, 25 June 1819.
35 NA-Hale (mf. A-1085), E.F. Hale to Lord Amherst, 19 October 1820.
36 UT-Hale, E.F. Hale to Lord Amherst, 27 December 1819; E.F. Hale to Lord Amherst, 6 July [1822].
37 ANQ-TR, Greffe Joseph-Casimir Dury, CN401–33.
38 NA-Hale (mf. A-1085), E.F. Hale to Lord Amherst (no date; late October 1820?).
39 Ibid., E.F. Hale to Lord Amherst (no date; 20 July 1820?).
40 UT-Hale, E.F. Hale to Lady Amherst, 17 July 1819.
41 Ibid., E.F. Hale to Lord Amherst, 21 August 1819.
42 Zeller, *Inventing Canada*, 3–9.
43 Hale, "Observations on Crickets in Canada," *Transactions of the Literary and Historical Society of Quebec*, 1: 254–5.
44 UT-Hale, E.F. Hale to Lord Amherst, 28 July 1819.
45 Daniels, "The Political Iconography of Woodland in Later Georgian England," in Cosgrove and Daniels, *The Iconography of Landscape*, 43.
46 UT-Hale, E.F. Hale to Lord Amherst, 27 December 1819.
47 NA-Hale (mf. A-1085), E.F. Hale to Lord Amherst (no date; late October 1820?).
48 Daniels, "The Political Iconography of Woodland," in Cosgrove and Daniels, *The Iconography of Landscape*, 48.
49 NA-Hale (mf. A-1085), E.F. Hale to Lord Amherst (no date; 20 July 1820?).
50 UT-Hale, E.F. Hale to Lord Amherst, 2 June 1822; NA-Hale, vol. 4, Jeffrey Hale to Mother, 17 June 1820, ff. 250–1.
51 UT-Hale, E.F. Hale to Lord Amherst, 29 October 1822; NA, Documentary Art Division, Hale Sketchbook, I-2 (C-1307), which shows that the hedges were planted to obscure a fence.
52 UT-Hale, E.F. Hale to Lord Amherst, 2 June 1822.
53 Ibid., E.F. Hale to Lady Amherst, 17 Sept 1819.
54 Bigsby, *The Shoe and Canoe*, 1: 48.
55 Clarke, "Taking Possession"; Harley, "Deconstructing the Map."
56 NA-Hale (mf. A-1085), E.F. Hale to Lord Amherst, 15 December 1820.
57 UT-Hale, E.F. Hale to Lord Amherst, 20 September [1819].
58 NA, Dalhousie Muniments, MG 24, A 12, mf. A-537, E.F. Hale to Lord Dalhousie, 5 April 1824.

59 Cooke, *W.H. Coverdale Collection of Canadiana*, 98. Gilbert Gignac provides an insightful discussion of the artistry of the sketchbook ("Elizabeth Frances Hale, 1774–1826," in Béland, *La peinture au Québec*, 277–82).

60 UT-Hale, E.F. Hale to Lord Amherst, 27 December 1819.

61 Prioul, "Les paysagistes britanniques au Québec," in Béland, *La peinture au Québec*, 51.

62 NA-Hale (mf. A-1085), E.F. Hale to Lord Amherst, 15 December 1820.

63 Ibid., E.F. Hale to Lord Amherst, 19 October 1820.

64 Ibid., E.F. Hale to Lord Amherst, 24 February 1820.

65 NA-Hale, vol. 4, J. Hale to Revd Richard Hale, 6 June 1824, f. 340.

66 Ibid., Jeffery Hale to John Hale, 7 January 1821, f. 259.

67 NA-Hale (mf. A-1085), E.F. Hale to Lord Amherst, 11 January 1820.

68 Ibid., E.F. Hale to Lord Amherst, 20 May 1823.

69 ANQ-TR, Greffe Joseph-Casimir Dury, CN401–33; ANQ-M, Greffe Augustin Trudel, CN401–91.

70 NA, Census of 1825 for Sainte-Anne (mf. C-718). Rather, the Chandlers purchased their own seigneury of Nicolet in 1821, with aspirations to establish an English community similar to those of the Hales (Richard Chabot, "Chandler, Kenelm Conor," *DCB*, 7: 165–7).

71 NA, Lower Canada Land Records, RG 1, L 3 L, vol. 100 (mf. C-2531), John Hale to Earl of Dalhousie, 10 March 1827, ff. 49453–4; "Report from Select Committee on Lower Canada," 3 July 1834, *British Parliamentary Papers*, 1: 144, 173.

72 Anglican Church of Canada, Quebec Diocesan Archives (Lennoxville), Three Rivers, B24, Parish Report, Rev. Sam Wood, 26 January 1833.

73 A memorial plaque dedicated years later in the Anglican cathedral in Quebec to four Hale patriarchs listed John Hale's status as seigneur before his government positions. In a similar vein, his obituary commented that he "lived some years at the Domain [of Sainte-Anne], on the best terms with the inhabitants, amongst whom he introduced several improvements" (*Quebec Gazette*, 26 December 1838).

74 McCord Museum, Hale Family Papers, M20483, Edward Hale [uncle] to Edward Hale, 26 November 1840.

75 Ibid., George Hale to Edward Hale, 16 April 1845.

76 Ibid., Edward Hale [uncle] to Edward Hale, 5 November 1844.

77 Harper, *Krieghoff*, 18.

78 Pratt, *Imperial Eyes*.

CONCLUSION

1 Testimony of Nicolas Vincent (Isawanhonhi), in *Journals of the House of Assembly of Lower Canada*, 1823–24, app. R, "Seventh Report from the Special

Committee ... [on] the Settlement of the Crown Lands," app. A (testimony), 9 December 1823.

2 Ingall, "Remarks on the Country lying between the Rivers St. Maurice and Saguenay," 219.

3 Thoreau, *A Yankee in Canada*, 75, 36.

4 Bernard, *Les Rouges*, 341–7.

5 *Gazette de Québec*, 5 décembre 1822.

6 Gallichan, *Honoré Mercier*, 57.

7 BJ, vol. 103, Moulin de la seigneurie, 1838–44, Requête des habitants propriétaires de la Seigneurie de Batiscan à John Stewart, 2 décembre 1838.

8 Bernard, *Les Rouges*, 341.

9 Anderson, *Imagined Communities*.

Bibliography

MANUSCRIPT SOURCES

ANGLICAN CHURCH OF CANADA, QUEBEC DIOCESAN ARCHIVES
(LENNOXVILLE)
Three Rivers, B24, Parish Reports.

ARCHIVES DE L'ARCHEVÊCHÉ DU QUÉBEC (AAQ)
Cahiers des visites pastorales, 69CD.
Notre-Dame-de-Québec, C1 CD.
Registres des insinuations ecclésiastiques, 12A.
Registres des lettres, 210A.
Registres des requêtes, 220A.
Vicaires généraux, 1CB.

ARCHIVES DU SÉMINAIRE DE QUÉBEC (ASQ)
Polygraphie.

ARCHIVES DU SÉMINAIRE DE TROIS-RIVIÈRES (ASTR)
Fonds fabrique de la paroisse Sainte-Geneviève de Batiscan, FN-287.
Fonds Paroisses, DR-285, no. 120, Saint-Stanislas.

ARCHIVES NATIONALES DU QUÉBEC À MONTRÉAL (ANQ-M)
Conseil supérieur, Registres, M9.
Greffe J.-B. Badeaux, CN401–55
Greffe Nicolas-Benjamin Doucet, CN601–134.

Greffe Nicolas Duclos, CN401–30.
Greffe Louis Guillet père, CN401–46.
Greffe Jacques de La Touche, CN401–28.
Greffe Augustin Trudel, CN401–91.
Pièces détachées de cours de justice de la Nouvelle-France, Juridiction sei-
gneuriale de Batiscan, M38/5.
Procès-verbaux des grands-voyers, E2.
Registres d'état civil:
Église protestante St-James, Trois-Rivières CE401–50.
Église Sainte-Anne de la Pérade, ZQ2–8.
Église Saint-François-Xavier de Batiscan, ZQ1–14.
Église Sainte-Geneviève de Batiscan, CE401–3.
Église Saint-Stanislas de Batiscan, CE401–43.
Seigneurie Batiscan, P220/1.

ARCHIVES NATIONALES DU QUÉBEC À QUÉBEC (ANQ-Q)
Archevêché de Québec, P332.
Collection des pièces judiciaires et notariales, M67.
Cour des plaidoyers communs, District de Québec, T50–301.
Cour supérieur de Québec, T11–1.
Fonds Seigneuries, P240.
Magdeleine Lonval, P-1000–1314.
Ministère de l'agriculture, E9.
Poll Books, M46.1.
Tarieu de Lanaudière, P244.
Terres et forêts, E21.
Verchères/Naudière – Procès avec le curé de Batiscan (photocopies), ZQ 27.

ARCHIVES NATIONALES DU QUÉBEC À TROIS-RIVIÈRES (ANQ-TR)
Cour du banc du roi (dossiers), T25.
Cour du banc du roi (plumitif), T25
Forges de Batiscan (copies), DR-8.
Greffe Joseph-Casimir Dury, CN401–33.

ARCHIVES OF ONTARIO
William Warren Baldwin and Robert Baldwin Papers, MS 88.

MCCORD MUSEUM
Hale Family Papers, M20483.

MCGILL UNIVERSITY, MCLENNAN LIBRARY, RARE BOOKS
DEPARTMENT
Joseph Frobisher, Diary, 1806–10, MS 433/2.
James L. Glennie, "Diary of a Journey Commencing 1st June [1800]."

NATIONAL ARCHIVES OF CANADA (NA)

Adjutant General, Lower Canada, Correspondence, RG 9, 1 A 1.

Earl Amherst Papers, MG 12, WO 34.

Baby Family Collection, Transcriptions, MG 24, L3.

British Military and Naval Records, RG 8, series C.

Censuses of New France, 1685–1739, série G1.

Census Returns, 1825, C-718.

Census Returns, 1831, C-723.

Civil and Provincial Secretary, Lower Canada, "S" series, RG 4, A 1.

Colonial Office Papers, Q series, MG 11, CO 42.

Dalhousie Muniments, MG 24 A12.

Thomas Dunn Letterbook, MG 24, B 10.

Executive Council and Land Committee, RG 1, L 7.

France, Archives des colonies, Correspondance générale, Canada, Transcriptions, MG 1, série C11A.

France, Archives des colonies, Des limites et des postes, Transcriptions, MG 1, série C11E.

France, Archives des colonies, Lettres envoyées, MG 1, série B.

Grand voyer, RG 1, E 17.

Haldimand Papers, MG 21 (British Library, Add. MSS 21884).

Hale Family Papers, MG 23 G11–18.

Lower Canada Land Papers, RG 1, L 3 L.

Neilson Collection, MG 24 B1.

Nouvelle-France, Archives judiciaires, Transcriptions, MG 8, B 4.

Nouvelle-France, Correspondance officielle, 3ᵉ série, MG 8, A 1.

Nouvelle-France, Ordonnances des intendants, Transcriptions, MG 8, A 6.

Quebec, Lower Canada, and Upper Canada, Petitions and Addresses, RG 1, E 16.

Sainte-Anne de la Pérade, Transcriptions, MG 8, F 83.

School Records, RG 4, B 30.

Selkirk Papers, MG 19, E 1.

NATIONAL ARCHIVES OF CANADA, DOCUMENTARY ART DIVISION

Hale Sketchbook.

"Report concerning Montreal in Kent a Seat of the Right Honorable Lord Amherst etc etc etc by H. Repton," 1812.

NATIONAL ARCHIVES OF CANADA, NATIONAL MAP COLLECTION (NMC)

Plan cadastral de Batiscan (ca. 1726), NMC-1724.

Plan cadastral de Batiscan (ca. 1726), NMC-1725.

Murray Map (1760), sections FF, FH, NMC-10842.

Sainte-Anne de la Pérade (1825), H2/325, NMC-8982.

Sainte-Anne de la Pérade (1830), H2/325, NMC-15665.

PARCS CANADA, RÉGION DE QUÉBEC (QUÉBEC)
Compagnie des forges de Batiscan, registre des lettres (now held at the NA)

TORONTO REFERENCE LIBRARY
Laurent Quetton de St-George Papers, s129.

UNIVERSITÉ DE MONTRÉAL, SERVICE DES COLLECTIONS
  PARTICULIÈRES
Collection Baby, p58.

UNIVERSITY OF TORONTO, THOMAS FISHER RARE BOOK
  LIBRARY (UT)
Hale Papers, Manuscript Collection no. 90.

OTHER SOURCES

Anderson, Benedict. *Imagined Communities: Reflections on the Origin and Spread of Nationalism*. Rev. ed. London: Verso 1991.
Arrêts et réglements du Conseil supérieur de Québec et ordonnances et jugements des intendants du Canada. Québec: E.R. Fréchette 1856.
Aubert de Gaspé, Philippe. *Mémoires*. Montréal: Fides 1971.
Audet, Pierre E. *Les officiers de justice: Des origines de la colonie jusqu'à nos jours*. Montréal: Wilson & Lafleur 1986.
Barkan, Leonard. *The Gods Made Flesh: Metamorphosis & the Pursuit of Paganism*. New Haven: Yale University Press 1986.
Barthe, J.B.M., ed. *Analyse des actes de François Trottain*. [n.p.: n.p., n.d.].
Bates, Réal. "Les conceptions prénuptiales dans la vallée du Saint-Laurent avant 1725." *RHAF* 40, no. 2 (1986): 253–72.
– "Stock, caractéristiques et mode de transmission des prénoms dans une population traditionnelle: L'exemple du Canada sous le Régime français." In *Actes du XVIe congrès international des sciences onomastiques (Québec, Université Laval, 16–22 août 1987)*, ed. Jean-Claude Boulanger. Québec: Les Presses de l'université Laval 1990.
Bégon, Élisabeth. *Lettres au cher fils: Correspondance d'Élisabeth Bégon avec son gendre (1748–1753)*. Montréal: Hurtubise HMH 1972.
Béland, Mario, ed. *La peinture au Québec, 1820–1850: Nouveaux regards, nouvelles perspectives*. Québec: Musée du Québec / Les Publications du Québec 1991.
Bernard, Jean-Paul. *Les Rouges: Libéralisme, nationalisme et anticléricalisme au milieu du xixe siècle*. Montréal: Presses de l'université du Québec 1971.
Bertrand, Georges. "Pour une histoire écologique de la France rurale." In *Histoire de la France rurale*, vol. 1, *La formation des campagnes françaises des origines au xive siècle*, ed. Georges Duby. Paris: Seuil 1975.
Bervin, George. *Québec au xixe siècle: L'activité économique des grands marchands*. Sillery: Les éditions du Septentrion 1991.

Biggar, H.P., ed. *The Works of Samuel de Champlain*. 6 vols. Toronto: Champlain Society 1920–36.

Bigsby, John J. *The Shoe and Canoe; or, Pictures of Travel in the Canadas*. Vol. 1. 1850; reprint, New York: Paladin Press 1965.

Boivin, B. "La flore du Canada en 1708: Étude et publication d'un manuscrit de Michel Sarrasin et Sébastien Vaillant." *Études littéraires* 10, no. 2 (1977): 221–97.

Boucher, Pierre. *Histoire véritable et naturelle des mœurs et productions du pays de la Nouvelle-France, vulgairement dite le Canada*. [n.p.]: Société historique de Boucherville 1964.

Bouchette, Joseph. *The British Dominions in North America*. Vol. 1. London: Henry Colburn and Richard Bentley 1831.

– *Description topographique de la province du Bas-Canada*. Montréal 1978.

– *A Topographical Dictionary of the Province of Lower Canada*. London 1832.

British Parliamentary Papers. Vol. 1. Shannon, Ireland: Irish University Press 1968.

Burke, Peter. *The Historical Anthropology of Early Modern Italy: Essays on Perception and Communication*. Cambridge: Cambridge University Press 1987.

– and Roy Porter, eds. *The Social History of Language*. Cambridge: Cambridge University Press 1987.

Caron, Ivanhoë. *La colonisation de la province de Québec: Débuts du régime anglais, 1760–1791*. Vol. 1. Québec: L'Action sociale, 1923.

Carter, Paul. *The Road to Botany Bay: An Exploration of Landscape and History*. New York: Alfred A. Knopf 1988.

Cartier, Jacques. *The Voyages of Jacques Cartier*. Introduction by Ramsay Cook. Toronto: University of Toronto Press 1993.

Charbonneau, Hubert, and Jacques Légaré, eds. *Répertoire des actes de baptême, mariage, sépulture et des recensements du Québec ancien*. Montréal: Presses de l'université de Montréal 1980–88.

Clark, G.N.G. "Taking Possession: The Cartouche as Cultural Text in Eighteenth-Century American Maps." *Word & Image* 4 (1988): 455–74.

Cliche, Marie-Aimée. "Filles-mères, familles et société sous le régime français." *Histoire sociale-Social History* 31, no. 41 (1988): 39–69.

– *Les pratiques de dévotion en Nouvelle-France: Comportements populaires et encadrement ecclésial dans le gouvernement de Québec*. Québec: Presses de l'université Laval 1988.

Coates, Colin M. "Authority and Illegitimacy in New France: The Burial of Bishop Saint-Vallier and Madeleine de Verchères vs. the Priest of Batiscan." *Histoire sociale-Social History* 22, no. 43 (1989): 65–90.

– "The Boundaries of Rural Society in Early Quebec: Batiscan and Sainte-Anne de la Pérade to 1825." PhD thesis, York University 1992.

– "Like 'The Thames towards Putney': The Appropriation of Landscape in Lower Canada" *CHR* 74, no. 3 (1993): 317–43.

Cohen, Anthony P. *The Symbolic Construction of Community*. London: Tavistock 1985.

Cohen, Marjorie. *Women's Work, Markets, and Economic Development in Nineteenth-Century Ontario.* Toronto: University of Toronto Press 1988.

Comaroff, John, and Simon Roberts. *Rules and Processes: The Cultural Logic of Dispute in an African Context.* Chicago: University of Chicago Press 1981.

Commentaire sur le discours de l'honorable Chas. Delanaudiere (qui a paru hier). Québec: William Moore 1792.

Complément des ordonnances et jugements des gouverneurs et intendants du Canada. Québec: E.R. Fréchette 1856.

Cook, G. Ramsay. "Cabbages not Kings: Towards an Ecological Interpretation of Early Canadian History." *Journal of Canadian Studies* 25, no. 4 (1990–91): 5–16.

Cooke, W. Martha E. *W.H. Coverdale Collection of Canadiana: Paintings, Watercolours and Drawings (Manoir Richelieu Collection).* Ottawa: Public Archives Canada 1983.

Cosgrove, Denis, and Stephen Daniels, eds. *The Iconography of Landscape: Essays on the Symbolic Representation, Design and Use of Past Environments.* Cambridge: Cambridge University Press 1987.

Courville, Serge, J.-C. Robert, and N. Séguin, *Atlas historique du Québec: Le pays laurentien au XIXᵉ siècle: Les morphologies de base.* Sainte-Foy: Presses de l'université Laval 1995.

Cronon, William. *Changes in the Land: Indians, Colonists, and the Ecology of New England.* New York: Hill and Wang 1983.

Crosby, Alfred. *Ecological Imperialism: The Biological Expansion of Europe, 900–1900.* Cambridge: Cambridge University Press 1986.

Dalton, Roy C. *The Jesuits' Estates Question, 1760–1888: A Study of the Background for the Agitation of 1889.* Toronto: University of Toronto Press 1968.

Dareau, François. *Traité des injures dans l'ordre judiciaire.* Paris: chez Prault père 1775.

Darnton, Robert. *The Great Cat Massacre and Other Episodes in French Cultural History.* New York: Basic Books 1984.

Day, Gordon M., and Bruce G. Trigger. "Algonquin." In *Handbook of North American Indians,* vol. 15, *Northeast,* ed. Bruce G. Trigger. Washington, DC: Smithsonian Institution 1978.

Dechêne, Louise. *Habitants and Merchants in Seventeenth Century Montreal.* Trans. Liana Vardi. Montreal: McGill-Queen's University Press, 1992.

– *Le partage des subsistances au Canada sous le régime français.* Montréal: Boréal 1994.

Dépatie, Sylvie, Mario Lalancette, and Christian Dessureault. *Contributions à l'étude du régime seigneurial canadien.* La Salle, Qué.: Hurtubise 1987.

Desbarats, Catherine. "Agriculture within the Seigneurial Regime of Eighteenth Century Canada: Some Thoughts on the Recent Literature." *CHR* 73, no. 2 (1992): 194–210.

Dessureault, Christian. "L'égalitarisme paysan dans l'ancienne société de la vallée du Saint-Laurent." *RHAF* 40, no. 3 (1987): 373–408.

- "Les fondements de la hiérarchie sociale au sein de la paysannerie: Le cas de Saint-Hyacinthe, 1760–1815." Thèse de doctorat, Université de Montréal 1985.

Dickinson, John A. *Justice et justiciables: La procédure civile à la prévôté de Québec, 1667–1759.* Québec: Presses de l'université Laval 1982.

- "La justice seigneuriale en Nouvelle-France: Le cas de Notre-Dame-des-Anges." RHAF 28, no. 3 (1974): 323–46.

- "Réflexions sur la police en Nouvelle-France." *McGill Law Journal – Revue de droit de McGill* 32 (1987): 496–522.

Dictionary of Canadian Biography. Vols 1-7. Toronto: University of Toronto Press 1966–88.

Dommergues, André. "La forêt en Nouvelle-France au dix-septième siècle." *Études canadiennes* 23 (décembre 1987): 53–64.

Doughty, Arthur G., ed. *An Historical Journal of the Campaigns in North American For the Years 1757, 1758, 1759, and 1760.* By Captain John Knox. Vol. 2. Toronto: Champlain Society 1914.

Douville, Raymond. "Les lents débuts d'une seigneurie des Jésuites." *Les Cahiers de Dix* 25 (1960): 249–76.

- *Les premiers seigneurs et colons de Sainte-Anne de la Pérade, 1667–1681.* Trois-Rivières: Éditions du Bien Public 1946.

Dufour, Jeanne. "Les forges et la forêt dans la Sarthe." *Revue géographique des Pyrénées et du Sud-Ouest* 55, fasc. 2 (1984): 219–30.

"Erster Feldzug der Braunschweiger in Kanada, im J[ahre] 1776." *August Wilhelm Schlözers Briefwechsel meist historischen und politischen Inhalts* 5, no. 29 (2nd ed., 1780): 267–79.

Fauteux, Joseph-Noël. *Essai sur l'industrie au Canada sous le régime français.* Québec: L.-A. Proulx 1927.

First Report of the Committee of the House of Assembly … which Relates to the Settlement of the Crown Lands. Quebec: John Neilson 1821.

Fortin, Claire-Andrée, and Benoît Gautier. "Aperçu de l'histoire des forges Saint-Tite et Batiscan et préliminaires à une analyse de l'évolution du secteur sidérurgique mauricien, 1793–1910." Rapport de recherche, Université du Québec à Trois-Rivières 1985.

Fournier, Marcel. *Les Européens au Canada des origines à 1765 (hors France).* Montréal: Éditions du Fleuve 1989.

Fowke, Vernon C. *Canadian Agricultural Policy: The Historical Pattern.* Toronto: University of Toronto Press 1946.

Franquet, Louis. *Voyages et mémoires sur le Canada.* Montréal: Éditions Elysée 1974.

Fyson, Donald. "Du pain au madère: L'alimentation à Montréal au début du XIXe siècle" RHAF 46, no. 1 (1992): 67–90.

Gadoury, Lorraine. *La noblesse de Nouvelle-France.* La Salle: Hurtubise HMH 1992.

Gagnon, Serge. *Mariage et famille au temps de Papineau.* Sainte-Foy: Presses de l'université Laval 1993.

Gallichan, Gilles. *Honoré Mercier: La politique et la culture*. Sillery: Les Éditions du Septentrion 1994.

Garrioch, David. *Neighbourhood and Community in Paris, 1740–1790*. Cambridge: Cambridge University Press 1986.

Gazette de Québec. 1766–1825.

Gosselin, Auguste. *L'église du Canada depuis Monseigneur de Laval jusqu'à la Conquête*. 3 vols. Québec: Laflamme & Proulx, 1911–14.

Goy, Joseph, and Jean-Pierre Wallot, eds. *Évolution et éclatement du monde rural: Structures, fonctionnement et évolution différentielle des sociétés rurales françaises et québécoises $xvii^e - xx^e$ siècles*. Montréal: Presses de l'université de Montréal 1986.

Gray, Hugh. *Letters from Canada, Written during a Residence There in the Years 1806, 1807, and 1808*. London: Longman, Hurst, Rees and Orme 1809.

Greer, Allan. "L'habitant, la paroisse rurale et la politique locale au xviiie siècle: Quelques cas dans la vallée du Richelieu." *Sessions d'études* 47 (1980): 19–33.

– *Patriots and the People: The Rebellion of 1837 in Rural Lower Canada*. Toronto: University of Toronto Press 1994.

– *Peasant, Lord, and Merchant: Rural Society in Three Quebec Parishes, 1740–1840*. Toronto: University of Toronto Press 1985.

Greer, Germaine. *The Obstacle Race: The Fortunes of Women Painters and Their Work*. New York: Farrar Straus Giroux 1979.

Hale, John. "Observations on Crickets in Canada." *Transactions of the Literary and Historical Society of Quebec* 1 (1829): 254–5.

Hamelin, Louis-Edmond. "Le rang d'arrière-fleuve en Nouvelle-France." *Géographe canadien / Canadian Geographer* 34, no. 2 (1990): 110–19.

Hardy, René. *La sidérurgie dans le monde rural: Les hauts fourneaux du Québec au xixe siècle*. Québec: Les presses de l'université Laval, 1995.

– Jean Roy, and Normand Séguin. "Une recherche en cours: le monde rural mauricien au 19e siècle." *Cahiers de géographie du Québec* 26, no. 67 (1982): 145–54.

– and Normand Séguin. *Forêt et société en Mauricie*. Montréal: Éditions du Boréal Express / Musée national de l'Homme 1984.

Hare, John. *Aux origines du parlementarisme québécois, 1791–1793*. Sillery: Les Éditions du Septentrion 1993.

Harley, J.B. "Deconstructing the Map." In *Writing Worlds: Discourse, Text & Metaphor in the Representation of Landscape*, ed. Trevor J. Barnes and James S. Duncan. New York: Routledge 1992.

Harper, J. Russell. *Krieghoff*. Toronto: University of Toronto Press 1979.

Harris, Richard Colebrook, ed. *Historical Atlas of Canada*. Vol. 1, *From the Beginning to 1800*. Toronto: University of Toronto Press 1987.

– *The Seigneurial System in Early Canada*. 2nd ed. Montreal: McGill-Queen's University Press 1984.

Haskell, Thomas. "Capitalism and the Origins of the Humanitarian Sensibility, Part II." *American Historical Review* 90, no. 3 (1985): 547–66.

Heriot, George. *Travels through the Canadas*. Edmonton: M.G. Hurtig 1971.

Hoffer, Peter Charles. "Honor and the Roots of American Litigiousness." *American Journal of Legal History* 33, no. 4 (1989): 295–319.

Hunter, William S., Jr. *Hunter's Panoramic Guide from Niagara Falls to Quebec*. Boston: John P. Jewett & Co. 1857.

Ingall, Lieutenant. "Remarks on the Country Lying between the Rivers St. Maurice and Saguenay, on the North Shore of the St. Lawrence." *Transactions of the Literary and Historical Society of Quebec* 2 (1831).

Innis, H.A., ed. *Select Documents in Canadian Economic History*. Toronto: University of Toronto Press 1929.

Isaac, Rhys. *The Transformation of Virginia, 1740–1790*. Chapel Hill: University of North Carolina Press 1982.

Jaenen, Cornelius. *The Role of the Church in New France*. Toronto: McGraw-Hill Ryerson 1976.

Jarnoux, Philippe. "La colonisation de la seigneurie de Batiscan aux 17e et 18e siècles: L'espace et les hommes." *RHAF* 40, no. 2 (1986): 163–91.

Jones, P.M. *Politics and Rural Society: The Southern Massif Central c. 1750–1880*. Cambridge: Cambridge University Press 1985.

Journals of the House of Assembly of Lower Canada. 1798–1830.

Lachance, André. *Crimes et criminels en Nouvelle France*. Montréal: Boréal Express 1984.

– *La justice criminelle du roi au Canada au XVIIIe siècle*. Québec: Presses de l'université Laval 1978.

Lacroix, Yvon. "Les origines de La Prairie, de 1667 à 1697." Mémoire de maîtrise, Université de Montréal 1980.

La Fleur, Mary Ann. "Seventeenth Century New England and New France in Comparative Perspective: Notre Dame des Anges, A Case Study." PhD thesis, University of New Hampshire 1987.

Lalou, Richard, and Mario Boleda. "Une source en friche: Les dénombrements sous le régime français." *RHAF* 42, no. 1 (1988): 47–71.

Lambert, John. *Travels through Canada, and the United States of North America, in the years 1806, 1807 & 1808*. 2nd ed. London: C. Cradock and W. Joy 1814.

Lange, Mr. *La nouvelle pratique civile, criminelle et beneficiale; ou, Le Nouveau praticien françois*. Paris: Jean & Michel Guignard 1708.

Lavallée, Louis. *La Prairie en Nouvelle-France, 1647–1760: Étude d'histoire sociale*. Montreal and Kingston: McGill-Queen's University Press 1992.

Legault, Roch. "Les aléas d'une carrière militaire pour les membres de la petite noblesse seigneuriale canadienne de la révolution américaine à la guerre de 1812–1815." Mémoire de maîtrise, Université de Montréal 1986.

Lemire, Maurice. "Champlain: Entre l'objectivité et la subjectivité." In *Scritti sulla Nouvelle-France nel Seicento*, ed. N. Doiron. Bari: Adriatica 1984.

Lévesque, René, F. Fitz Osborne, and J.V. Wright. *Le gisement de Batiscan: Notes sur des vestiges laissés par une peuplade de culture sylvicole inférieure dans la vallée du Saint-Laurent*. Ottawa: Imprimeur de la Reine 1964.

Lockridge, Kenneth A. *A New England Town: The First Hundred Years: Dedham, Massachusetts, 1636–1736*. Expanded ed. New York: W.W. Norton 1985.

Lunn, Alice Jean E. *Développement économique de la Nouvelle-France, 1713–1760*. Trans. Brigitte Monel-Nish. Montréal: Presses de l'université de Montréal 1986.

Macdonald, Norman. "Hemp and Imperial Defense." CHR 17, no. 4 (1936): 385–98.

Mann, Bruce H. *Neighbors and Strangers: Law and Community in Early Connecticut*. Chapel Hill: University of North Carolina Press 1987.

Massicotte, E.Z. "Des loteries à Montréal en 1701." BRH 24 (1918): 180–1.

Milobar, David. "The Origins of British-Quebec Merchant Ideology: New France, the British Atlantic and the Constitutional Periphery, 1720–70." *Journal of Imperial and Commonwealth History* 24, 3 (1996): 364–90.

Mintz, Sidney, and Eric Wolf. "An Analysis of Ritual Co-Parentage (Compadrazgo)." In *Peasant Society: A Reader*, ed. Jack Potter, May Diaz, and George Foster. Boston: Little, Brown and Co. 1967.

Moogk, Peter. "'Thieving Buggers' and 'Stupid Sluts': Insults and Popular Culture in New France." *William & Mary Quarterly*, 3rd ser., 36, no. 4 (1979): 524–47.

Morissonneau, Christian. *Le langage géographique de Cartier et de Champlain: Choronymie, vocabulaire et perception*. Québec: Presses de l'université Laval 1978.

Munro, W.B., ed. *Documents Relating to the Seigniorial Tenure in Canada, 1598–1854*. Toronto: Champlain Society 1908.

Nelson, William E. *Dispute and Conflict Resolution in Plymouth County, Massachusetts, 1725–1825*. Chapel Hill: University of North Carolina Press 1981.

Noël, Françoise. *The Christie Seigneuries: Estate Management and Settlement in the Upper Richelieu Valley, 1760–1854*. Montreal and Kingston: McGill-Queen's University Press 1992.

– "La gestion des seigneuries de Gabriel Christie dans la vallée du Richelieu (1760–1845)." RHAF 40, no. 4 (1987): 561–82.

Ouellet, Fernand. *Le Bas-Canada, 1791–1840: Changements structuraux et crise*. Ottawa: Presses de l'université d'Ottawa 1980.

– "Dualité économique et changement technologique au Québec (1760–1790)." *Histoire sociale / Social History* 9, no. 18 (1976): 256–96.

– *Economy, Class, & Nation in Quebec: Interpretive Essays*. Ed. and trans. Jacques Barbier. Toronto: Copp Clark Pitman 1991.

– *Éléments d'histoire sociale du Bas-Canada*. Montréal: Hurtubise 1972.

– *Histoire économique et sociale du Québec, 1760–1850*. Montréal: Fides 1971.

- "Officiers de milice et structure sociale au Québec (1660–1815)." *Histoire sociale / Social History* 12, no. 23 (1979): 37–65.
- , J. Hamelin, and R. Chabot. "Les prix agricoles dans les villes et les campagnes du Québec d'avant 1850: Aperçus quantitatifs." *Histoire sociale / Social History* 15, no. 29 (mai 1982): 83–127.

Ovid. *Metamorphoses*. Trans. Thomas Orger. London 1811.

Paquette, Lynne, and Réal Bates. "Les naissances illégitimes sur les rives du Saint-Laurent avant 1730." RHAF 40, no. 2 (1986): 239–52.

Pearcy, Lee T. *The Mediated Muse: English Translations of Ovid, 1560–1700*. Hamden, Conn.: Archon Books 1984.

Pièces et documents relatifs à la tenure seigneuriale. Québec: E.R. Fréchette 1852.

Porter, Roy. *English Society in the Eighteenth Century*. London: Penguin Books 1982.

Pratt, Mary Louise. *Imperial Eyes: Travel Writing and Transculturation*. New York, Routledge 1992.

Provost, Honorius. "Le régime des cures au Canada français." *Rapport de la Société canadienne de l'histoire de l'Église catholique*, 1954–55, 85–103.

Rapport de l'archiviste de la province de Québec. Various years.

Report concerning Canadian Archives. Various years.

Robertson, J. Ross, ed. *The Diary of Mrs John Graves Simcoe*. Toronto: William Briggs 1911.

Rosen, Lawrence. *Bargaining for Reality: The Construction of Social Relations in a Muslim Community*. Chicago: University of Chicago Press 1984.
- "Islamic 'Case Law' and the Logic of Consequence." In *History and Power in the Study of Law: New Directions in Legal Anthropology*, ed. June Starr and Jane Collier. Ithaca: Cornell University Press 1989.

Roy, P.-G. *La famille Tarieu de Lanaudière*. Lévis: [n.p.] 1922.
- "Madeleine de Verchères, plaideuse." *Mémoires de la Société royale du Canada*, 3ᵉ sér., 15 (1921): 63–72.
- éd. *Ordonnances, commissions, etc, etc, des gouverneurs et intendants de la Nouvelle-France, 1639–1706*. 2 vols. Beauceville: L'Éclaireur 1924.

Rutman, Darrett B. "Assessing the Little Communities of Early America." *William & Mary Quarterly*, 3rd ser., 43, no. 2 (1986): 163–78.

Sabean, David Warren. *Power in the Blood: Popular Culture and Village Discourse in Early Modern Germany*. Cambridge: Cambridge University Press 1984.
- *Property, Production, and Family in Neckarhausen, 1700–1870*. Cambridge: Cambridge University Press 1990.

Saint-Pierre, Jacques. "L'aménagement de l'espace rural en Nouvelle-France: Les seigneuries de la Côte du Sud." In *Peuplement colonisateur aux XVIIᵉ et XVIIIᵉ siècles*, ed. Jacques Mathieu and Serge Courville. Québec: Cahiers du Célat 1987.

Saint-Vallier, Jean-Baptiste de. *Rituel du diocèse de Québec, publié par l'ordre de Mgr de Saint-Vallier*. Paris: chez Simon Langlois 1703.

Sanfaçon, Roland. "La construction du premier chemin Québec-Montréal et le problème des corvées." *RHAF* 12 (1958–59): 3–29.

Sansom, Joseph. *Sketches of Lower Canada, Historical and Descriptive.* New York: Kirk & Mercein 1817.

Sansom, Roch. "Une industrie avant l'industrialisation: Le cas des Forges du Saint-Maurice." *Anthropologies et Sociétés* 10, no. 1 (1986): 85–107.

Stansbury, P. *A Pedestrian Tour of Two Thousand Three Hundred Miles, in North America ... Performed in the Autumn of 1821.* New York: J.D. Myers & W. Smith 1822.

Tebbenhof, Edward H. "Tacit Rules and Hidden Family Structures: Naming Practices and Godparentage in Schenectady, New York, 1680–1800." *Journal of Social History* 18 (1985): 541–66.

Têtu, H., and C.-O. Gagnon, eds. *Mandements, lettres pastorales et circulaires des évêques du Québec.* Vol. 3. Québec: Imprimerie générale A. Coté 1888.

Thomas, Keith. *Man and the Natural World: Changing Attitudes in England, 1500–1800.* London: Allen Lane 1983.

Thompson, E.P. *Whigs and Hunters: The Origin of the Black Act.* Harmondsworth: Penguin 1977.

Thoreau, Henry D. *A Yankee in Canada.* 1866; reprint, Montreal: Harvest House 1961.

Thwaites, Reuben Gold, ed. *The Jesuit Relations and Allied Documents.* 74 vols. Cleveland: Burrows Brothers 1896–1901.

Tippett, Maria. *By a Woman: Celebrating Three Centuries of Art by Canadian Women.* Toronto: University of Toronto Press 1992.

Todorov, Tzvetan. *The Conquest of America: The Question of the Other.* Trans. Richard Howard. New York: Harper & Row 1984.

Tousignant, Pierre. "Problématique pour une nouvelle approche de la Constitution de 1791." *RHAF* 27, no. 2 (1973): 181–234.

Trudel, Marcel. *Atlas de la Nouvelle-France / An Atlas of New France.* Québec: Presses de l'université Laval 1968.

– *Les débuts du régime seigneurial au Canada.* Montréal: Fides 1974.

– *Dictionnaire des esclaves et de leurs propriétaires au Canada français.* Montréal: Hurtubise HMH 1990.

– *L'esclavage au Canada français: Histoire et conditions de l'esclavage.* Québec: Presses de l'université Laval 1960.

– *Initiation à la Nouvelle-France.* Montréal: Éditions HRW 1968.

– *Le régime militaire dans le gouvernement des Trois-Rivières, 1760–1764.* Trois-Rivières: Éditions du Bien Public 1952.

Les Ursulines des Trois-Rivières depuis leur établissement jusqu'à nos jours. Vol. 2. Trois-Rivières: P.V. Ayotte 1892.

Vance, Norman. "Ovid and the Nineteenth Century." In *Ovid Renewed: Ovidian Influences of Literature and Art from the Middle Ages to the Twentieth Century,* ed. Charles Martindale. Cambridge: Cambridge University Press 1988.

"Vertrauliche Briefe aus Kanada. S[ainte]-Anne, 9 März – 20 Apr[il] 1777." *August Wilhelm Schlözers Briefwechsel meist historischen und politischen Inhalts* 4, no. 23 (2nd ed., 1780): 288–323.

"Von Kanada, aus Briefen eines deutschen StabsOfficiers, dat[iert] Batiscamp (einer Paroisse in Kanada) den 2. Novemb[er] 1776." *August Wilhelm Schlözers Briefwechsel meist historischen und politischen Inhalts* 3, no. 18 (3rd ed., 1780): 320–40.

Weld, Isaac, Jr. *Travels through the States of North America, and the Provinces of Upper and Lower Canada, during the Years 1795, 1796, and 1797.* London: John Stockdale 1799.

White, Richard. *Land Use, Environment, and Social Change: The Shaping of Island County, Washington.* Seattle: University of Washington Press 1980.

Whitelaw, Marjory, ed., *The Dalhousie Journals.* 3 vols. Ottawa: Oberon Press 1981–82.

Wien, William Thomas. "Peasant Accumulation in a Context of Colonization: Rivière-du-Sud, Canada, 1720–1775." PhD thesis, McGill University 1988.

– " 'Les travaux pressants': Calendrier agricole, assolement et productivité au Canada au XVIIIe siècle." *RHAF* 43, no. 4 (1990): 535–58.

Wilhelmy, Jean-Pierre. *Les mercenaires allemands au Québec du XVIIIe siècle et leur apport à la population.* Beloil: Maison de mots 1984.

Wright, Louis B., and Marion Tinling, eds. *Quebec to Carolina in 1785–1786: Being the Travel Diary and Observations of Robert Hunter, Jr., a Young Merchant of London.* San Marino, Calif.: The Huntington Library 1943.

Zeller, Suzanne. *Inventing Canada: Early Victorian Science and the Idea of a Transcontinental Nation.* Toronto: University of Toronto Press 1987.

Index

Acadians, 56
Adam, Marie-Anne, habitant, 64, 109
agricultural society: in Trois-Rivières, 53–4
agriculture: and forestry, 128–9
Algonquins, 7–8, 10
American invasion in 1775, 23, 93–5, 115
Amerindians, 6–8, 10–11, 15, 57, 170n14. *See also* Algonquins; Hurons; Iroquois
Amherst, Jeffery, general, 27–8, 146
Amherst, William Pitt, 28, 30, 146–7
animals, indigenous, 38–41
archaeological evidence, 7
Aubry, Laurent, priest of Sainte-Geneviève and Saint-Stanislas, 89–92, 94, 119, 170n14, 192n89
aveu et dénombrement, 18, 28, 36
Ayotte, François, habitant, 59

Badeaux, Joseph, agent for Commission of Jesuit Estates, 97, 138–9, 141
bailiffs: *huissiers*, 105; replacing militia captains, 90, 93
Baribault, Jean-Baptiste, fur trader, 103
Baril, Catherine, habitant, 63
Baril, François, miller, 103–4, 111
Bates, Joshua, employee of Batiscan Iron Works, 130
Batiscan Iron Works, 125–43, 164; closure of, 162; described by travellers, 146; fire at, 131; founding of, 29–30, 62, 127, 129–30; impact of, 136–43; land, 175n76; products, 132–4; store, 136; supplies, 135–6; workers, 67, 130–1
Batiscan seigneury: concessions in, 17, 26, 29, 33–5; early settlement by Europeans, 10–11, 55–6, 86; grant to Jesuit order,

15–17; legal possession of, 10, 15; maps, 2, 16, 27; name, 13–14. *See also* mills; seigneurial dues
Bayard, Nicolas, manager of Batiscan Iron Works, 131, 133–4, 136, 202n26
Beauharnois, Charles de, governor, 82–3
Bédard, Abbé Thomas-Laurent, 25
Bégon, Michel, intendant, 43, 61, 117–18
Bell, Mathew, owner of Saint-Maurice ironworks, 97, 133–4, 147
Bigot, François, intendant, 21, 44
Bigsby, John, traveller, 98, 152
Board of Commissioners of the Jesuit Estates: experimental farm, 54; interested in hemp, 45; local influence, 96; management of Batiscan seigneury, 34, 121–2, 128, 138–9, 141; takes over Jesuit estates, 30